D1569288

# What A Wonderful Time!

4/29/05 Jonas & Ruth Scheffel

# Other Books By Bob Terrell

* All Aboard! The Story of Charlie (Choo Choo) Justice
* Diamonds in the Dust
* Grandpa's Town
* Historic Asheville
* Prison Bars to Shining Stars
* The Reluctant Lawman
* The Spiderweb Trail
* Trouble on his Trail
* The Wolf Creek Incident (with Preston Roberts)
* The Will Harris Murders
* The Old Ball Yard — Home of Memories
J. D. Sumner — Gospel Music is my Life!
Fun is Where You Find It!
Holy Land:  A Journey Into Time
A Touch of Terrell
Billy Graham in Hungary
Woody (with Barbara Shelton)
Old Gold
The Peace That Passeth Understanding (with Connie Hopper)
Disorder in the Court (with Marcellus Buchanan)
Billy Graham in the Soviet Union
Keep 'em Laughing
Papa Coke (with Sanders Rowland)
The Ralph Sexton Story
The Chuck Wagon Gang — A Legend Lives On
The Music Men
Plenty More in the Pot (with Udean Burke)
Elvis — His Love for Gospel Music (with J. D. Sumner)
Who Are These Iraqis?
A Nickel's Worth of Hope (with Andre Vandenberg)
McCormick Field — Home of Reality
The Legacy of Buck and Dottie Rambo
Givens Estates — A History
The Life and Times of J. D. Sumner

*Published by WorldComm® / Alexander Books™

# *What A Wonderful Time!*

## The Story of the Inspirations
### Or
### How Four Students and their Teacher
### Stormed the Heights of Gospel Music

# Bob Terrell

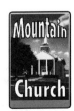

Publisher: Ralph Roberts
Vice-President: Pat Roberts

Editors: Vivian Terrell, Pat Roberts

Cover Design: Gayle Graham
Interior Design & Electronic Page Assembly: **WorldComm**®
Front Cover Photograph: J&E Photography, Rt. 5 Box 711, Grove OK 74344
Back Cover Photograph provided by: Singing News Magazine.
Interior photographs as indicated

10  9  8  7  6  5  4  3  2  1

### Library of Congress Catalog Number: 99-066728

Trade Paper
ISBN  1-57090-095-7
Case Bound
ISBN  1-57090-096-5

The author and publisher have made every effort in the preparation of this book to ensure
the accuracy of the information. However, the information in this book is sold without
warranty, either express or implied. Neither the author nor **Mountain Church**™ will be liable
for any damages caused or alleged to be caused directly, indirectly, incidentally, or
consequentially by the information in this book.

The opinions expressed in this book are solely those of the author and are not necessarily
those of **Mountain Church**™.

**Trademarks:** Names of products mentioned in this book known to be a, or suspected of
being trademarks or service marks are capitalized. The usage of a trademark or service
mark in this book should not be regarded as affecting the validity of any trademark or
service mark.

**Mountain Church**™—a division of Creativity, Inc.—is a full–service publisher located at
65 Macedonia Road, Alexander NC 28701. Phone (828) 252–9515, Fax (828) 255–8719.
For orders only: 1-800-472-0438. Visa and MasterCard accepted.

**Mountain Church**™ is distributed to the trade by **Alexander Books**™ 65 Macedonia Road,
Alexander NC 28701. Phone (828) 252–9515, Fax (828) 255–8719.

This book is also available on the internet in the **Publishers CyberMall.** Set your
browser to http://www.abooks.com and enjoy the many fine values there.

This book is dedicated
with respect and love
to our wives and children,
who made the sacrifices
and paid the price
for us to sing.

—The  Inspirations

The  Inspirations
PO Drawer JJ
Bryson City NC 28713
Telephone:  828/488-2865
Web  site:   theinspirations.com

# CONTENTS

# Foreword

I know the Inspirations in the capacities of fan, friend, colleague, and fellow-Christian. As singers, musicians, and gentlemen, I love them and hold them in highest esteem. I consider myself to be extremely fortunate to have witnessed their amazing careers first-hand. They have given me unlimited access to their professional and personal lives, and for that, I'm grateful.

Having the honor of naming this book makes me especially proud. "What A Wonderful Time" it has been for me and thousands, perhaps even millions of other gospel music enthusiasts because of the Inspirations. As a writer for the *Singing News*, I constantly hear of the tremendous respect and admiration the Inspirations command from their peers and fans.

My first recollection of the Inspirations was watching them on the *Gospel Singing Jubilee* television program. They were heroes of my youth and have become even more so in my adulthood.

They have always displayed great professionalism, but I consider their most admirable traits to be that they live what they sing, and they do things the right way. I've traveled many miles with them, been with them in their homes, churches, and other settings on a regular basis, so I know this to be a fact. I'm sure anyone else who knows them well would agree.

Since their formation, the Inspirations have capti-vated gospel music with a mystique and appeal that was never seen before and has not been witnessed since. They have remained the same throughout their illustrious careers. They became the hottest group on the road, storming to the top of their profession with a beautiful, unmistakable sound. They are one of the most revered groups of all time, as well as one of the most recognizable groups of any musical genre. Their reign of consistency is astounding and will probably never be duplicated.

The Inspirations are due thanks from all gospel music lovers for the class manner in which they have always presented themselves, as well as the many positive contributions they have made to the field. They have helped springboard as many singers as any group in the industry and have continually blessed people and helped change lives for the better.

My friend and colleague Bob Terrell has done a masterful job writing this account of one of our greatest gospel music groups. I believe you will enjoy it immensely.

Tim Gardner
670 Old Hanging Rock Road
Newland, North Carolina 28657
828/765-7819
June, 1999

# Introduction

To me, and I am sure to thousands of other long-time fans of the Inspirations, it seems that they should still be teen-agers. I suppose they are held in this light because of their dynamite success in gospel music as four high school boys and their teacher.

That some of them have crossed the half-century mark and Martin is old enough to draw early Social Security seems impossible.

There has never been a quartet, not even the Statesmen, that achieved success so quickly as the Inspirations. I am sure that a part of the reason was their youth. When they came to sing at a concert with the greatest quartets in the world, it was like a tiny David going up against Goliath again, and just as occurred in the biblical story, David prevailed again.

In eight short years, the Inspirations rose from the bottom of the briar patch to the pinnacle of gospel music, voted in 1972 by fans across the nation as America's Favorite Gospel Group in a poll conducted annually by the *Singing News*. No other quartet ever scaled the heights so quickly.

There were reasons for such a rapid rise: dedication to their task, the tremendous harmony they generated from the start, their youth, of course, and the presence of the Holy Spirit in their midst. You can add to that the fact that they have always maintained good physical condition, which has given them the stamina to meet their challenges.

Like all other quartets, they jest and throw barbs at each other on the bus, but they do walk the straight and narrow, and the moment they step on stage to face an audience, they become very, very serious. They sincerely feel that their task is not to further the reputation of the Inspirations, but to uphold and magnify the Kingdom of God, and for this reason alone, any quartet would be blessed.

This book is their story. It has been a long time coming, but now that it is here, all you have to do is sit back, relax, read the book, and enjoy one of America's greatest success stories.

Bob Terrell
PO Box 66
Asheville NC 28802
828/236-2120

I

# Atlanta

They were like five big-eyed rabbits in a carrot patch, those four high school boys and their teacher, rolling toward Atlanta in a Chevrolet Greenbriar van.

The teacher spoke: "Boys, do you feel like General Sherman?"

They looked at him blankly, and he chuckled.

"Like the general," the teacher said, "we've got to take Atlanta by storm!"

And that's what they did.

This was their big chance and they had no intention of flubbing it! June 10, 1966. Five thousand people came to the auditorium that evening, many of whom had been listening to the Inspirations sing in churches around Atlanta and didn't want to miss their big league debut. Those fans had prodded Promoter J. G. Whitfield to let the Inspirations sing on the big show in Atlanta, and Whitfield had relented.

They had been singing together for two years, starting in the basement of the teacher's home. What helped make these fellows appealing was that the bass was fourteen years old; the tenor and lead, seventeen; the baritone, twenty-one; and the teacher, twenty-nine—and they had the audacity to challenge for a position among the giants of gospel music.

They were the Inspirations, five young fellows, most of them still wet behind the ears, from the mountains of North Carolina. The teacher was Martin Cook, who taught physics and chemistry at Swain County High School in Bryson City, a small town tucked away in the hills beside Fontana Lake and the Great Smoky Mountains. The singers were Archie Watkins, tenor; Ronnie Hutchins, lead; Jack Laws, baritone; and Troy Burns, bass.

By June of 1966, after the Inspirations had been singing together two years, folks around Atlanta, where the quartet had sung in more churches than anywhere else, began to demand that Whitfield put them on one of his huge sings in the downtown Atlanta City Auditorium. Whit resisted for a while, not willing to gamble on such a young, nonprofessional quartet, but people continued to twist his arm, purely aggravating him to let the Inspirations sing.

On a Monday morning in May, 1966, after singing with the Inspirations in Bryson City, Les Beasley, manager of the Florida Boys, telephoned Whit, who had at one time sung with Les and the Florida Boys.

"Whit," Les began, "we sang up in the Smoky Mountains Saturday night and I heard a little group from Bryson City. They're called the Inspirations and they are good. They've got a little old boy named Archie singing tenor that nobody likes but the people. But he *can* sing tenor and this group *is* going to do something."

"Is that the quartet I've been hearing about?" Whit asked.

"I guess it is," Les said. "They sing in a lot of churches around Atlanta, and what makes this group so unusual is they're all still in high school. One of their teachers is the pianist. His name is Martin Cook."

"How can I get in touch with them?"

"I thought you might ask that," Les replied. "I've got their telephone number for you."

Before that Saturday night, Les Beasley had never seen the Inspirations, and he was mightily impressed with them.

Whit called Martin immediately and booked the Inspirations.

They had parked their van near the auditorium, alongside the glittering, customized motorcoaches of the Swanee River Boys, the Smitty Gatlin Trio, the Travelers, the Dixie Echoes and Happy Goodman Family, who were also on the program.

A hush settled over the auditorium as Whitfield walked on stage to introduce the Inspirations as the opening quartet. They came with a rush, and almost before Martin seated himself at the piano, the four youngsters launched into their "coming on" song, an attention-grabber titled *On The Sunny Banks*, and when Archie's high tenor voice began to ring in the rafters, the crowd came alive, shouting, stomping, whistling, and cheering for these country boys from the mountains.

The louder the cheers, the harder the youngsters sang. They had the place rocking before they finished their first song, and they kept it going until they sang their "going off" song.

Besides introducing each other and each giving a very short personal testimony, the Inspirations did nothing but sing, sing, sing.

Indeed, Atlanta felt that it hadn't been hit with so big a wallop since Sherman passed through!

"We stood in awe that night," Archie said. "We were never frightened, because we handled our singing as a ministry, and the Lord always took care of that. Before we went on, we prayed and sang a few songs in the dressing room, and generally got ourselves ready."

"The boys were never scared, despite the size of the crowd," Martin said about that night. "We had been tense coming down the road and maybe we felt some pressure, but we were never scared. Once we got on and started doing our work, our concentration was such that we didn't have a chance to fear the big crowd.

"Mr. Whitfield had given us twenty minutes to sing, and when we stopped, the crowd kept applauding and cheering, and we had to sing some more. We even left the stage and had to come back on.

"Archie really busted the high notes that night," Martin added. "We sang *He Looked Beyond My Faults and Saw My Need*, and our harmony was perfect."

Whitfield came to Martin and shook his hand when the Inspirations finally got off stage. "If ever a quartet made a splash in one place," he said, "you did it tonight."

Everyone in gospel music learned during the next week that a group of kids called the Inspirations had built a fire in Atlanta.

That reception shoved the Inspirations into the big-time. Whether they wanted it or not, their lives were changed that evening. They had grabbed the golden ring and to this day, thirty-five years later, they haven't turned it loose.

The Inspirations became Atlanta's favorite group. The second time the quartet sang there, fans brought cow bells and whistles and went wild again. Another time, the Inspirations wore bibbed overalls.

"They probably liked us," Archie said, "because we were country boys. Or maybe," he added with a wink, "they felt sorry for us."

Whitfield knew that he had brought a headline group to the gospel stage.

Even General Sherman would have been proud of the way the Inspirations took Atlanta!

# 2

# Martin

M artin Cook was born at the head of the creek, eight and a half miles up Caney Fork in Jackson County, deep in the Balsam Mountains of North Carolina. As most mountaineers were, he was born at home; a midwife, his Aunt Suzie, delivered him. Archie Watkins once said Martin lived in the last house at the end of the longest road, and to sum it up correctly, you could say he lived in the backwoods of Western North Carolina.

He lived where his great-grandpa, Ethan Allen Cook, had lived. Martin's father was John Cook and his mother, Ellen. Both lived on Caney Fork all their lives. One of his uncles, Ben Cook, was a fire and brimstone mountain preacher who brought many a lost soul to the foot of the cross.

Like their preceding generations, the Cooks lived in the midst of nature because they wanted elbow room and the freedom to holler or spit without disturbing the neighbors. Also, hunting and fishing were excellent there, and the Cooks were outdoorsmen of the first class.

Martin's great-grandfather Ethan, along with Ethan's brother Solomon Cook and a number of other backwoodsmen, had crossed the mountains from Haywood County sometime in the 1800s, traversing the divide where tourists now study nature in the beauty of the

Balsams from the Blue Ridge Parkway. They came walking or on horseback with worldly goods loaded in sleds pulled by powerful horses. They pushed into the head of the Caney Fork of the Tuckaseegee River. Coops of chickens rested on the sled loads, and two or three cows were tied to the rear of the sleds. In that faraway time, there were no wagon roads on which to negotiate the mountains.

At some far distant time, the land was crinkled by geologic upheaval, and much of it was pitched on end, ringing the land with tall, rugged mountain peaks. When the Cooks moved into Caney Fork, huge stands of virgin hickory, poplar, pine, oak, and chestnut provided succor for a great population of bear, deer, turkey, and smaller game. Whitewater streams rushed down the mountains, filled with rainbow-striped trout. Truly it was an Eden in which large families lived off the land in comfort.

For many years, their outlet to civilization lay not down the creek in Jackson County, where a good road carries residents out today, but back across the mountains from whence they came to the growing town of Waynesville, a high country horseback journey of nine rough miles.

The land they occupied was rugged and wild. It was a huge mountain range that drained several hundred square miles into the Tuckaseegee River along creeks with colorful names like Rough Butt Creek, Piney Mountain Creek, Sugar Creek, and Beechflat Creek, some of which the Cooks helped name. The mountain peaks thereabout were called by intriguing names: Sugarloaf, Doubletop, Yellowface, Rich Mountain, and Rough Butt Bald.

Ethan Allen Cook was a Civil War veteran who had seen enough of life in and near large towns to know he didn't like it. His dad, Martin's great-great-granddaddy, Hancey Cook, lies buried in the Ochre Hill churchyard cemetery a few miles from Caney Fork, giving the family a long sense of permanency in their neck of the woods.

About the time the Cooks crossed the ridgelines, Martin's mother's people—his grandmother and grandfather, Bill and Mary Wood Watson—also moved to the head of Caney Fork, crossing the mountains as their predecessors had by horseback and sled. They came from Waynesville across Old Bald Mountain and down into their promised land.

The major attraction for both families was that this was primeval forest land in which hunting and fishing were excellent and all manner of outdoor life abounded. A good rifleman could keep his family fed forever on Caney Fork without having to raise a single head of cattle, unless, of course, the kids had a taste for good beef.

Martin was born June 29, 1936, after his family had occupied Caney Fork for four generations. By that time, their remote community was linked with the Jackson County seat of Sylva by a good road running down the creek and northwest along the Tuckaseegee River.

Near the confluence of Caney Fork and the Tuckaseegee was the community of Cullowhee where Western Carolina Teachers College had grown to good size and would play a role in Martin's musical development.

Martin grew up in a strong Christian home infused with the old-time religion that adhered strictly to spiritual and family values. Everyone pitched in to help with chores. They grew or hunted everything they ate. The women canned fruits, vegetables, and hog meat, gathered eggs, and had their sons and daughters extract plenty of milk directly from their cows. Most days, Martin milked the cow before he went to school, even to college. His mother made clothes, except for a few items, for her three children, Martin, Candler, and their sister Arbie. They went to the store only for things they couldn't grow, like sugar, soda, salt, and coffee, and they usually took dozens of eggs to exchange for those staples.

"I had a bicycle with a basket on the front," Martin said, "and I took eggs to the store for Mama and traded for things she needed. It was a good life."

He went to school six years at John's Creek schoolhouse on Caney Fork, and then, still in grammar school, transferred to Camp Laboratory School, a part of WCTC in which teachers were trained. Going to grammar school on the college campus was a lucky stroke for a growing boy who loved music and was already playing the piano. He had taken lessons from an excellent musician, Mrs. Ila Jackson of the nearby Tuckaseigee community, who had studied music in England. Through the seventh and eighth grades he took music lessons twice a week in the front of Hoey Auditorium from Mrs. H.P. Smith, whose husband, Dr. H.P. Smith, whom students called "Horse Power," taught in the college's history department.

Martin had played the piano publicly a few times before he moved to school in Cullowhee. His dad was singing leader in their community and their church, Balsam Grove Baptist. In the evenings, neighbors gathered in the Cook home and sang ballads and hymns to the accompaniment of an old pump organ which Martin's sister, Arbie, played. When Martin was a small child, more often than  not, the last thing he heard before going to sleep was the strains of old hymns from the living room.

When a neighbor died, strict mountain custom prevailed. The body was brought home from the funeral parlor the day before the funeral and lay in state all night. Everybody from the countryside gathered in and sang hymns until midnight or later. And then, one or more people stayed up all night, "sitting up" with the corpse.

"That was the custom," Martin said many years later. "That was the way we did."

Built on land given by Martin's grandfather, the church was down the lane from the Cook home, and anyone who came to visit had to come through the churchyard. Sunday was a holy day—a day of rest and church-going, of restoking body and soul for the week of hard work ahead. After church, people came to the Cook home for dinner about 1:30 in the afternoon. Folks ate breakfast, dinner, and supper then. When all had eaten, they spent a portion of the afternoon singing. Arbie played and sang with her father and two other fellows in a quartet. She also played for the church choir and other community quartets, and for Riley Smith and the Tonemasters of Asheville in concerts with the best quartets in the business.

Most of the songs they sang, especially in the years around the start of World War II, were gospel songs. Many great gospel songs came out of the depression. The Stamps-Baxter Music Company promoted its songbooks heavily in rural areas and new songbooks came out every quarter. "We would gather together," Martin said, "and start at the front of a new book and go through the entire book, singing each song. Everyone turned down the pages of the songs they liked best. Today, Martin has a picture on his piano at home of his father's quartet, singing out of Stamps-Baxter books.

That was how Martin came to love—and really how he got into—gospel music. His was a clear case of osmosis.

Martin finished the grammar grades at Camp Lab School and in 1950 enrolled in high school at Cullowhee High, which was also on the campus of Western Carolina. At the time, probably no mountain school could boast of having a swimming pool, but the students at Cullowhee High had access to the college pool on the lower level of Breeze Gymnasium. "Swimming was a course like algebra or English," Martin said. "We all got to take it if we wanted, and got to take a lot of other special courses offered because of the college."

He was a serious student, eager to learn, so eager, in fact, that he finished a four-year college course and qualified for a teaching degree in two and a half years. He enrolled at Western Carolina in January of 1955 and graduated the summer of 1957. Living at home, Martin was a day student who commuted the few miles to school. He went to college the year round with the exception of one six-weeks' summer school session during which there were no courses offered that he needed.

He did not go straight to college from high school. Graduating in the spring of 1954, he waited until January '55 to enroll in college because he wanted to work for his tuition money.

Coming out of high school he got a job picking apples in the huge Barber's Orchard near Waynesville in Haywood County. Barber's had a snub-nosed, two-ton truck with a canopy over its bed, and an air horn that could be heard all over Caney Fork. It came around about five o'clock every morning and picked up Barber's pickers. The truck took them by Sylva, across Balsam Mountain, and down to the orchard, and then hauled them home again late in the day. Martin grew tired of riding the truck every day, found a room to rent near the orchard, and rode the truck over on Monday morning and home again Friday evening, spending the weekends at home and avoiding the forty-four-mile round trip every day. When apple-picking season ended, Martin and his brother Candler worked in the woods, getting out logs and locust posts. Martin saved his money for the education years ahead.

He did not study music in college, concentrating instead on a degree in mathematics and science. At that time he had no thought of music as a vocation.

He had a taste of playing piano for the public in the seventh or eighth grade. His sister Arbie got a job and moved to Asheville that fall and was unable to play the piano in their church's revival, so Martin filled in, making his first public appearances as a musician in his own church. "There was no one else to play," he said. "It was up to me, so I played and enjoyed it."

Through college Martin took some music courses that broadened his musical knowledge, but he did not take piano lessons.

"My best music study," he said, "was probably engineering physics, where we studied sound wave lengths and frequencies, learning how musical chords and scales are built on certain frequency relationships and how sound waves interact to make beautiful harmonics."

Martin made additional money for tuition, however, by teaching piano to community kids in his home. Between all those jobs—picking apples, logging, and teaching piano—he financed his education.

At Western Carolina, he was an exceptional student whom the college allowed to take as many as twenty-three quarter hours when eighteen made up the normal student load.

Martin's first contact with Bryson City, about thirty miles west of Caney Fork, came in 1950 when he was fourteen years old. A man from Bryson City named Walter Laws drove a Royal Crown Cola truck on a route that included stops in Cullowhee, Tuckaseigee, and on Caney Fork.

Walter was an exceptional talent in gospel singing. Having grown up with gospel as his favorite music, he became an outstanding singer. He had no desire, though, to exploit his talent on the professional gospel circuit, which was then beginning to spread widely across the South, thanks largely to Wally Fowler's All-Night Sings that had begun in 1948. Like many others—Martin included—from the far western part of North Carolina, Walter would drive to Asheville on occasion to hear the big quartets when they came to town, groups like the Rangers Quartet, the Homeland Harmony, the Harmoneers, the LeFevre Trio, the Blackwood Brothers, and the Statesmen, who grew to become almost everyone's favorite singing group.

Martin, too, was already in love with gospel singing, having sung in his country church and in community sings since he could remember. On weekends, he hitched a ride to Bryson City with students who attended Western Carolina. He often sang with Walter Laws in the Smoky Mountain Quartet, enjoying the weekends and grounding himself in the rudiments of quartet singing. On Sunday evening, one of the Bryson City singers drove him home to Caney Fork. Now and then, the Smoky Mountain Quartet came to Caney Fork and sang on Sunday afternoon, and the neighborhood gathered to listen.

Walter Laws was the uncle of Jack Laws and Archie Watkins, who later became original members of the Inspirations.

After graduation from college in 1957, Martin took a teaching job at Crabtree High School, down the Pigeon River in Haywood County. He played on weekends for the Silvertones, a quartet in the Haywood County town of Canton. Ray Dean Reese, who has sung bass with the Kingsmen Quartet for many years now, sang bass for the Silvertones.

In Canton, Martin met a weekend singer, Raymond McKinney, who married a girl named Ruby, a sister to the wife of Martin's first cousin, Ed Cook. Martin helped Raymond paint the house that Raymond and Ruby moved into after their wedding.

Raymond and his brothers, Reece and Lewis, and a friend named Frank Cutshall started a weekend quartet called the Kingsmen Quartet. They asked Martin to play for them, and he became the first pianist for this Asheville quartet that later became the number one quartet in the nation in a poll of gospel singing fans conducted by an industry magazine, the *Singing News*.

"We met and practiced," Martin said, "at Ed Cook's father-in-law's house in Canton, across the road from the Champion Papers plant."

On weekends, especially Sunday afternoons, the Kingsmen sang wherever they could, often at a mobile home park in Georgia. They quickly became so good they sang on the Bob Poole television show in

Greenville, South Carolina, on Channel 4, WFBC-TV. Poole's show was a springboard for a lot of good singers and singing groups.

Military service separated Martin from the Kingsmen. As a physics and chemistry teacher, he was exempt from the draft. The nation was not at war and with no conflict in sight, many teachers were exempt, but never one to shirk responsibilities, Martin thought he should not be an exception, so he joined the army in 1958. He spent two years in the army, including thirteen months in Korea as an artillery surveyor.

With two weeks remaining on his army hitch, Martin came home for a weekend and married Ora Blanche Shuler, "the little girl next door."

"She lived around the hill from us," he said, "and had always been the prettiest little girl I ever saw. She graduated from high school one day and we got married the next day." Their wedding day was June 3, 1960.

After the wedding Martin and Ora Blanche drove to Fort Benning in Columbus, Georgia, and there spent their honeymoon and his last two weeks in service.

Martin's sister, Arbie, is six years older than he, and his brother, Candler, is three years older. When Martin came out of the army in 1960, Arbie was teaching in Buncombe County, and Martin and Candler accepted teaching jobs at Swain County High School in Bryson City. Jerry Rice, a Western Carolina graduate shortly after the end of World War II, was principal of the Swain County school. Before Martin was discharged, Dr. Rice offered him a teaching position, and by return mail Martin accepted the job.

"I had not intended to go back to teaching," he said, "but I didn't know what else to do. I did not have music in mind for a career at that time. Music was just something we did, a part of our lives. It never occurred to me that I should look at it for a career."

Martin and Ora Blanche had $55 between them when they moved to Bryson City. "We didn't have a thing," he confessed. "But we went home on weekends and Mom gave us eggs and Granny Shuler gave us milk, and they loaded us up with so much food that we didn't have to buy many groceries."

While he taught at Swain, Martin went to night school at Western Carolina and earned a Master's Degree, which increased his teaching income and gave him a better chance for promotion in any school system.

He spent summers working as a ranger-naturalist for the National Park Service, a job for which he was eminently suited because of his outdoor upbringing. Assigned to Mammoth Cave National Park in southwestern Kentucky, Martin enjoyed that vast, strange area of enormous caverns and underground rivers.

He loved living in Bryson City, located about seventy miles west of Asheville, and about the same distance from Knoxville, Tennessee, and Atlanta, Georgia. His love, however, was not for proximity to cities but for distance from them. He loved the Great Outdoors, and Bryson City stood on the eastern end of vast Fontana Lake and the southern side of the Great Smoky Mountains National Park.

Martin thought he was in Paradise.

# 3

# Birth of the Inspirations

In the spring of 1964, before Martin went to Mammoth
Cave to work through the summer, he and Jack and
Archie were already singing together. By that time
he realized that if he tried to stay away from music, he
would have found it impossible. He and Walter Laws had
spent so many hours in Martin's basement singing for
pleasure that Martin could feel music stirring deeply in
his soul. Others would often drop by and join in, but if
no one else showed up, just the two would sing.

Fast friends by then, Martin and Walter usually went
downtown and got a hot fudge cake to go. Back home,
they took a couple of R.C. Colas off Walter's truck, and
after they ate, they would begin to sing.

Taking the newest gospel songbook—Stamps-Baxter,
Vaughan Music Company, or Tennessee Music Company—they would start at one end of the book and go
through it, singing every song, turning down the pages
of the ones they liked best, just as the Caney Fork
singers had done when Martin was a pup. Walter was
a top-quality high tenor or lead singer, and Martin sang
what other part they needed for the best harmony.
Martin also played the piano.

"I couldn't sing much," Martin said. "I had to sit to
play the piano, and I never could sing very well sitting
down. I know the parts, knew them then. I knew the sound

of each note and knew how to hit it. I can hit them even today, but I just never sang much. I prefer playing the piano. That way, I can hear each part being sung, and if someone is off a bit, I can get him back on pitch." That knowledge proved important in the development of the Inspirations into a quality professional quartet.

One thing happened at Mammoth Cave that registered on Martin's mind. He attended the Brownsville, Kentucky, Baptist Church one Sunday in the summer of '64. The preacher chose divine inspiration as his subject and before the sermon ended, the idea came to Martin to name the quartet they had started the Inspirations.

At that time, the embryo of the Inspirations began to come together.

Jack Laws' father, Wayne, often came and sang. Like Walter, he was a good singer. One evening, Walter Laws said, "Jack can sing harmony. I think I'll bring him up here." Martin encouraged him to bring Jack. He knew Walter was a fine singer and trusted his judgment. This was before Archie came in March of '64.

Jack had been in one of Martin's classes at Swain County High. The first night he showed up, Martin helped him find his first low "sol." He hit the note right in the middle, and today, thirty-five years later, he sings the low sol as well as anyone in gospel music. Jack first came to Martin's house-singing in early January, 1964, and he liked singing so well he quickly became a regular. He was not a neophyte, having sung in church for several years, with the Bryson City Quartet, and, most helpful of all, with his family, all of whom were accomplished singers and musicians.

Others dropped in just for the fun of singing, but no one had in mind organizing a quartet just yet. Sometimes there were a half-dozen singers taking part in the evening sessions.

Archie Watkins was next to join the group. One afternoon in March of '64 when Archie was a freshman in high school, he went home with Jack to spend the night, and Jack brought him to Martin's house. Walter Laws didn't show up, and no one was on hand to sing high tenor. The only three there that evening were Martin, Jack, and Archie. Archie was fifteen and like Jack, he had sung before, mostly in church and occasionally with the Bryson City Quartet. That quartet was not really organized as far as public appearances went; it was a matter of "let's get together and sing some tonight"—but that's how many good singers learned to sing.

Martin had never heard Archie sing, or try to; Archie was a warm body sitting on the couch, and Martin thought "any port in a storm."

"Archie, why don't you sing with us?" Martin invited. "Hit this," and he began playing the old song, *In The Sweet Forever*. To Martin's surprise, Archie hit the notes and their harmony sounded good that evening.

"He was squeaky," Martin said, "but he was pretty good."

Archie has been singing with Martin since—for thirty-five years now they have not been separated singing.

"He has stuck in there, Archie has," Martin said recently, with pride in his voice.

So the early weeks of 1964 drifted by and the harmony in Martin's basement improved by the day. Others still came to sing. A young man named Jerry Bowers started singing lead, and Martin had only to play the piano. But when their nightly sessions began to stretch to midnight and one a.m., Bowers balked. "I can't do this," he said. He enjoyed singing but he drove a milk truck and had to get up at four o'clock in the morning. He was excused.

And then at school one day, Martin discovered quality in the voice of Ronnie Hutchins, a youngster in his home room. Ronnie was a sophomore in high school. He was fifteen, the same age as Archie.

An English teacher, John Wikle, conducted assembly programs at Swain High. Wikle uncovered so much talent in the student body that he began turning assemblies into variety shows. He found real talent, people who could sing, people who could speak, people who had different talents and could do different things.

One day in assembly, Ronnie Hutchins went on stage and narrated a dramatization of "Little Red Riding Hood," and Martin, seated in the auditorium, suddenly perked up and listened with full attention, watching Ronnie closely.

"I thought, Man!" Martin said, "that boy has talent. He made eye contact, he had all the things it takes to perform on stage, and he had a good, promising voice. He ought to be able to sing!"

When Ronnie came off stage, he walked back and took the seat beside Martin because it was handy and empty.

"Ronnie," Martin said to him, "why don't you come up to the house tonight and sing with us?"

Martin didn't know whether Ronnie had ever sung, even in the shower, but actually, Ronnie was acquainted with music. He had sung in the choir at Arlington Baptist Church.

Ronnie thought a moment and said softly, "What do you mean, sing?"

"We sing of a night at my house," Martin returned. "Come on up there."

Ronnie came that evening, and sure enough, he fit perfectly with the group. He began singing the lead and took to music like a flea to one of Martin's hounds. That was early in the fall of 1964.

A young man from the community, Dean Robinson, not a student, showed up rather regularly and sang bass with Archie, Jack, and Ronnie, and Martin suddenly had a full-fledged quartet on his hands. The four sounded good together. So Martin called the group the Inspirations and they made a few appearances in churches and on John Wikle's variety shows. An early appearance was at the Swain High May Day program in '64, put on by a teacher, Phyllis Claxton. They sang the old cowboy song, "Cool Water," popularized by the Sons of the Pioneers.

A 1964 newspaper clipping, from the *Smoky Mountain Times,* shows Archie, Ronnie, Martin, Jack, and Dean Robinson—Archie and Ronnie in professorial horn-rimmed glasses—who were scheduled to sing in a benefit Jamboree the following night in the school auditorium for the Bryson City Woman's Club and the Junior Women's Club.

"We didn't know that much about singing," Archie said, "but we could tell if we were harmonizing. We just started singing and had the best time in the world. Somebody would say, 'Let's get together again tomorrow night,' and we'd all say, 'Okay.' So we did." They had no notion they were drawing maps of their lives.

"We just kept getting together and singing," Archie said. "A guy like Dean Robinson had more love and desire to sing than anybody. He wanted to sing every night, and he probably had the least talent of all."

One evening early in 1966, Dean didn't show up. Someone complained that they needed a bass singer, and Jack said, "Martin, you remember Troy Burns?" Troy had been to Martin's house a couple of times the year before when he was thirteen, and his voice popped and cracked a lot.

"Yeah, I remember him," Martin said.

"He's almost fourteen now," Jack said, "and his voice has changed and he's going to make a real bass singer. He can bust the low notes right now."

"Well, bring him up here," Martin said, and the following night Troy came along. Jack was right; Troy could sing. Despite his youth, he had a rather strong bass voice. He fit in with the Inspirations like a glove.

"Those are the ones who cut our first record as the Inspirations Quartet," Martin said. "Archie, Ronnie, Jack, and Troy are the ones I call the original Inspirations. That's how we came together, and it took a while to boil the singers down to those four. We sang wherever we could get somebody to listen, and I think that's the way it was with some of those groups who say they've been singing for sixty years. A lot of their early singing was like ours, around the house and down at the church."

# 4

# Coming of Age

When it finally occurred that Martin and the boys had something they couldn't turn loose, they began to get serious. A stickler for detail, and for getting things right—partly because of his teaching background—Martin began helping the kids with what they needed to know. They were dedicated, church-going Christian boys, eager to learn.

At Martin's house in the evenings, after the quartet's personnel had become fixed with Archie, Ronnie, Jack, and Troy, they often worked into the wee hours of the morning. They learned the rudiments of good singing. Martin showed each note on the piano, one by one, and they would work all night on one chorus of one song, learning it correctly. They would get the vowels, the enunciation, and the harmony—the whole bit—just right, and then move on to something else.

"We even wrote down exactly what we wanted the Inspirations to sound like," Martin said. "We didn't want a lot of vibrato, not a bluegrass sound, but some clean, new sound with a message."

That was in the mid-1960s and they thought there was a place for a group to present the gospel in such a manner that people could hear it, understand it, enjoy it, and get from it a good, perhaps life-enriching feeling.

"We were looking for a clean sound," Martin said, "that the guy driving a pickup truck would like. He's not a big music fan, not a hardcore type for any music, but he knows what he enjoys hearing. Give him a good, fast sound that he likes, and he'll turn the radio up. That's what we went for. We developed that sound, and we've had it thirty-five years without changing it."

Martin did not return to Mammoth Cave that summer. The U. S. Park Service transferred him home to work in the Great Smoky Mountains National Park. His primary job was to lecture groups visiting the park to help them understand what they were experiencing and also to help them appreciate it.

"We sang about every night," Archie said, "and sometimes we enjoyed it so much we sang till one o'clock in the morning. We just loved it."

One of the things the Inspirations did early on was work on inverting the harmony of songs, something that any successful quartet today must be able to do. Martin had also done that with the Silvertones and Kingsmen. Most good gospel groups had learned to invert harmony on the last chorus of a song, but the Inspirations went a step further because of Archie's capabilities.

The regular melody would be done by the lead singer all the way through the first verse, and then the quartet would invert the harmony for the remainder of the song. The tenor took over the melody for a final chorus.

"Remember the song *I Wouldn't Take Nothing for my Journey Now*?" Martin asked. "Not the mixed group version with soprano and alto, but the male quartet version with first tenor and lead. When they did that song they'd sing it through and then change and the first tenor would take the melody and do a couple of choruses. All the quartets did it that way. When the Statesmen really drove a song, they inverted the melody that way."

Martin said, "Archie had the ability to sing those B-flats all the way through a song, and he is the only guy I've ever known who had it. The B-flat would be the top note and he could hit it over and over and over. It didn't strain his voice because it was in his range. *On The Sunny Banks* was the first song we put in E-flat, and we did it as an experiment. The song had been around a long time with the second tenor doing the melody, but Archie did it all the way through from the beginning. When he hit those high B-flats, the sound really had a ring to it.

"That's one of the things we've capitalized on," Martin added, "and the fact that Archie could take the melody song after song really helped us. Most tenors could do it on a couple of choruses, maybe twice in a stand, but then they were through. They could do it for three or four years, but few could sing it longer than that. That's because most sing in falsetto, out of their range. Archie, though, could stand up there and sing it all night, night after night, year after year, without hurting his voice—and after thirty-five years he's still doing it. That's because we keep the songs within his voice range. Like *Amazing Grace*, the way it's written, the second tenor sings the melody. I never heard it done any other way, but Archie does it. He and whoever is singing the lead invert the harmony through the entire song."

With an inverted harmony, the Inspirations later helped Squire Parsons put his great song, *Beulahland*, before the public. Squire often went to Bryson City from his home near Asheville for practice sessions, and one day he was scratching around on a shelf at home and a piece of paper on which he had scribbled the words of *Beulahland* fell to the floor. He had written the words sometime before but hadn't gotten around to finishing the song. "Hmmm," Squire mused. "I'll just take this with me." He and Archie began fooling around with it. Archie started doing the melody and everyone liked it. So the Inspirations worked it up, took it to the "Gospel Singing Jubilee," the 1960s-'70s television show that carried gospel music coast to coast, and put it on every program for about two months. *Beulahland* became one of the great songs of the year.

The Inspirations' sound, which is different from that of most male quartets, did not come about accidentally. The quartet went about the development of sound and style methodically, writing down what they wanted their sound to be and then working toward that goal.

From the beginning, because of the way they pitched their songs, they had the makings of the sound they wanted.

The secret of their early triumph in sound lay primarily with Martin. He knew piano, he knew sound, he knew how to sing each part, he coached the others meticulously, and the boys, eager to learn, established the sound.

A big factor was Martin's learning music so well, and teaching piano lessons at home through college made him thoroughly familiar with different keys. Many of gospel's pianists play only in four or five keys. Martin can play in any key and because of his expertise, the quartet was able to pitch songs the way they needed or wanted to pitch them rather than where Martin could play them. If a song needed to be in a certain key and they wanted to sing it a certain way, they could do it that way. He could even play in B, a key that very few gospel pianists play. Often the boys worked out their own arrangements, and Martin gave them the leeway.

*Touring The City* is in B, which is the best place for Archie to sing it. Almost any other pianist would have played it in another key, and the song wouldn't have sounded the same. The Inspirations put it exactly where they thought the song sounded best. The main thing is that the man featured on the melody has the song pitched where he can sing it. There it will sound the best. Before settling on the key of B for *Touring The City*, Martin asked Archie, "Is that where you can do it best?"

Archie replied yes.

"Then you sing it there," Martin said. "Really sing it."

Each member of the quartet learned how to say each vowel and each word, and that has always been a mainstay of the Inspirations. Anyone who listens to an Inspirations' song can understand the words. The Inspirations wanted bell-clear singing, and they perfected it!

Early on, Martin found the voice range of each of the quartet members. Their best range, he discovered, was with Archie's top note an A flat. Ronnie sang the next part down, and it was best for both of them.

When Archie hits an A flat and Ronnie an F, that's a sound that cannot be duplicated on any other notes. They learned to do it that way together. They didn't copy anyone else, they figured it out for themselves. It's a sound that can't be copied by anyone else. They started singing together in the tenth grade. Sometimes when Archie hits an A flat and Ronnie the E flat it produced another sound that has not been duplicated. Those sounds are made by the blend of their particular voices, not by others.

"There's a ring to that sound that does something to you," Martin said. "It's caused because they started out as kids and their voices locked together on those notes. It's hard to duplicate a family sound because they usually start singing as kids working around the house, and they grow into their sound. Archie and Ronnie hadn't sung enough to develop an independent pattern, so they learned to do that together."

Which brought up another point—Jack Laws's harmony.

"Nobody ever sang harmony better than Jack," Martin said. "There may be better singers, singers who would be better in other groups, far better even, but Jack knows exactly how to put that sound together, how much volume, how to say the words—or, possibly, how *not* to say them. I taught Jack, and still tell him, not to say the words too strongly. The main thing we want from Jack is the tone. The other boys are in better position to pronounce the vowel and make it clear.

"Jack will put that tone in there on songs that he doesn't even know the words to," Martin added. "It isn't necessary for him to know the words. All he has to do is make the tone to the sound that the other boys make. That's what harmony is, a blend of voices. Harmony comes naturally to Jack. Maybe he couldn't do it as well in another group, but he mastered the Inspirations' sound a long time ago."

No one in the Inspirations is allowed to sing above, or try to sing below, his natural range. Martin told the boys collectively that he would not allow anyone to sing beyond his range, creating cracking, popping, and especially screeching sounds, and no one wanted to. These singers were perfectionists almost before they got out of diapers.

"It worked very well," Martin said later. "When we inverted the harmony, we went to E-flat, and then later on, when we began to sing *Jesus Is Coming Soon*, we dropped everything a step. We went to A-flat and D-flat. A-flat was the key we sang *Jesus Is Coming Soon* in, and when Ronnie took the melody it was in A-flat, and then we inverted to D-flat. There the 'do' becomes the 'sol' and Archie was singing it.

For example, if Ronnie were doing the first three notes of *Amazing Grace* in the key of A flat, his first three notes would be E flat, F, and A flat (the 5, 6, 8 notes). When Archie does the same beginning of *Amazing Grace*, he starts on the excact same note Ronnie stopped on and goes A flat, B flat, D flat. These are the 6, 7, 8 notes, but in the key of D flat, like the *Beulahland* key and other great songs we have done. Sometimes we raise a song an octave, such as *Hide Me Rock of Ages*. The first verse starts with Matt on G (sol), Jack on mi (E) below Matt, and Archie on middle C above Matt. The last verse starts with Archie taking Matt's G an octave higher, Matt getting Jack's E an octave higher, while Jack is left to get the middle C that Archie left behind.

"Gospel music is usually written for soprano, alto, tenor, and bass parts. The Chuck Wagon Gang, the Speers, and choirs could sing it right off the page since they had the soprano singer.  It is more difficult for a male group to get it right off the page.  There are some general guidelines that help.  First, the melody (soprano on top note on the trebel cleff) is usually dropped an octave and the lead singer sings it.  The first tenor then takes the first harmony note above the lead, and the baritone takes the first harmony note under the lead singer.  A good portion of the time, that is the pattern.

"From the music, first tenor or baritone will do the alto line or bottom note on the treble clef.  When the baritone sings the alto line, he does it an octave low.  The verses of *No Tears in Heaven* are a good example of where the baritone may sing the alto line an octave low.  On the other hand, with first tenor singing the alto line, *Softly and Tenderly* may be sung as it is written in most books, probably in A flat, by just dropping the melody notes an octave for the lead singer.  There are many variations and that's where the work comes in.

"I realize this is very technical, but those who know music will understand, and perhaps it will help some quartet.

"Singing out of range," Martin said, "will ruin a voice. We almost messed Archie up a few years ago. Three of our guys—Eddie Deitz, Troy when he was singing lead, and Archie—would do a couple of numbers a night as the Smoky Mountain Trio and they would move into high harmony about a step above Archie's range. Suddenly Archie began having voice problems, and it wasn't a thing in the world but singing falsetto, singing above his voice. There were times when Archie could sing as high as anybody, but he didn't need to because he sounds better in his range.

"That's one good thing about playing the piano," Martin added. "I'm not in the singing. If I were singing, my mind would play tricks on me and I'd try to make it sound how I want it to sound. But I'm over there, out of it, and I can really tell how it sounds. I can look at the guys' singing and be totally objective. When we learn a new song, we'll pitch it in three different keys, and I'll listen and choose the one that sounds best. And it won't be one with someone singing out of his range. We will not do that!"

Basically, the Inspirations chose, with variations, of course, the sound of the Old Hickory Singers, the Jordanaires, and Wally Fowler and the original Oak Ridge Quartet. They sang the original sounds of gospel music, usually soft and smooth but driving when a song demanded it.

"We and the McKameys and another group or two have been accused of trying to change the sound of gospel music," Martin said, "but that's not so. We've just gone back to what the sound was like in the beginning, and people like it."

Few who sit in the audience realize how much effort and how much work the Inspirations put into developing songs to fit their sound or how much they practice the song. Not any of the perfection they achieve on stage has come by accident.

The newest member of the Inspirations, as of this writing, lead singer Matt Dibler of Easley, South Carolina, who joined the quartet in 1998, discovered how deep the professional musicality of the Inspirations runs.

"There is a lot more to singing with the Inspirations than I thought there would be," he said. "I've always been a big Inspirations fan. I listened to them, I loved to go to their singings, I loved just being around them. Our family used to sing in the kitchen, singing songs the Inspirations sang."

Matt memorized their songs, memorized all three parts but the bass, and he could sing along with an Inspirations' tape and blend in. A Baptist preacher, Matt was pastor of the Open Door Baptist Church in Easley from 1987 till 1999, and when he attended Inspirations' concerts, it was natural that he become friends with Mike Holcomb, the bass singer who is also a Baptist preacher.

"The first time Mike came to sing and preach in our church," Matt said, "my wife told him that I was going to sing with the Inspirations one day. For ten years I had prayed for an opportunity to do just that, and the Lord opened the door.

"I thought it would be nice just to go to Bryson City and sing. That's the way I thought it would be, that I would go up there and just sing. In my mind, they were hillbillies on stage singing, but when you travel and work with them, you suddenly realize that these are very thorough, very professional singers who know exactly what they're doing.

"I didn't realize how technical their singing was. I was used to just standing up and singing, paying no attention to vowels and where I closed a word, and the breathing. I didn't know that was what made their sound, and I didn't know how much work they put into keeping their singing sharp. I hadn't thought much about timing and rhythm. I thought that just happened, but it doesn't, not with a truly professional quartet like the Inspirations. They work at it! They work hard at it! And they work on it all the time."

# 5

# Starting Out

All the preliminaries had been done by early 1965. The quartet had developed a unique sound, harmony, and enunciation, and it was evident from their singing that they had worked tremendously hard. They had been singing around Bryson City, in churches, especially in Victory Baptist Church, the Rev. Tom Harris, pastor, where most of them by then were members, and at social functions and benefits.

Now it was time to hit the road.

There was never a time when Martin addressed the group and said, "Now, fellows, the time has come. You're ready." It was not like training a basketball team or an infantry unit. Neither Martin nor the singers had control of that. It was demand that started them on a trail that led them almost three million miles around America, Canada, Mexico, the Caribbean, and various other places, in the next thirty-five years.

"About every two months," Martin said, "we would sing someplace, and when people got to telling other people about us, we began to get more frequent invitations."

Their first singing on the road was at Goshen Baptist Church in North Wilkesboro in the fall of 1964. The guys loaded into Martin's four-door Dodge and drove close to 150 miles for that church service, and they were well received. Clay Crisp, who had come from the little mountain town of Stecoah, farther west than Bryson City, had heard the Inspirations and liked them so well, he invited them to his church.

Dean Robinson was still singing bass when they went to North Wilkesboro that first time.

They were so well received that they were invited to sing in other churches around North Wilkesboro and before long they were making that trip once a month and sometimes every two weeks.

One weekend they got Ray Dean Reese to go with them and sing bass. Ray Dean has now been singing bass for the Kingsmen Quartet of Asheville for many years. But at that time he told the Inspirations he couldn't sing with them any more. He had a good job with a coffee company. It wasn't a big decision for him because the Inspirations weren't doing anything big. They hadn't made a record, and they were still singing for fun.

That was when they got Troy Burns to sing bass, and only a few days after that when they made their first record, called *Our Pioneer Heritage*, at Mark V in Greenville, South Carolina.

They cut the record on a Saturday and late that afternoon drove to Georgia and sang at Poplar Grove Baptist Church in the Royston area that night. They sang at Bethlehem Baptist Church in Dahlonega on Sunday morning, and later that day at Wahoo Baptist Church in the same area.

"I tell you," Martin said, "we enjoyed it. The people responded to our quartet of 'little boys.' Troy was fourteen; Archie and Ronnie seventeen, and Jack was twenty-one."

A weekend or so later, they sang at Poplar Springs Baptist Church in the Dahlonega area.

"Yes, we got paid," Martin said. "Sometimes we'd get fifteen dollars and sometimes twenty. The first thing we'd do after singing was go to Shoney's and eat, and generally we got enough money to eat on."

No one worried or even thought about money at that point. They just wanted to sing.

Word spread. Other Georgia churches invited them to sing, and before long they were singing in churches in Atlanta.

The boys had to work at odd jobs to buy their first sport coats. They always dressed nicely to sing, wearing jackets and ties. They were so young and so pure in their singing that the public began to clamor for more. They ran the wheels off Martin's Dodge and replaced it with a '64 Buick, which saw such use that its engine boiled over and melted down coming up Black Mountain east of Asheville. Their next vehicle was a van, a Chevrolet Greenbriar, which, although small, gave them more room than an automobile.

They sang every weekend and sometimes through the week, if not on the road, then around Bryson City. When they walked down the streets of Bryson City, people knew them, and all would speak with mountain hospitality in their voices. Folks in Bryson City began to love their little Inspirations.

The guys were still going to school, still involved in everything around home, still with their parents. Mom and Dad were still the bosses.

About all they did, except for weekend appearances was practice at night and make records. But all this time they were working hard and improving.

"Other groups would try to make fun of us," Archie said. "They called us a military unit. Martin was the drill sergeant and we were his little soldiers, but it wasn't like that at all. When we started singing, we were so strict among ourselves because we didn't want anything to blemish our reputations, that we must have appeared military to other groups.

"But, I'll tell you this," Archie added, "We just wouldn't allow anything that might detract from our seriousness. If a girl wanted to carry on an extended conversation with one of us, we were protective of each other. We just wouldn't let that happen. We would either call him over to help us, or a couple of us would go to him and get him away with some excuse that the girl wouldn't take offense to."

One of the things the Inspirations didn't worry about in those early days was money. When they began to get a lot of invitations to sing in churches, they were approached several times by well-meaning people who wanted to support them financially.

"If you will set up a tax-free religious tax shelter, we'll support you regularly," they were told.

"They wanted to give us money," Archie said, "and deduct it off their taxes. But we felt that ours was a business, not a church, and we never did that. I believe that has been a vital part of our success. I believe the Lord blessed us for that. We could have got around paying a lot of taxes, but we didn't, and today our consciences are clear. I've thought about that a lot of times. We felt that dodging taxes, regardless of how legally we did it, wouldn't be representing what we really were and what we were about."

Martin taught physics and chemistry at Swain County High for six years until 1966, and the boys attended classes every day. But every night they sang, if not in public then in Martin's basement. He lived on a hill above the schoolhouse.

In 1966 Martin accepted a teaching position at Camp Lab School on the Western Carolina College campus and for three years taught chemistry and physics, and in the summer tested for Dr. C.D. Killian's gifted student program.

Singing became a priority with the Inspirations, evident by two things that happened. First, they left their high school prom one evening, piled in the van, and drove to Mountain City, Georgia, to sing.

The second thing had to do with Archie's athletic ability. He had all the makings of an outstanding athlete at Swain High. But when singing and sports began to rub, Archie's mind may have been troubled, feeling a tug in both directions, but it wasn't troubled for long.

"I loved to play sports," he said, "but I wanted to sing more than I wanted to play football. Football was in the summer and fall when we could sing the most, so I quit playing football in my sophomore year."

He continued to play basketball. It was a winter sport when there was little singing to do except practice, and he was finished with basketball practice before singing time in the evenings. In his junior year, Archie had to miss a couple of basketball practices because of singing, and his coach, Swede Frauson, a former all-state star at Western Carolina College, gave him an ultimatum, saying, "Archie, you've come to the point where you've got to decide whether you want to sing or play ball."

"Okay, coach," Archie responded quickly. "I'm going to sing." The answer came automatically, without thought or study. Frauson today laughs about the incident and says he thinks Archie made the right choice.

Swede left Swain High after that year, and a new coach, Reggie High, replaced him. Carroll Wright, the football coach, told the new coach that Archie was a point guard and that he needed to get him to play, but when the basketball coach approached Archie and asked him to come back on the team, Archie said, "I can't, coach. I'm singing, and singing's first."

"If you play," the coach said, "and you have to miss some time, it will never be mentioned. We can work this out. If you need to miss, you just miss."

Archie missed two games that season, and nothing was said. Swain had a good season, winning more than half of their games in the tough Smoky Mountain Conference. Archie was co-captain of the team.

"We beat Franklin 52-51," Archie said, "and I shot two free throws at the buzzer and won the game. I scored twenty-six points that night, exactly half of our points. I'll never forget that. It was the biggest thing I did in sports."

He played so well that season that he was voted to the all-conference team.

Without missing a beat, though, he had continued to sing.

Archie also drove a school bus, and occasionally singing conflicted with that. His supervisor, Vaughan Davis, told him one morning, "Archie, you're going to waste your time with singing till you won't amount to anything." But Archie insisted on singing and they, too, worked out a compromise. Archie continued to drive the bus through high school, and in the summers he worked with the poverty program in Swain County.

In later years, Davis often mentioned that conversation to Archie, who got a kick out of it. Davis would laugh and tell others how he wanted Archie to quit singing so he could drive a school bus.

Although they were just singing, with no real thought of turning professional, the quartet loved singing so much they thought they would never stop. One day in the fall of 1964 they made a commitment to themselves and to God that they would sing together for twenty-five years They said they would sing however, wherever, and whenever they were asked.

"I did realize then," Martin said, "that there was a place for us, and that we were good enough to fill it. I've been a gospel singing fan since I could sit up all night listening to the Grand Ole Opry, hoping that Wally Fowler and the Oak Ridge Quartet would sing one song on there, or the Foggy River Boys, or somebody, anybody. I loved the music, and I knew that the Inspirations had what it takes to make it.

"I had seen groups I loved fall by the wayside. They changed the kind of singing, of presentation, that the audiences really loved and started doing something else."

Before he was married, when Martin attended concerts in Asheville, singing was something he and a lot of others lived for. They would go to Asheville and see Dad and Mom Speer, and the Statesmen and Blackwood Brothers.

"Man, that was as high as you could get," Martin exclaimed. "I hadn't been to a concert in three or four years when I came back from Korea at the end of my stay in the army. One Saturday night they were having a sing in Asheville and I told Ora we had to go, that she would enjoy it so much.

"Well, I've never been so disappointed. I realized later that that evening was a revelation to me. Because I had been away from it for so long, I saw how much gospel singing had changed, and I don't think many groups realized it. It was unbelievable how much time the quartets spent selling songbooks and records. I don't mean just selling them, I mean talking about them on stage. They would sing a song and spend three or four minutes talking about songbooks and records.

"Ora and I spent four hours there, and when we left we had heard about an hour and a half of singing altogether, if that much. I couldn't believe how much singing had changed in three or four years. Real gospel music was where you'd go out and sing and people would get happy and shout. They would enjoy themselves, get emotional, clap their hands, and some would shout up and down the aisles. Back then you had to get there early to get in the building.

"Dad Speer was a major factor in that. He put force into gospel music, and when he dropped out, it changed. With his presence and presentation, you couldn't do much of anything else but listen, enjoy yourself, and if you got happy enough, shout in the aisles. When the Speers came on stage and sang *Won't We be Happy in Heaven*, the quartets didn't do much else that night—they couldn't top that. You had to be a clear idiot if you tried anything else.

"I had been going to the Asheville sings for many years. I was there from the time Betty Johnson sang in the late 1940s, and that's where I first heard Gordon Stoker and the Jordanaires. How they sang! How they sang!

"But when we left the singing that night, I explained to my wife all the way home that what she saw really wasn't the way it was, that it was different than what gospel singing was the last time I went. I saw how commercialization was destroying gospel singing, each quartet outdoing the other, one selling three records for five, the next selling four for five, and the third selling so many for ten. I saw it destroy the best music America has ever known."

That is why the Inspirations never sell from stage. They never do commercials, and no one else sells from stage in the concerts promoted by the Inspirations. "We don't mind their telling they've got a new album, or a new book," Martin said, "but they can't make a sales pitch on stage."

Most of the Inspirations, other than Martin, had never heard a professional gospel group sing until after they began to practice. They began driving to Asheville to the gospel sings in City Auditorium and there heard the best professional quartets in the country. The Asheville promotions were joint ventures of J.G. Whitfield and the Kingsmen Quartet. Their promotions usually featured the Kingsmen, Florida Boys, the Dixie Echoes, the Thrasher Brothers, the Singing Rambos, and some others who were regulars on Whitfield's promotions around the South. Now and then, the Blackwood Brothers and the Statesmen were booked and always filled the auditorium.

"The first time I heard the Blackwood Brothers," Archie said, "J.D. Sumner was already gone and was running the Stamps Quartet, and when I first heard the Statesmen, Jake Hess was gone."

Although they were just kids in school, the Inspirations began to take note of things at concerts they didn't think represented gospel music very well. They had already decided they were going to minister with their singing.

After each concert in Asheville or elsewhere, they went back home and hashed out what they had observed.

"Let's talk over what we liked and what we didn't," someone said, and they would dissect the concert.

Archie said, "Boys, I saw one of those singers stand and talk to a lady a long time, and I don't think that looked good."

Someone wrote that point down.

"I don't like their long hair," Jack said. "It didn't look good. And some weren't dressed neat and conservative."

Those points were also written down.

Troy said, "Well, I didn't like the drums."

"I didn't, either," Archie said.

"They were loud," Jack said, "and I heard a lot of people say they were so loud they couldn't hear the singers."

They put that point on paper.

From time to time, after attending singings elsewhere, the Inspirations added to their list. They didn't enumerate things they liked because they had already outlined what they wanted to look and sound like, and, besides, they weren't looking for pluses; they were studying minuses.

Archie bought a one dollar record at a singing and when he returned to his seat and looked it over, it had everything on it except what the quartet had represented.

"I took it back," Archie said, "and got my dollar back."

After that singing, the Inspirations added to their list that they would not make cheap albums.

Rex Nelon was friendly with the kid singers, talked with them at a concert about singing, and spent considerable time with them.

At their post-singing session, Archie said, "Did you notice how friendly Rex Nelon was to us? We're going to be friendly with the people who come to hear us sing. Write that down."

They worked out things to do and things to avoid in a democratic way.

"Let's just make these our by-laws," Martin suggested. "They'll be rules we'll live by."

The others hashed it out and agreed.

"Anything within reason that anybody in the quartet wants," Archie said, "we'll do. Whatever anybody objects to, we won't. And if the things are reasonable and we think they're for the good of the group, we'll make them our by-laws.

"We said if a man wants to fool with a woman or drink alcohol, there won't be any questions asked. He'll just walk away from the quartet."

They wrote nothing about money into that rule.

Frank Cutshall had left the Kingsmen not long before the Inspirations had promoted a singing with the Kingsmen in Bryson City. One of the Kingsmen mentioned Frank's leaving and said, 'Boy, that was a hard thing to do, buy Frank out'."

"We really didn't think there was anything in our quartet to buy out," Archie said. "So we said we would take care of that. At that time we wrote down that anybody who leaves because he gets in trouble, will leave without compensation. He'll just walk off and leave the quartet hands down, because we're not going to hock everything we have to buy him out. He'll leave and we'll get somebody else to sing."

This rule was later amended, after the Inspirations accumulated a wealth of recordings and paraphernalia like a bus and other things a working quartet needed.

Archie added, "I want to emphasize that Frank Cutshall was not in trouble. He left because he didn't want to sing, or wasn't able to sing, or something like that."

The Inspirations added that rule to their by-laws, and when they became more interested in becoming a professional quartet, they incorporated in the early 1970s and adopted their rules into the incorporation papers.

Here, verbatim, were their rules:

BY-LAWS OF INSPIRATIONS INCORPORATED

In the following paragraphs you will find set forth the purpose and operational procedures of the Inspirations Incorporated.

The Inspirations are grounded and were founded in the heart of God's Word and Will. A known fact exists, that God would have the human race salvaged and inspired by His Grace and Spirit. But how can the world hear and know this Grace and Spirit unless there be a messenger of the Word? Upon this basis, The Inspirations were organized that they might be an inspiration to people throughout the world.

In order to be pleasing to God and influential to society, the Inspirations have set the following by-laws by which all who sing must abide:

(1) Each person should be saved and living for God.

(2) Each member must be, when before the public, clean shaven, freshly bathed, moderately dressed, and above all must always maintain a neat appearance in his hair style.

(3) When in public each person should live a life worthy of being called a Christian. He must have a clean mouth, no vulgarity nor profanity practiced habitually, a clean mind, and a clean heart filled with love and compassion for lost humanity.

SOME MAY NOT ABIDE BY THESE LAWS. IF NOT, LISTED IS THE DISMISSAL PROCEDURE OF THE INSPIRATIONS.

(1) The president of the corporation will have the authority to dismiss any member of Inspirations Incorporated on any of the following charges:

(a) Adultery or being overly friendly to any woman at a public place, this including your wife.

(b) The selling or use of any type of alcoholic beverages.

(c) The pushing or use of any type of narcotics.

(d) Use of tobacco while in a public place, a building where the Inspirations will sing, or while on a quartet-owned vehicle, and thereby influencing and disappointing Inspirations followers.

(e) Repeated use of vile language.

(f) Embezzlement of quartet funds.

(g) Repeating classified quartet business outside the corporation meetings.

(2) INSUBORDINATION

  (a) The refusal to obey a direct order from the president can result in dismissal.

  (b) The failure to make an appointment without a proven reason.

  (c) Leading in agitation in order to cause friction within or to attempt to undermine the group.

(3)  INEFFICIENCY

If someone does not do his job, then by a vote of the corporation he can be dismissed from the corporation.

HOWEVER, if a person wants to sing and make this a career, he can work in the Inspirations and always have a comfortable living and a secure future.

Signed:
        Martin A. Cook
        Archie Thomas Watkins
        Troy L. Burns
        Eddie T. Deitz
        Jack Laws
        Mike Holcomb

Witness my hand and Notarial Seal, this the 12th day of September, 1973.
        Pat Fortner
        Notary Public.

The other guys saw Troy spit-shining his shoes one evening before a concert, and someone said, "Boy, that looks good," and the entire quartet began spit-shining shoes before engagements.

"Everybody's gonna wear spit-shined shoes," one of the singers said, "because they really make us stand out. They're sharp."

Invariably, someone from another quartet would say, "There are those military boys." Spit-shining shoes was widely adopted in the military.

"That was fine," Archie said. "We didn't mind. It showed others that we had discipline, and that's what we all wanted. We surely were gung-ho in those days. . . ."

From their earliest days, the Inspirations have promoted gospel music concerts. When they had just begun to sing, they promoted sings in the Swain County High School auditorium, and after thirty-five years, Martin vividly recalls an incident that occurred at one of those sings.

The Chuck Wagon Gang of Fort Worth, Texas, were special guests on one of the Inspirations' promotions in 1965 or '66. A furniture factory in Bryson City, wanting to help the Inspirations make good, agreed to buy singing tickets for all of its employees and purchased hundreds of tickets. "That way," the factory manager said, "you can't lose."

The building was filled to hear the Chuck Wagon Gang, and Martin and Roy Carter, who managed the Gang, had agreed on a percentage split.

After the singing, Martin and Archie went backstage with Roy and Howard Gordon and counted the money. Martin gave Roy the percentage they had agreed on, and was counting out the Inspirations' money, when Roy, who had never seen Martin or the Inspirations before that night, suddenly put several hundred dollars back on the table. "Martin," he said, "you boys will need that, so you keep it. That's too much money for us for a Thursday night."

Martin was shocked, and many years later he said, "I had never had that happen before, and I have never had it happen since." And Archie added, "I've been a fan of the Chuck Wagon Gang since."

Another fellow, a promoter, has been unusual in his booking of the Inspirations all these years. Richard Carper of Lancaster, Pennsylvania, president of Garden

Spot Promotions, Inc., has continually raised the amount of money he pays the Inspirations for singing on his promotions.

"We have worked for him for twenty-five years longer, and he has regularly given us raises."

Once Martin telephoned James Blackwood at his home in Memphis, and said, "James, we've recorded an old convention song that you own. How do you want us to pay your royalties on it?"

James mused a moment and said, "The fellow who wrote that song has never gotten any money out of it, Martin; just send whatever royalties there are to him." The grateful writer was Roscoe Reed and the song was *Far Better Than This.*

The Inspirations continued to promote concerts to make traveling money. Singing in churches for free will offerings was no way to make ends meet, and the concert promotions earned the quartet enough to meet expenses on the road.

# 6

# Ralph Sexton

In the summer of 1967, Ralph Sexton, Sr., of Asheville, one of the sages of evangelism, pitched a huge gospel tent on an abandoned airport near Beta in Jackson County, about three miles east of Sylva.

He launched a tent revival that turned out to be one of the most unusual meetings he had ever conducted. Night after night, he preached the gospel to crowds that never filled the tent.

"It was hard," Ralph said many years later. "When I say the word hard, I mean the meeting was slow getting started. It was as if we were battling something we couldn't see. We preached as hard as we could, and passed the offering plate each night, and we prayed constantly, but things got tougher and tougher. We were about to fall behind in expenses. There are many expenses involved in moving to a town and putting up a tent. We were almost to the point of not knowing whether we could continue."

And then, one evening, Ralph saw a little white Chevrolet Greenbriar van roll up and park, and a man and several boys got out and came into the tent. They said they were the Inspirations Quartet of Bryson City, and they had come to help us with the meeting. "It was a wonderful gesture on their part," Ralph said. "We needed help; we really did."

The Inspirations took the platform and began to sing, and the crowd perked up. So did Ralph Sexton. "They seemed to put life into that meeting," he said, and he thought maybe this was what they needed to turn that revival around.

For several evenings the Inspirations came and sang and things began to happen. "The people who loved God realized that we were in rather difficult circumstances," Ralph said, "but God is sovereign, so he sent us help."

Several of the quartet members attended Victory Baptist Church in Bryson City. The church was saving money to buy new pews, but the membership agreed to give $500 of the pew money to the tent revival and the pastor, Tom Harris, brought the check to the meeting.

"You've heard of a shot in the arm?" Ralph said. "Well, that was a shot in the spiritual arm. God used it. And then the Inspirations, in their singing, really helped to get that meeting going."

A late Sunday afternoon service at that revival remains in Sexton's mind. It was a beautiful, sunlit summer day, and a good-sized crowd filled most of the tent for the three o'clock service. Jess Oakley, an evangelist from Kentucky, was with Ralph that day, and when the service began everything seemed to go well.

Ralph was basking in the light of the Lord, thinking how could anything get better than this? "Then the Inspirations got up and Archie began to sing *Little is Much if God is in It*, and I want you to know, praise God, heaven moved in. God in his mercy came and showered that meeting with his presence. The revival opened up and it was wonderful. I don't believe I have ever heard anyone sing *Little is Much* like Archie sang it that evening."

When the revival at Sylva ended, Ralph took his tent on to Bryson City and pitched it there. The Inspirations supported that meeting, and it, too, was successful.

"I appreciate Brother Martin Cook and the Inspirations," Ralph said. "God has used him to help those young men. He has required that those boys live clean, holy lives, and I think that's one reason God has blessed the Inspirations so. They didn't compromise. When the long hair and all of that compromise came along and some of the quartets went to contemporary and rock beat, almost like putting on a show, Martin and the Inspirations steered away from that. They still looked like gentlemen, clean on the outside, clean on the inside, and I know that's one reason God has made the Inspirations such a success. They are highly revered across the land."

Ralph and the Inspirations became close friends and have remained so for thirty-five years. They have sung in Ralph's tent meetings, in his church, and anywhere he asked them to sing. One of those tent meetings, all because of a puff of wind and a clap of thunder, became a hilarious melee one June evening in 1970.

Dr. Sexton had pitched his tent on the school ground in Leicester, a few miles northwest of Asheville. Meeting time was seven o'clock. The Inspirations had come to sing at the meeting that evening. The night was hot and Ralph and his brother Leroy had rolled up the sides of the tent, but the tent was packed with people sitting close together, and from the front you could look over the crowd and see dozens of fans waving back and forth.

Dr. Sexton's sermon was going to be on the gates of Jerusalem, in which he would introduce a gate and talk about it, and the Inspirations would sing a song about that gate.

After the Inspirations sang their preliminary song, Brother Sexton stood to the pulpit and began to preach. The harsh light of a raw bulb lent deep shadows to his face, but the Word came strong from his heart.

Near the beginning of the sermon, a small wind rose in the north. Far back in Madison County it gathered force, flowed across Spring Creek, and came down Sandy Mush with a gentle rush. Finally, the breeze reached inside Ralph Sexton's tent and gave the canvas a tug.

Suddenly Ralph hushed. He watched the canvas ripple for a moment, felt the wind cool on his face, and then it was gone and all was still again. Ralph stood silent for a moment, carried back across twenty-five years to a spot near Hammond, Indiana, on the shores of Lake Michigan. He began to tell the crowd at Leicester the story of one eventful day in that Hammond revival.

The meeting was going well. One afternoon Ralph walked down to the tent on the shore of the lake and found his brother, Leroy, gazing out over the waters.

"Brother Ralph," Leroy said, breaking his reverie, "we're gonna lose the tent tonight."

"What?"

"She's gonna blow away."

Ralph looked at the sky and there wasn't a cloud in sight. Not a breeze stirred, not a ripple on the water.

"How do you know that, Brother Leroy?"

"I don't know how I know it. All I know is she's going tonight."

All afternoon Ralph watched the weather, which gave no indication of a blow. The air was still, the sky serene, as if touched by God's own hand.

It can't be, Ralph thought; Leroy is wrong.

That night the tent was filled to capacity. Leroy sat very still, casting furtive glances across the lake, his ears tuned for any sound beyond the usual.

Just as Ralph began his sermon, a hard wind came off the lake with a blast, and the canvas began to shake. He looked for Leroy who had taken up a song book and had begun to sing the old hymn, *Is Not This The Land of Beulah?*

The wind grew stronger, flowing off the lake with a steady roar. The whole tent began to rock. Ralph looked up at the center pole and saw the canvas split. "Lord help us," Ralph shouted. "Brother Leroy was right."

In the back of the tent a preacher leaped to his feet. "Have faith in God!" he shouted.

"That's right, brother," Ralph shouted into the microphone. "Have faith in God, but when God says it's more expedient to run than sit still—RUN!"

The crowd bolted out the sides of the tent and headed for a nearby church. Leroy backed up to the canvas at the rear of the tent, stretching his hands as if trying to hold up the tent, still singing. The blow hit just at Leroy's back and knocked him twenty feet down the aisle, heels over head.

Then the tent came down.

Ralph was outside, peering anxiously toward the place where he last saw Leroy, and just before the canvas hit bottom, Leroy came crawling out. The brothers then made it to the church from where they looked back in time to see their tent shredded by the wind.

Ralph told his congregation at Leicester that night: "Not a soul was hurt. The Lord was with us."

A few minutes later, Brother Sexton learned how strong is the power of suggestion. He went on with his sermon in the tent in Leicester, and as he neared the end, a hard clap of thunder came from back toward Sandy Mush, a great streak of lightning rent the sky, and a puff of wind flapped the canvas for a few seconds. A hundred people in the crowd rose as one and bolted through the rolled-up sides of the tent, straight into the parking lot, and Ralph and the Inspirations looked with startled expressions as dozens of car engines came alive and automobiles fled the parking lot, headed away from the tent, full speed ahead.

After the service ended and the remainder of the crowd dispersed, Martin Cook strode up to Dr. Sexton and, with a twinkle in his eye, said, "Preacher, I'll bet that's the last time you'll tell that story at a tent meeting."

"If you took a survey today," Ralph Sexton said, "of the top five quartets in America, the Inspirations would be there. They have lived clean, separated lives. I have had them in my church, in my tent, on television with me, and people love to hear them. People still feel their anointing, and when I'm with them I feel it, too.

"Thirty-five years is a long time to sing," he concluded.

"Thirty-five in the Bible is the number of hope and joy. Down through the years, God has used the Inspirations to bring hope and joy to his Church and to his people.

"I must say there is no doubt in my mind that God raised up these young boys to sing his praises. I also believe that God gave them their name—the Inspirations—because they have been an inspiration to so many."

Martin Cook calls that tent revival near Sylva "one of the best things that ever happened to the Inspirations."

"We sang in about every service from the time we showed up till the end of the revival."

Sexton became one of the real supporters of those early Inspirations.

"After that Sylva revival," Martin said, "Brother Ralph would have us as guests on his television show (a 30-minute Sunday morning service on WLOS-TV, Channel 13, in Asheville) and that was a big, big boost at the time we really needed a boost. Oftentimes, he would just let us have the thirty minutes for ourselves. He wouldn't even be there. We would do the show live, and I would do his mail pitch and everything. Not only was that good exposure, it was good experience for us."

Another evangelist who helped spread the Inspirations' fame in those early days was Maze Jackson. "Maze had a radio program all over the country, and in it he had a special program for truck drivers. We were the only quartet he ever had on his program. Maze and Ralph Sexton both offered our videos for sale on their programs. We sold the videos to them at cost."

Both of those evangelists, as others came to do in future years, recognized the spirituality and sincerity, not to speak of the talent, of the Inspirations from the start.

# 7

# Things Happen Quickly

The Inspirations suddenly found their world exploding around them—all of it for good.

From the vantage of thirty-five years of singing, when Archie takes a retrospective look at the early days of the quartet, he points a finger at two reasons for the Inspirations' meteoric rise in gospel music.

First, the Spirit was there, and secondly, harmony was present.

Others would point to a third reason, the youth of the quartet, which made the group unusual. Here were four high school boys and their teacher who could really sing and who were serious about the solid Christian impression they made on audiences.

"Harmony and the Spirit had to come simultaneously before either would work," Archie said. "The harmony can be good and people will enjoy it, but it's not nearly as good if the Spirit's not there. The Spirit is something we feel on stage, and also something the people feel out there in the seats.

"We've seen it happen time and time again," he added. "After we sang a few songs, things would get very quiet, and all of a sudden it would erupt. People would start clapping and hollering. In Atlanta they rang cowbells. Not the first time we were there because many at that first singing didn't know who we were. But when we'd go back, there were times when they would ring cowbells and blow whistles and shout and holler, demanding that we sing more of each song.

"We didn't know what we were doing—what we were creating—and we didn't know where we were going. We had no idea. But we soon knew that wherever it was, the crowd would go with us."

Keeping harmony and the Spirit in mind, three other things propelled the Inspirations to stardom, giving them a huge push after the Atlanta singing and establishing them in the big-time. One was the song, *Jesus Is Coming Soon;* another was the Gospel Singing Jubilee, a syndicated coast-to-coast television show started by and featuring Les Beasley and the Florida Boys; and the third was a seven-minute feature on the Inspirations on the CBS Weekend News in 1970.

The song came first. Actually, *Jesus Is Coming Soon* was in the songbooks a long time before someone discovered how good a song it really was.

"Most good songs," Martin said, "are written on real-life experiences. People experience things and songs come out of those experiences."

R. E. Winsett wrote *Jesus Is Coming Soon* during World War II when times were dark and young men were being killed on firing lines around the world.

"The song was about the nation's condition during the war," Martin said, "and it had come from Mr. Winsett's heart. He read of all the mayhem and killing around the world and apparently thought that peace would not reign again until Jesus came back to earth."

Winsett must have been disappointed when his song didn't hit. It was published in one of the gospel songbooks and a few quartets may have sung it, but it never really got off the ground.

"Timing of a song is important," Martin said, "and to be most effective, a song must be sung during its time."

This one, however, was an exception to the rule. It lay virtually unnoticed for a quarter of a century, and

Winsett died without realizing that he had written a smash hit. But when it was introduced to the Inspirations, the song was appropriate for the day, because the nation was troubled with the burgeoning threat of war in Vietnam.

It could be said, if one wished to be technical, that the Inspirations rode that one song into the big-time. On the other hand, it could be noted that the Inspirations were basically responsible for turning that song into the top gospel song of the year—and into one of the best gospel songs ever.

"It was the best song we ever had," Archie said.

Eva Mae LeFevre said it was the Song of the Century. Others agreed. Others still agree. The Inspirations had to work on the song before they sang it, though. It had always been done the way Winsett wrote it, with the lead doing a straight melody, but the Inspirations turned it over and inverted the harmony so that Archie sang the melody.

The Inspirations recorded the song in 1968 and it swept the country, winning the 1969 Dove Award as the best gospel song of the year. The Inspirations put it on record several months before any other group recorded it. When they saw the extreme popularity of the song, almost every gospel group began singing it, and most used the Inspirations' arrangement.

The George Shelton Family gave the song to the Inspirations before it really became popular. The Inspirations and the Sheltons were close friends and once when the Sheltons stopped off in Bryson City on their way to Nashville to cut a record, the two quartets got together at Martin's house. George Shelton said they wanted the Inspirations to hear the songs they were going to record. That was in the days when quartets put twelve songs on each recording, and the Sheltons had twelve or fourteen songs ready to record, with a couple more in reserve.

When they finished singing the songs they intended to record, George Shelton said, "We've got another song we can sing if we need to. It's called *Jesus Is Coming Soon.*"

"Let's hear it," Martin said.

The Sheltons sang it, and Jack Laws flipped. He thought it was the best song he'd ever heard.

"We gotta record that!" Jack exclaimed. "We just got to!"

Martin asked the Sheltons what they thought about letting the Inspirations record it, and George replied, "We don't care. We probably won't put it on our record anyway."

The song fit the Inspirations' style and sound to a "T."

As soon as the Inspirations put *Jesus Is Coming Soon* on the Gospel Singing Jubilee, it really hit. All the major quartets recorded it, and disc jockeys around the country gave it a huge amount of air time.

The song hit WACT in Gordo, Alabama, like an atomic bomb, just as hard as the Inspirations had hit Atlanta a couple of years before. Jack Ham was the guy who played it on WACT, and the switchboard lit up like a Christmas tree when he put the song on the air. Calls came in from Gordo and surrounding towns, including Tuscaloosa, twenty-five miles away.

In Atlanta—actually in Decatur, Georgia—Wes Gilmer's Suppertime Show on WGUN, called "Big Gun," was a program that most folks listened to late in the afternoon. The station reached all the way into North Carolina, at least to Bryson City. It covered most of Georgia, and parts of Alabama, South Carolina, and North Carolina, and possibly the Tennessee area around Chattanooga.

"Wes pushed *Jesus Is Coming Soon* and he pushed the Inspirations," Martin said, "just like we were his own kids. He was the backbone of J.G. Whitfield's all-night sings in Atlanta, and with his great voice, did all of Whit's emceeing."

With air time like that all around the gospel singing world, the song couldn't have missed the charts.

The Gospel Singing Jubilee was carried on television stations in every section of the United States and in most parts of Canada. It was a full hour of top-quality gospel singing featuring the Florida Boys, Dixie Echoes, and Happy Goodman Family.

Les Beasley had been watching the Inspirations' progress, and after appearing on one of the Inspirations' promotions in Bryson City, he invited the youthful quartet to sing on the Jubilee.

They accepted and sang *Jesus Is Coming Soon* on the Jubilee, which brought in a bag of mail from all around the country, written by people who enjoyed hearing the Inspirations and begged for them to return to the show.

"The show was taped in Nashville on Monday, Tuesday, and Wednesday," Archie said. "We enjoyed doing the Jubilee so much that we told Les to call us anytime day or night, if a group could not make the taping. We would be glad to come on a moment's notice and do the show as a substitute for any group that couldn't fulfill its booking. We told him we didn't care when he called, even in the middle of the night, and we would be in Nashville by noon the following day."

Les didn't have to call. Knowing a winner when he saw one, he booked the Inspirations often on the Jubilee until they became regulars on the show. They sang as regular members of the cast for a dozen years

The Jubilee was taped at Channel 2 in Nashville, and gave the Inspirations excellent exposure all over the country. The program was telecast into four million homes from Philadelphia to Seattle, covering every television market in the United States. It ran for a full hour and was usually shown on Sunday mornings.

"The Jubilee was probably the biggest thing we ever did," Martin said. "Les Beasley certainly helped put us on the map by including us on the Gospel Singing Jubilee, and we delivered the goods. We had something he needed. We had *Jesus Is Coming Soon* and we were a little different from other quartets.

"Archie received more mail and more response from that television show than any other individual on the

Jubilee," Martin concluded, "mostly because he was featured on *Jesus Is Coming Soon.*"

The CBS Weekend News segment, a prime time Saturday night news clip aired in December of 1970, was the simple story of Southern gospel music, and almost any quartet could have been used to anchor it, but the Inspirations were chosen. How and why they were chosen was through a friend, Warren Roberts of Atlanta. Dell Hall of CBS contacted Roberts to discuss an idea for using a gospel quartet on a segment of the Weekend News.

When Hall told Roberts what he had in mind, Roberts said, "You need to check on these boys, the Inspirations, from up in the mountains. They would be ideal." He told Hall of the Inspirations' youth and popularity, and Hall contacted Martin and arranged to get together. When they did, Hall liked what he saw and invited them to participate in the news clip.

Foster Davis of Atlanta headed the film crew that shot the video in the heart of Dixie on the weekend of November 20-22, 1970. The crew set up certain shots, like shooting from a cornfield as the Inspirations passed by in their bus, but they correctly focused the heart of the newscast on singing. They filmed hours of video on stage and in churches and school auditorium. Davis filmed the huddle the Inspirations always went into to pray before going out to perform, and that shot was featured prominently on the show.

When they had finished filming, the Inspirations apparently had made a good impression on the crew members, one of whom said, "I believe these boys have a sincere desire to help people."

The Inspirations represented gospel music well on the national news that night. They got their points across and made a lot of new fans for the quartet-singing world.

Roger Mudd presented the story straightforward without casting either reflections or undue praise on the Inspirations. For years afterward, when the Inspirations sang in a new town, someone there would usually say,

"I saw you on the news."

Such exposure to the nation couldn't have been bought.

Bill Hefner, maestro of the Harvesters Quartet on WBTV in Charlotte, who later became a United States Congressman after the Harvesters went out of business, promoted gospel sings in Winston-Salem. He brought in big names—the Statesmen and Blackwood Brothers, J.D. Sumner and the Stamps Quartet, the LeFevres, the Imperials, and other top-rated groups.

The Inspirations desperately wanted to get on Hefner's promotion. They practically begged him until he relented. For one of his 1968 programs, he invited the Inspirations to a Sunday singing and filled the auditorium with fans waiting to hear the Blackwood Brothers and Statesmen.

Hefner's Sunday programs were long. Quartets would sing from two to six o'clock in the afternoon, take a break for supper, and come back and sing till late Sunday night.

The Inspirations led off at two o'clock. Hefner came to them and said, "Fellows, we've got a lot of power lined up to sing today; so I'm going to let you open the show and you can sing from two to two-twenty and that's it. Twenty minutes! Martin and the boys took no offense. At that time, many promoters booked them to open their programs and explicitly limited them to fifteen or twenty minutes.

"That was all right," Archie said. "We had our punches right in line. Our program for those kinds of dates was like this: We'd start out with *Daniel Prayed* and then maybe *He'll Hold My Hand* or something like that, and do a couple of others, maybe *Stroll Over Heaven* and *Reunion in Heaven (What a Wonderful Time)*. Next to last, we would feature Troy on *When They Ring Those Golden Bells*, and wind up with our going-off song, *Jesus Is Coming Soon*. That was our program to open a concert, six or seven songs."

After their fourth song on the Winston-Salem program, the Inspirations gave their testimony. Nobody had said a word on stage until then. And they kept their testimonies short. Martin would say simply, "We're glad to be here. Troy Burns is our bass," and Troy would say a short testimony and finish with, "Our baritone is Jack Laws," and Jack would give his testimony and pass it on down the line. Then they would finish singing their program. They did not do any commercial type of record pitches from stage. They might mention that they had a new album but would say nothing more to describe it.

"When we finished *Jesus Is Coming Soon*," Archie said, "we'd just leave. We were happy to be there, just to be a part of that singing."

That afternoon, though, the quartet had to do *Jesus Is Coming Soon* six times. The crowd kept yelling for more and the Inspirations responded with encores. The people were tearing down the building.

Hefner was trying to please the big crowd and wanting to get on to the Statesmen, Blackwoods, LeFevres, and Stamps. He had a lot of great talent there and he was worried. He had contracted them for big money and people had paid to come and hear them, but the crowd, going wild, kept the Inspirations on stage.

"That's how powerful the song was," Archie said. "It wasn't us, it was the power and the spirit of the song. It was the fact that the Spirit had come over the place and people were getting something out of it. They felt something."

All the singers were standing in the wings, watching that performance by the Inspirations, and one, a big-time professional singer, was moved to mention to a colleague, "What in the world is it? What do those boys have? What've they got?" and the other answered, "It's the Spirit. They've got the Spirit of the Lord."

"I appreciate that more than anything else," Archie added. "If the Spirit's not in it, it's no good."

In 1968, the Inspirations made their debut in Asheville, nearest large singing city to Bryson City, and were a hit with *Jesus Is Coming Soon*, singing in their animated style. They have been favorites in Asheville since.

During that time, a promoter, Clyde Baker, started a gospel television show on Channel 12 in Winston-Salem. He called it "Inspiration Time," with no reference to the Inspirations Quartet. The show became popular in the Tar Heel Piedmont, and quartets were happy to be invited for guest appearances. The Inspirations and the Hopper Brothers and Connie anchored the show, and it gave the Bryson City quartet good exposure in the central part of their home state.

The Inspirations have as much trouble finding new songs as any other quartet. They are constantly on the lookout for new material and have discovered that great songs come from unexpected places—and many at unexpected times.

On a Monday in 1973 the Inspirations were in Nashville to tape the Gospel Singing Jubilee. They were making preparations to cut a new album and needed some songs.

Archie asked Ben Speer if he had any good material lying around.

"Yes, we do," Ben replied. "I'll bring some tomorrow."

When he arrived the next day, Ben had a song called *Touring The City*. He sat at the piano. "I'm going to play this for you," he said, "and it may be one that fits your style.

"We've had this song six years," he said. "Hinkle Little, a preacher from Taylorsville, North Carolina, came to Dad's funeral six or seven years ago and while talking to Mom and some of the rest of us, he said, 'Some day we'll be there touring the city together.'"

Harold Lane, with the Speers at the time, heard Little's comment and wrote a song about it.

"We don't like it," Ben said, "because it doesn't fit us, so I want to see if you like it."

He began to play and sing the song.

"Before he finished," Archie said, "that song tore me all to pieces. All the other guys felt the same way. I just flipped over it and it really blessed me."

Ben gave the song to the Inspirations. It had three verses. The Inspirations loved the first verse, but the second and third were not up to the first. So Archie rewrote those two verses into one, and the entire song was strengthened.

"I had really prayed that the Lord would send us a song," Archie said. "I had a burden about our singing because Ronnie had just left the quartet, and we seemed to be kind of bogged down. I was worried, and I prayed that if we didn't get a good song we'd be in trouble. I was really burdened about this."

The Inspirations rehearsed the song the rest of that day and put it on the Jubilee the next morning.

After the taping, Archie asked Les Beasley what he thought of the song.

"I'll be honest, Archie," Les said, "it doesn't do much for me." He *was* honest about it. The song wouldn't have fit the Florida Boys' style, but it was tailor-made for the Inspirations.

They recorded the song immediately and began using it for their closer. In just a few months they recorded a song called *Wake Up to Sleep No More*, which also became a blockbuster for them. In November of 1973 the Inspirations sang at the University of Alabama in Tuscaloosa and tried the song out and the audience responded with encore cheers. The next night they sang the song in Atlanta and the reception was the same. They knew they had another hit on their hands.

Through most of 1973 and the entirety of 1974 the Inspirations and the Happy Goodman Family sang together every Friday and Saturday night in a "Battle of Songs."

The Inspirations hired Roger Fortner of Bryson City to play the bass in late 1973 and Dale Jones of Akron, Ohio, to play the steel in 1976, getting ready for the "Battle of Songs." At the time Jack was playing the flat-top guitar and didn't like it, so in agreement with Roger and the rest of the quartet, he took over the bass and Roger played electric guitar. The quartet was composed of Archie on the high tenor, Troy singing lead, Eddie Deitz the baritone, and Mike Holcomb the bass. With Martin at the piano, that was the makeup of the quartet for the next five years.

Going into the Battle of Songs with the Happy Goodman Family was a challenge for the Inspirations. The Goodmans were extremely popular wherever they went—and they could sing! The Inspirations knew they had a tussle on their hands, and they decided that one way to measure up was to stay in good physical shape. They played basketball and softball, worked out in gyms every chance they got, and stayed in good physical condition all year.

"When we had spare time," Archie laughed, "the Goodmans would go lay up in the motel and we would head for the YMCA. We felt it was to our advantage to stay in shape physically. Exercising and playing ball has been a godsend for us all these years. It's hard, staying on the road. Those who have a tendency to stay on the bus or in the motel room get out of shape and it affects their singing."

For about two years, most of the Inspirations' singing dates included the Happy Goodmans. "Mr. Whitfield found that by putting us together," Martin said, "we would draw more people than if he had us and the Goodmans and two other groups. That's hard to believe, but it's a fact. Whit and W.B. Nowlin promoted the Battle of Songs all across the country, from California to Virginia."

No doubt such wide exposure contributed to the popularity of both groups and their songs. The Inspirations concentrated on two great songs, and at the end of the year *Touring The City* was the number one song in gospel music and *Wake Up to Sleep No More* was number two. They led the top twenty that year.

"A lot of that success," Archie said, "was because of our conditioning regimen."

The Battle of Songs had been so enthusiastically accepted across the country that the Inspirations wanted to do more specialized programming, so in 1975 they came up with the idea of *A Night of Inspiration*, and W.B. Nowlin quickly saw its potential and agreed to sponsor it across the country as he had the Battle of Songs.

"This was a night that featured the Inspirations," Martin said, "and sometimes a guest group. The Primitives often sang with us, and the Florida Boys and Governor Jimmie Davis were our guests at times, but most of the time we were paired with the Galileans, and some way our two styles meshed and people loved that program. We liked to work with the Galileans. They were such good people and very good to work with.

"A lot of nights, though, we would do the program alone, and the people seemed to like that.

"W.B. promoted the programs for us and we paid him a percentage of the gate. We paid the rate on the building, paid the insurance, and paid all the help and other items. That turned out to be a good deal for W.B. and the Inspirations both. W.B. promoted these programs across the northern states from Pennsylvania to Ohio, and in the major markets of Oklahoma City, Houston, Lakeland, Memphis, and many, many more cities. In Chattanooga we sang to the largest crowd I've ever seen in that building, about three thousand people. We were the only group there and sang the whole program, and we really had a good time.

"We stopped the *Night of Inspiration* in 1984 when we worked out a deal in Gatlinburg and spent the summer and most of the fall singing there."

Another enjoyable promotion of the Inspirations' early years were a series of airplane tours to Hawaii. Wilcox World Tours of Asheville sent huge numbers of chartered airliners filled with tourists to the islands for several summers, and the Inspirations, through Maurice Templeton, current owner of the *Singing News* and then a travel agent for Wilcox, filled some of the planes with their fans.

Hawaiian vacationing was a large operation. In one summer, Wilcox filled twenty-two airliners. From 1975 to 1985, the Inspirations sold spaces to their fans on these tours and took twelve groups, singing to them both in midair and at resorts in Hawaii.

On one trip, the Inspirations attracted such a large number of fans they filled one plane with 238 passengers and put a large overflow on commercial airliners.

On many of those trips, the Inspirations sang on Al Harrington's luau show in the Hilton Dome in Honolulu. This was a culture show in which 2,500 people would participate in a giant luau and then gather in the dome to listen to different genres of music, sometimes island music from Haiti, and at other times mountain music or western shows, and the like.

Harrington enjoyed having the Inspirations because they were different and they presented a different kind of music from his usual shows.

He would introduce the quartet with, "And now, from the Appalachian mountains of North Carolina, the Inspirations are going to give you some of the music they enjoy there."

"We'd walk out and sing *Amazing Grace*," Martin said, "and get the best applause of the evening. We really enjoyed doing those shows because we reached a lot of people who had never heard gospel music. Of course, a lot of our fans would be there to hear us, too."

"We would sing our hit songs on that show," Martin added, "and every time we went to Hawaii, if we couldn't sing on the Harrington show, he would be disappointed."

The Inspirations' Hawaii trips ended when they contracted to sing in Gatlinburg during the summers.

The National Quartet Convention is something else the Inspirations like to do, but they had a hard time getting on it in their early years.

"We begged to get on the convention," Martin said. "When *Jesus Is Coming Soon* was our strong song, we wanted to sing on the convention, but they wouldn't invite us. J.D. Sumner started the convention as a Blackwood Brothers promotion and I called him repeatedly, but for some reason we were not included in the invitees.

"We didn't get to sing at the convention until J.G. Whitfield bought it, probably about 1970, but when he took over, he put us right on. We might never have been on it otherwise."

The Inspirations sang at the convention for a few years, and the current group of owners bought it from Whitfield, and the Inspirations were excluded again.

"We didn't go," Martin said, "because we weren't invited, and we decided not to beg to get on any program. I don't know why, but about four years ago they began inviting us again.

"I enjoy the convention and think it's a good thing. We get to rub elbows with large numbers of people, some of whom are our people and some who are not. We have a booth but don't do much business. We talk to promoters and agencies, and to other singers and our fans and have a thoroughly enjoyable time."

In the early years, Martin, who has a good head for figuring angles, set up an arbitrary triangle with

Chattanooga, Birmingham, and Atlanta on its points and most of its interior lying in Alabama, including that greatest of gospel singing areas, Sand Mountain. He told the rest of the Inspirations, "We are going to hit every place in that triangle." And they did. Every city, town, and hamlet large enough to support a gospel sing found the Inspirations coming to their place once, twice, or three or four times in the next few years.

In later years, he explained, "It wasn't hard to figure that triangle. Most gospel records were sold within its limits. Most gospel music took place within two hundred fifty miles of that triangle. Marvin Norcross showed us that most gospel records are sold from the Mississippi River through the triangle. It still happens there. If it doesn't happen in that area, it doesn't happen at all! I'm told that more Bibles are sold there than any other place."

Asheville is not in that triangle, but at that time, it was considered one of gospel music's hottest towns. "Mr. Whitfield and Eldridge Fox promoted sings in City Auditorium in Asheville," Martin said, "but we had trouble getting booked there at first. I don't know why. We got into Birmingham before Asheville, and Asheville was the nearest big singing town to Bryson City. I would say our first Asheville date was in the last part of 1968, right before we recorded *Jesus is Coming Soon.* I remember one of the songs we sang was *Surely Goodness and Mercy.*"

Actually, the Inspirations had sung once before that in Asheville, but it was an appearance they'd rather forget. That appearance was not on a gospel promotion, but on some other kind.

"I remember they had a horse and monkey act before us," Archie laughed.

"Yeah," Jack added, "and halfway through our performance they pulled the curtain because the crowd was so small and the stage hands hadn't been paid."

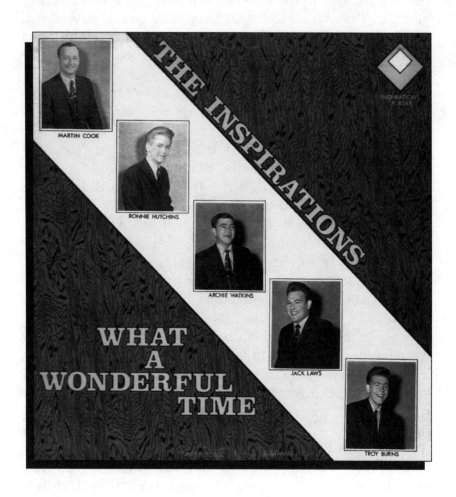

# 8

# On the Road

Until J.D. Sumner built the first customized bus in 1955, transportation for gospel quartets was a problem. At first, they used private automobiles, packing the trunk full of instruments, songbooks, recordings, and other things, with five men trying to make themselves comfortable in the seats. On long hauls, that was an impossibility. Some quartets rode in the back of pickup trucks until they could afford an automobile.

The first improvement on that was adoption of the limousine. Some of the more affluent quartets bought limousines, and after that it was the dream of every quartet to be able to purchase its own limousine. A limousine could accommodate more than five, giving quartets the luxury of carrying more musicians than just a piano player. Some of the groups hitched trailers to the rear of limousines to transport records and sound equipment. They felt they were traveling in style because each man had more leg room.

But the day in 1955 when J.D. finished transforming an old 1938 bus into a rolling apartment, complete with chairs, tables, beds, closets, and other comforts of home, and the Blackwood Brothers proved it would pay for itself, the quartet world changed over quickly and everyone bought buses. Then buses spread into rock and country, even into popular music, and to John Madden, the pro football analyst who won't fly, and Muhammad Ali, the heavyweight boxing champion of the world.

The Inspirations bypassed limousines, unable to afford one on a part-time singing basis. However, before motorcoaches, they did what they could to provide comfort for themselves when they grew weary of travel.

They moved from riding Martin's Buick, which had melted down on Old Fort Mountain, to a used Chevrolet Greenbriar van in 1966. The van had three seats, two of which would fold down to give the guys a flat sleeping area.

"We didn't change the inside arrangement in the van for sleeping," Martin said, "because the back two seats would fold down so the guys could sleep stretched out."

"That van," Archie said, "had manifold problems. The manifold was always coming loose. Once, we left a singing in Ohio, piled in the van bound for Knoxville to sing at Brother C.J. Holt's church on Sunday morning, and the manifold gasket blew out.

The engine was in the rear of the Greenbriar, beneath the floor where the guys slept, and the fumes were so strong they had to let the windows down. To keep from freezing, they bundled up with all the clothes they could stand and piled the rest of their suits on top. One would drive and the others huddle up.

"We couldn't stop," he said, "else we'd never get the van started again. It was winter and cold as ice and we had to ride from Ohio to Knoxville with the windows down. It's a wonder it didn't kill us all."

That was a miserable trip, but they made it on time.

"I guess that proves if you want to sing bad enough," Archie said, "you'll find a way."

Like any other quartet, the Inspirations are often forced to entertain themselves on the road. On the bus, they have television and radio and a state-of-the-arts sound system, but there are times when men who travel together need to vent their boredom on something nonelectronic.

When the Inspirations were kids, they especially loved to get on the same program with Wendy Bagwell and the Sunliters and with almost any mixed group. Usually women would find a convenient place backstage for their purses, and, kidlike, the Inspirations thought it hilarious to wire those pocketbooks with coat hangers so tightly the ladies couldn't get them open. They would even wire them to whatever they were hanging on so the women couldn't get them loose. When caught, the Inspirations would say, "We just wanted to keep somebody from carrying them off."

Probably the toughest joke they played on anyone on the road was on one of their own. Jack Laws loved to wallow in his bunk, catching up on sleep he'd probably lost while bear-hunting, and when the bus stopped for a snack or quick lunch, Jack would roll over and say to the fellows getting off the bus, "How about bringing me a cup of coffee and a good hamburger."

Riding that old 4104 through Pennsylvania one day, bound for a singing engagement with evangelist Maze Jackson, the bus pulled into a diner and the group began to unload.

"Bring me a hot cup of coffee and a good hamburger," Jack said to Archie.

No one should say that the Lord had it worked out for the boys to pull a major league joke on Jack. In this case, you'd be nearer the truth saying the devil made them do it.

Anyway, Archie bought the coffee and hamburger to go, and when he arrived at the cash register to pay, he saw a container of boxes of Ex-Lax in the glass counter.

"Those boxes each had two layers," Archie said, "about three inches square."

"We ought to fix him up," Troy said, and he and Archie and Eddie bought a box of Ex-Lax. The strength of that much laxative didn't cross their minds. They put one layer on Jack's steaming hamburger and the other layer in his coffee, and Eddie took them to him.

Jack was so hungry he didn't notice that his food had a peculiar taste. He ate every bite and licked his fingers, sacking out again for the remainder of the ride.

Late that afternoon, the Inspirations rolled up to a mobile home where they would have supper with a family of their fans.

"We were fellowshipping at the table," Archie said, "and all of us were keeping an eye on Jack."

Suddenly Jack paled. He arose quickly and asked for the bathroom and was directed down the hall. Seated so he could see the hall, Archie watched Jack go into the bathroom, and moments later he bolted out and rushed through the side door of the trailer.

Jack did not return to the table, and the quartet and their hosts finished eating, all the Inspirations straining not to burst out laughing. Entering the bus, they saw Jack sitting in a front seat, pale as a ghost.

"Boys," Jack said, "something's tore my stomach all to pieces. I've ruined everything I've got."

He had darted into the bus and taken a whole roll of copies of the *Singing News* (it was printed in tabloid newspaper form then) and rushed to the barn.

"That was on Thursday afternoon," Archie said. "We sang the whole weekend and Jack never got off the bus."

He lay in bed all the way home and feebly left the bus and headed home. On his way, Jack stopped by Carl Fox's house. Carl was Troy Burns's grandpa.

They swapped greetings and Carl asked Jack how he was.

"I'm sick as a bird," Jack said. "I can't keep nothing on my stomach. I've had bad diarrhea for almost four days now, and I'm about to die."

"Tell you what I'll do," Carl said. "I'll he'p you with that." He opened the kitchen cabinet and brought out a jar of clear corn whiskey, moonshine variety, the ages-old mountain remedy for whatever ails you. Carl shook the jar and a handsome bead rose in the contents.

The old fellow poured a saucer full of moonshine, struck a match, and lit the stuff. It burned with a soothing blue blaze, and when Carl blew it out, Jack drank what was left.

Next morning, his tummy felt fine.

Some mountain folks believe like Granny Clampett, that all it takes to cure the common cold is a slug of moonshine and two weeks of rest. Few people have grown up in the Smoky Mountains area without being dosed with moonshine, asafetida, castor oil, and ramps—not necessarily in a row, or even anywhere near each other.

The moonshine works. Ask Jack.

Quite possibly the most hilarious incident on the road occurred to the Inspirations early on. It was an accident to which the solution was readily apparent. The punch line was an old joke, but owing to the excitement and anxiety of the moment, not any of the singers thought of the remedy.

The Inspirations were in the process of purchasing their first new bus in 1971, the Silver Eagle they retired from the road in 1998 after riding it more than two million miles. The quartet had a singing date at the Sunday morning service at Temple Baptist Church in Chattanooga, the Rev. T.D. Burgess's church. When the service was completed, Martin was going to fly to Dallas, buy the bus, and fly back to Knoxville where Eddie Dietz and his wife, Sandy, would pick him up and bring him on home to Bryson City. Marlin Shubert, the bass singer, would drive the old 4104 to Birmingham and Mark Lowery, who had bought it, would take possession.

When they reached Chattanooga, Burgess told them there had been a mistake and they were not scheduled to sing that Sunday. It worked out well for the Inspirations, who got a jump on their bus-selling and buying chores. Martin flew to Texas, the Inspirations unloaded all their possessions from the 4104 into a U-Haul truck, and Marlin headed for Birmingham in the old bus.

Eddie drove the truck. In it with him were Ronnie, Archie, Jack, and Troy. Ronnie sat up front with Eddie, and Archie, Jack, and Troy got in the back of the truck, spread a mattress on the floor, and sacked out to sleep all the way home. They raised the loading door of the truck about four inches to get fresh air.

Eddie cruised into Cleveland, Tennessee, and halfway through town came to a railroad underpass. There was no height clearance sign at the underpass so Eddie went into it at about thirty-five miles an hour.

Suddenly, there was a tremendous crash and a mighty jolt! The guys on the mattress were tumbled about when the truck came to a sudden halt, and the top of the truck peeled back until they could see blue sky and the concrete of the railroad overpass.

"Oh, Lord," Jack yelled, "we hit that trussel!" (Mountain folk call a trestle a trussel.)

All the guys were scared to death except Ronnie, who was in the front seat. He knew exactly what had happened, and he came up with a brilliant idea. "Eddie," he said, "just rev it up and floorboard it and we'll go on through." Eddie revved up the engine, let go the clutch, and the truck slammed forward a few inches and wedged itself tighter.

About that time a train came across the overpass and shook the guys in the truck severely.

Everyone managed to get out of the truck and milled about, trying to figure what to do. Finally, Archie suggested, "Eddie, see if it'll back out of there." So Eddie climbed back in the truck, revved up the engine again, put it in reverse, and let go the clutch, but the truck wouldn't budge.

They thought of more ways to free the truck, but abandoned them one by one.

At the side of the underpass an old man sat in a straight-backed chair, propped against the wall of a small gasoline station.

"He walked over to us," Archie said. "He was kinda goofy looking, but it turned out he wasn't as goofy as we were."

The old man peered around the truck as the guys discussed calling a wrecker. The fellow said, "Boys, you don't need a wrecker. You want me to tell you how to get that truck out of there?" and the Inspirations, as one, chorused, "Tell us!"

"Why, if you'll let the air out of them tars, boys," he said, "you can back that truck outta there."

It was as simple as that. The guys looked at each other sheepishly and let the air out of the tires. Eddie climbed back in the cab, and backed the truck out of the opening. They looked around and found that the low clearance sign had been knocked down out of sight. The quartet drove the truck on to Bryson City but there was no sleeping in the back as the air whistled through.

Driving to Knoxville to pick up Martin at the airport the following day, Eddie dreaded telling him about the truck. Martin got in Eddie's car laughing and carrying on, happy as a lark, and about twenty miles down the road, he noticed that Eddie was extremely quiet.

"What is it, Eddie?" he asked. "What's wrong?"

Eddie decided to play it straight.

"Two things," he said. "First, we had a little problem with that truck. You know that underpass in Cleveland. Well, somehow I sort of run the truck under it and got it stuck."

Martin laughed and said, "Well, that ain't no problem. You got insurance, didn't you?"

"That's the second problem," Eddie said. "I didn't take out insurance."

The quartet didn't have to pay for damage to the truck, however, because the clearance signs had been knocked down and there was nothing to warn Eddie of the low clearance.

There was a strange ending to that story. Chris Smith of Cleveland, Tennessee, who later sang for three years with the Inspirations, was a small boy at the time, and he and his father happened to drive by and saw the truck wedged into the underpass.

The news that Eddie hadn't taken out insurance on the bus didn't dampen Martin's spirits. He had been successful in Dallas in purchasing a new Eagle bus for the quartet to replace the old 4104.

The first bus, a 1954 model General Motors 4104, had been bought in 1968 from Valley Bus Lines in Knoxville for $11,000. Bryson Citians, proud of their Inspirations, have always been willing and eager to help the quartet. Johnny Cope, a Chevrolet dealer in Bryson City, financed the bus through GMAC, the same as if he had sold the bus. It was a regular bus filled with seats, and several people helped gut the insides and customize it. Others contributed time and materials.

It gave fairly good service for three years, but by that time the quartet had reached the point that it had to have new wheels to keep up with its ever-increasing schedule. The Inspirations still hadn't reached the financial solidity, however, where the bus could be bought in the quartet's name. Everything at that time was bought in Martin Cook's name, so he had added incentive in making the quartet a success.

"I had to put up everything I owned to get the bus," Martin said. "That's one reason I was delighted to incorporate later that year, glad to get all of that off my back."

The new bus was built in Belgium, brand, spanking new, and would be delivered by ship into Gaston, Mississippi, directly from the Belgium factory.

The Inspirations paid $57,000 for the bus to the Eagle Bus Company, owned by Continental Trailways and headquartered in Dallas. Archie and Martin flew to Mississippi and drove the new vehicle home.

When the Inspirations retired it from the road in late 1998, it still had its original configuration of rooms for quartet members and had the original bunks that Archie and Troy had built in, with help from others.

The Inspirations have always had their weather eyes peeled for fun. Ronnie got some of his fun out of aggravating the other guys. Although the fellows were known as conservatively dressed men on stage, Ronnie had always been the stylist of the group.

"He kept up with all the styles," Archie said. "He was a little ahead of us—let's put it that way to be nice. He bought a pair of Jesus sandals that none of us cared to see him wear. We felt they were hippie shoes and we didn't like that. We sang in Toccoa, Georgia, one evening and Troy and I sneaked Ronnie's sandals out of the bus and wired them to the back bumper with a coat hanger. They dragged the highway all the way home, and when we got to Bryson City, nothing was left but two or three strips of leather."

Everybody laughed at the joke, even Ronnie, but it turned out to be a joke that backfired and then backfired again.

The next weekend when the quartet hit the road, Ronnie had another laugh. He had purchased a pair of white and brown, high-heeled oxfords. "He did that just to aggravate us," Archie said, "and, boy! it just about killed us."

Archie was driving that old 4104 from Chatsworth, Georgia, to Dalton on a winding, country road that had no traffic that evening. "It wasn't a bad road," Archie said. "It was paved but it was awful winding, and we hadn't met a car since we left Chatsworth."

Suddenly, someone tapped Archie on the shoulder. It was Ronnie, who said, "I need to stop." That bus did not have a bathroom. Archie stopped and opened the door and when Ronnie got off, Archie saw that he was wearing only his underwear and those brown and white, high-heeled shoes.

"It was the shoes that did it," Archie said. "They put me in the wrong frame of mind." When he saw Ronnie walk off a few paces and stop, he quickly closed the door and drove away.

Archie looked in the rear-view side mirror and saw Ronnie galloping after the bus, high-heeled shoes pumping like pistons as he ran.

"All you could see in the reflection of the taillights," Troy said, "were those two big white and brown saddle oxfords chasing us."

When Ronnie fell off the pace and shook his fist at the bus, Archie pulled over and opened the door and let Ronnie in. He was so relieved to get back on the bus he didn't even scold Archie.

All of the Inspirations' driving incidents weren't that funny. Some had a serious side.

For the most part, the quartet has employed regular drivers. Archie's brother, Donald, has probably driven their bus a million miles. David Shuler drove for a while, and P.R. Vandeburg for a while. All the quartet members learned to drive and each has taken many turns at the wheel.

Mike Holcomb was driving on an interstate one night, and Archie, asleep in his compartment, woke and realized the bus was not moving. He got up to see why and saw Mike sitting in the driver's seat with his head down on his arms on the steering wheel.

"I thought he was praying," Archie said, "and I guess he was."

When Archie got to the driver's seat, he saw an old yellow Ford LTD with its sides scratched and dented, stopped in front of the bus.

"Mike must have gotten a little drowsy," Archie said, "and had squeezed to the left enough to run a carload of black folks into the concrete median. Not any of them was hurt, but, boy! were they hot!"

Mike's prayers were answered, however. One of the men was very nice and understanding and he quieted the rest to the point of reasonableness. The Inspirations paid for the damage to the car and everyone went his way.

The quartet recorded the first album Eddie sang on at Mark V Studios in Greenville, South Carolina, probably about 1965 or '66. Eddie had never driven a bus, nor had he ever thought of driving one. They recorded all day and most of the night and someone drove the bus to a little all-night restaurant where they ate.

Going back to the bus, Eddie said, "Fellows, when we get to my mother-in-law's house, wake me up and let me off the bus. His mother-in-law was Edith Bryson, married to Claude Bryson, uncle of the author. They lived in Dillardtown in Sylva.

Collectively, the guys said "okay" and took off running like they were trying to steal home in a baseball game. They all dashed onto the bus before Eddie got there, and when Eddie climbed aboard, all had disappeared into the back of the bus and were piling into their bunks to sleep.

Eddie stood for a minute, thinking, "What am I going to do? Somebody has to drive the bus."

So he got under the wheel and cranked it up.

"Scared to death, I got it in first gear," he said, "and got it back on the road. After a while, I got it in second gear, and I was trembling all over. Finally, I managed to get it in third gear and drove the rest of the way home in that gear, afraid to take it out.

"By the time I got to my mother-in-law's house, I was mad and I could have killed them all. Actually, it's a wonder I didn't, not knowing any more than I did about driving a bus, but it was late and there was little traffic on the road. They stayed in bed all the way home and I pulled off the road and parked at my mother-in-law's house and got off the bus. I don't know when they got up or who drove on home. I guess they were lying back there praying all the way, but they got their rest.

"And," he added, "I guess you could say I sort of learned to drive the bus. But I sure was mad at the other fellows for making me learn like that."

Martin laughed. "We didn't make him drive it," he said. "It was his choice. We all beat him to bed and he chose to drive the bus rather than spend the night where we sat."

An almost identical incident occurred with Reagan Riddle of the Primitives, who traveled on the bus with the Inspirations for eighteen months.

Both quartets had had a long, hard day, and that night, on a long haul, Martin was driving and everyone else was asleep, with the exception of Reagan. He sat up talking with Martin, making sure he didn't fall asleep at the wheel.

Around two o'clock, Martin, apparently wearing out, asked, "Reagan, can you drive a bus?"

"I don't know," Reagan answered, "I never tried."

"Come over here and look," Martin said. "There's nothing to it."

Reagan moved over beside Martin. "Here," Martin said, "all you've got to do is be careful when you pass a car and cut back in. Make sure you're past him."

Reagan gave Martin a blank look. Surely, he thought, he's not going to ask me to drive.

"You know how to double clutch, don't you?" Martin asked.

"Well, no," Reagan replied. "I really don't."

"Get under the wheel when I slip out," Martin said, "and hold it in the road."

Reagan thought Martin wanted to visit the men's room, but when Martin stood and stretched, he waited a minute and saw that Reagan still had the bus in the road—so he went to bed!

"That's right," Reagan said later, "he put me under the wheel and went to bed. I didn't have any idea where we were or what I was doing, but somehow we got where we were going. I must have driven the rest of the night, and I found that double-clutching wasn't as hard as I thought."

When they reached their destination, Reagan slowed and pulled off the road into a shopping mall parking lot.

"I got the bus stopped," he said, "and put on the air brake—and I went to bed."

He felt rather proud when he woke up later. He had driven the bus for many miles. "I really had," he said.

Muhammad Ali, the great heavyweight boxing champion, had a fear of flying and rode from place to place in a customized bus.

Once, late at night, David Shuler drove the Inspirations through South Georgia and a customized bus with "Muhammad Ali" painted on the side passed him. The Ali bus soon pulled into a truck stop, and David followed.

Ali was still up and David met him. Ali liked the appearance of the Inspirations' coach and asked David if he could see inside it.

All the Inspirations were sleeping in their cubby-sized rooms, and Ali opened their doors one by one, jumped inside each room, brandishing his fists, yelling, "I'm the Greatest!"

Jolted out of sleep, each Inspiration woke up frightened and wondering who this big, black guy was who threatened them with huge fists.

When Ali burst into Martin's room, Martin leaped out of bed still half asleep and put up his fists to fight, but when he saw who his opponent was, he quickly backed down.

On his way to Miami to train for a title fight, Ali liked the inside of the Inspirations' bus so well he asked Troy if he would send him the floor plan and gave Troy his address and telephone number.

# 9

# The Great Blizzard of '93

There are dangers to all gospel quartets who ride buses across the nation. Gospel singers have been killed in roadway crashes. Some dangers on the road come from Mother Nature, others from Man, and some come from both.

This was one from the latter category when Nature and Man teamed up against the Inspirations.

During the Great Blizzard of 1993, which blanketed Western North Carolina with more than twenty inches of snow, the Inspirations found themselves snowbound aboard their bus on Interstate 26 coming up Saluda Mountain from Spartanburg, South Carolina, to Asheville.

They had sung in LaGrange, Georgia, and snow was falling heavily when they left. Instead of taking U.S. 441 to Bryson City, which was their usual route from Georgia, they decided to stay with Interstate 85 to Spartanburg and come up Saluda Mountain on 26. Their thinking was that there would be enough traffic on the interstate so vehicles could keep moving into Asheville at least.

"It was kinda like coming in the back side to Bryson City," Eddie explained.

They might have made it except for a red Cadillac, which came flying up behind them, passed the bus, and just in front of it began to spin in circles on the slick pavement.

Donald Watkins, who was driving, had been easing up the road beside the median, holding traction, and doing very well, considering the condition of the road, but when the Caddy went into a series of spins, he had to brake to a stop—and that did it. They couldn't get enough traction then to get the bus moving and it stalled on the steepest part of Interstate 26.

Conditions couldn't have been worse. The snow was already a foot and a half deep and more was coming down rapidly. Visibility was not good because so many cars had stalled in and beside the road.

A man in a Suburban came down the mountain on the other side of the median and somehow Archie managed to stop him. The Suburban had been moving fairly well and Archie talked the fellow into turning around and driving the quartet to a motel up the road. The guys left Donald with the bus, knowing that snow plows would open the road the next morning, and gratefully piled into the Suburban.

Archie sat up front with the driver and the others made themselves as comfortable as possible in a jumble of shovels, picks, and other tools in the back. There were no seats in the rear of the vehicle.

"I noticed right off that the man was nervous," Archie said, "and I laid it to having to drive in that blizzard and on the wrong side of the interstate."

Neither the driver nor Archie could see any distance ahead, no more than several feet. It was snowing so heavily that Archie could barely see the side of the road, but by that he guided the driver.

"Get over to your left a little bit," Archie keyed the driver. "Now come back to your right a little."

The driver obeyed Archie's commands and the car crept along at a snail's pace.

All the guys were scared silly and so was the driver. The snow became deeper by the minute.

After a few minutes, the man said, "Whew! I can't take this! Boys, I've got to have something to calm my nerves."

Reaching behind the seat, he opened a cooler and withdrew a can of Bud Light and popped it open.

Archie saw the beer and thought, Dear God, he's not only nervous, he's drinking. He didn't seem in bad shape, but combined with his nervousness, the drinking would have a dulling effect.

Not any of the Inspirations drink, and it almost blew their minds, especially Eddie's. "I thought my greatest fear was going to be realized," Eddie said. "He's going to wreck and kill all of us, and tomorrow they'll find us lying in this Suburban with beer cans everywhere, and that's the way the Inspirations are going to be remembered."

"I had a bird's eye view of everybody in the car," Archie said. "The guys were lying back there in those tools, and they looked like a bunch of hobos. You ought to have seen the shock on their faces."

The driver took one slug of beer and said again, "My nerves are shot, boys, but this'll calm 'em." Then he put the can down and didn't drink any more.

Archie begged the driver to let him drive. "If you're getting too nervous," he said, "pull over and let me drive."

"I'll make 'er," the driver said—and through the grace of God and very little traffic, he did. On the wrong side of the road, he plowed several miles through the storm until they came to a motel on the interstate at Hendersonville, and it was with immense joy that the Inspirations alighted from that car.

When the Suburban stopped at the motel, the blizzard was so terrible that they barely got in the motel, but they took rooms. And then the power went off! But they could put up with that. At least they were warm and safe from the storm—and from the Good beer-drinking Samaritan.

They remained in the motel that night and most of the next day.

Donald got the bus going and somehow he and Archie got together as he came through Hendersonville and had such a hard time maneuvering around Asheville that they got home to Bryson City about the same time the rest of the quartet did. Archie's brother-in-law, Don Simonds, had taken Martin's Jeep and gone after the rest of the guys.

Approaching Asheville on his way to rescue the quartet, Simonds stopped and picked up a hitch-hiker. The heat had been running high in the Jeep and Simonds had not yet figured out how to turn it down, but the old boy he'd picked up rubbed his hands together and exclaimed, "Boy, this is the warmest I've been since it started snowing!"

That's when Eddie came up with the suggestion that they make a rule of the road: 1. Never leave the bus. 2. Don't let the bus leave you. 3. If you get left in or by the bus, go back to Rule No. 1.

A man who drove into the Inspirations' bus didn't need help from Mother Nature. He had already received the help he needed from John Barleycorn. He was the only fatality recorded in many more than two million miles on the road by the Inspirations.

The quartet was coming through an open country road outside of Selma, Alabama, with David Shuler driving. Martin was seated up front and saw the whole thing.

"It was dark," Martin said, "but in the edge of the bus's headlight beams I saw this car do a doughnut in a parking lot, and it shot straight out in front of the bus. The driver didn't have his headlights on, and he came at full speed. David didn't see him until he was in front of us. David crammed on the brakes so hard the jolt of the brakes was greater than when the car hit the bus, but it hit on the driver's side."

The man never regained consciousness. He died on the spot. The Inspirations were absolved of any blame, but the incident put the guys into an unusual calm for several days.

The Inspirations and the George Shelton Family had sung in Roy Knight's church in South Carolina one evening and left the church after such a fine service that they were all walking on cloud nine. They were still in the Greenbriar van. Martin was driving.

They topped a hill and went down the far side, all talking and enjoying each other, and suddenly they came to a crossroads. The right-of-way had not been cleared and the stop sign was covered with brush. When Martin saw the intersection, he slammed on the brakes.

The van was so loaded that, powerful as Martin's legs are, the van wouldn't stop, and it slid into the intersection. A car came through the intersection and struck the van on the right side.

"I think I would have made it through," Martin said, "if I had opened the throttle instead of hitting the brakes. The van just didn't have the kind of brakes that would have stopped such a load, especially on a downgrade."

Thankfully, no one was injured, and damage to the van looked to be much more extensive than it really was. They managed to drive it on home to Bryson City.

The INSPIRATIONS SING

from the HEART of the
GREAT SMOKIES

# 10

# Into the Wild Blue Yonder

Only on occasion have the Inspirations flown. They never flew to a date on the road, but occasionally they had to fly home to arrive in time for a local appearance.

"Years ago," Eddie said, "we'd try to sing at each other's homecomings every year. Those dates would come on certain days of the year, like the fourth Sunday in August or the second Sunday in September, and we'd try to sing at all of them.

"We were in Oklahoma City and had to fly out of Dallas on a red-eye to get to the homecoming at my church," Eddie continued. "It was going to be an all-night flight, and Martin decided to wear his suit. That was a mistake. We had to waste some time sitting in airports, and sleep in the cramped seats of the airplane, and when we got home sometime Sunday morning, Martin was a mess. Archie's mom pressed his suit at the Inspirations Motel, and we made it to the church in time for the homecoming.

"We'd do that," Eddie finished. "We would fly all night just to sing at somebody's homecoming."

Three or four rough flights finally weaned the Inspirations of flying. The quartet drove into Atlanta about seven o'clock one Sunday morning, and Martin and the singers transferred to Atlanta's Hartsfield Airport to fly to Asheville in order to get home for a homecoming.

When they left Atlanta, the weather was foggy, but soon the plane climbed above the overcast. However, as they approached Asheville, that airport, too, was fogged in. After circling for a while, the plane was diverted to Charleston, West Virginia, which was also socked in. Back to Atlanta the plane went, and found that the airport there had been temporarily closed to incoming traffic because of heavy fog. After a few minutes of circling, the pilot was informed that Asheville was open, so he made the thirty-minute flight to the Land of the Sky and landed safely. They had flown three hours.

"We finally got home," Archie said, "and found that we just beat the bus in."

The next flying incident also came in Atlanta. Roaring down the runway, full speed ahead, the plane began to bounce a little, like planes do when they are ready to fly. Instead of pulling the nose of the plane up, however, the pilot shoved the yoke forward and the plane almost nose-dived into the asphalt runway.

"I mean, man, he just cut it off," Archie said later.

The plane came to a stop before the runway ended, and the captain came on the intercom and apologized for the rough handling. "We caught a flight of blackbirds in one of our engines," he said, "and blew the engine. We will replace it as quickly as we can and then make the flight to Asheville."

Disembarking, when the Inspirations passed the captain standing in the doorway speaking to all passengers as they exited, his knees were shaking.

That put fear in the quartet again, and inside the terminal, even though the airline offered to put the fellows on another flight, they decided to pass up the chance. They rented a car and drove home to Bryson City.

There was another time when fog interrupted their journey. They flew from Atlanta to Asheville, only to find the airport closed because of fog, so they flew to Charleston, West Virginia, where they couldn't land for fog. Back to Atlanta they went and found fog engulfing the airport there. They circled a few minutes and went back to Asheville, couldn't land, back to Charleston the second time and landed long enough to refuel. They headed back to Asheville and found the airport still covered with heavy fog, but fortunately, after they circled Asheville for forty-five minutes, the fog lifted and they were able to land.

"We were scared," Eddie said. "We flew for more than four hours and I missed church that morning We got home about twelve."

The next week when Eddie was at his grandma Jamison's house in Dillardtown, she told him an unusual story.

"The strangest thing happened to me last week," she said. "I was praying on Sunday morning and the Lord put a heavy burden on my heart. He told me I needed to pray hard, that somebody was in trouble in the air. So I prayed and prayed until I got relief."

The time her relief came, Eddie remembered, was about the time the quartet landed in Asheville.

Two misguided old men once twanged the Inspirations' fragile flying nerves on a Sunday afternoon flight in 1970. CBS News spent a weekend with the quartet, filming for the seven-minute documentary for Roger Mudd's segment on the CBS Weekend News.

The Inspirations sang Sunday morning in a church in Tuscaloosa, Alabama, with cameramen filming the service. They had to be at a theater in Corinth, Mississippi, for an appearance that afternoon.

Having to fly to get there on time, the guys rented a small airplane that seated six, including the pilot. Since there were six men in the quartet at the time, one had to get another way to Corinth, so Jack chose to ride the bus.

Martin, Eddie, Archie, Ronnie, and Marlin Shubert crammed into the six-seater with the pilot.

Archie was scared; he hates to fly.

"Before we leave," Archie said to the pilot, "I want to know if you are prepared to die."

"That's not what's important," the pilot replied.

"What's important?" Archie asked.

The pilot answered, "What's important is, are *you* prepared to die?"

When they reached Corinth, the pilot was bringing the plane in on its final leg and suddenly he cursed, hauled back on the yoke, and turned the nose of the plane back into the sky.

"What's wrong?" someone yelled.

"Look down there," the pilot pointed toward the landing strip when he leveled off again, and a car was motoring blissfully down the runway.

Two old men trying to get to a decoration day ceremony at a cemetery near the airport had mistaken the landing strip for the road to the graveyard and were driving leisurely down the runway as the plane came in to land. Fortunately, the pilot saw them in time and managed to avert catastrophe by aborting the landing.

"That's what weaned us," Martin said, "incidents like that."

Jack once caused the quartet to cancel a scheduled flight. They had sung in Allentown, Pennsylvania, and headed home, but on the outskirts of Allentown, the bus lost its transmission. The guys needed to get home quickly and decided to fly. Donald Watkins, the driver, stayed with the bus, and Ronnie stayed with him.

At the airport the quartet approached the ticket counter when Jack suddenly paled and called Martin to one side.

"Look here," Jack said, opening his suitcase to show Martin his .357 Magnum pistol packed inside with his clothes.

Someone said, "Boys, Jack's got his .357 in his suitcase."

"That made us mad," Martin said. "We couldn't fly home with his gun in his suitcase, and we couldn't leave him there."

"If we left him," Archie said, tongue in cheek, "we knew he'd never get home."

"He wouldn't be there yet," Eddie laughed.

They discussed how to get home with the gun and decided to ride the train, but they could only get as far as Greensboro. No passenger service ran into Asheville.

They took a bus from Harrisburg to Washington and caught the train. A preacher, Wallace Griggs, who had come to Archie's house from Florida, drove to Greensboro, picked up the quartet, and brought the guys home to Bryson City.

"That was a smooth ride on that train," Archie said. "We enjoyed it even if we did spend all night and all day getting home."

The road that professional quartets travel is long and winding. Folks who don't like to be together should never enter the quartet field.

On a weekday in February, 1999, Martin Cook described how even the best of friends get a bellyful of each other's company. Regardless of how much they may enjoy it, they simply have to find some down time alone.

"The first day on the road," Martin said, "everybody sits together joking and laughing, and the last day one sits here, another over there, somebody else back yonder, sick of each other.

"Take this last weekend," he added. "We sang in Columbia, South Carolina, on Thursday and in Jacksonville, Florida, Friday and Saturday. When we got on the bus to leave on Thursday we were all joking and sitting together. We had gotten a card from a lady who has a truck stop on Saluda Mountain, inviting us to stop on the eleventh and she would give us a meal. We stopped and all sat together at one big table, talking at the same time, joking and laughing, having a good time.

"When we finished in Jacksonville Saturday night, three or four of us went to the Waffle House to eat. Somebody and I sat at this table, and Archie and somebody else at a table over in the corner, and Mike and another one or two went to Denny's across the street. We weren't mad at each other. We didn't tell each other we needed to separate like that. The thing I'm trying to say is that someway or another we've learned how to get along with each other."

# 11

# Superlatives

Martin Cook has been in gospel music all his life, as a pianist, as a singer, and as a spectator. He knows music. He knows what it takes to be a good singer, and he knows what is required of one who carries star status in the world of gospel music.

Martin is a lifelong student of gospel music, and when asked who he thought was the best of all time, he began to talk of superlatives, the best this, the best that, his favorite singer, those he admired the most. We ruled out his inclusion of any of the Inspirations in these categories.

James Blackwood is his favorite singer.

"There's nobody in James Blackwood's class in gospel music," he said. "Nobody was in Albert Brumley's class as a songwriter. He was a designer, a genius, the Thomas Edison of gospel music.

"Then you've got the Chuck Wagon Gang. They were pioneers. If it hadn't been for the Chuck Wagon Gang we wouldn't have had the music we've had and be at the level we are today. Without the Chuck Wagon Gang, a lot of our songs would never have been known to the extent they are. The Chuck Wagon Gang's style of singing was not the style of the Inspirations, but their style was good for the people. The Chuck Wagon Gang probably had more influence on the culture of America, on the life of the people, on the long-range effect than any other singing outfit in any medium, except for Elvis.

"The Chuck Wagon Gang introduced to America the music that was sung in church and in everyday life during the depression when they began singing. When times are bad, folks want uplifting music. That's what the Chuck Wagon Gang gave them. A lot of other kinds of music were never sung in everyday life where people lived. Now they talk about country music and bluegrass and such—it just wasn't sung except in certain areas by certain people.

"The Chuck Wagon Gang did more than anybody else to change our music from Sacred Harp, a four-note system, to a seven-note scale that everybody could sing. Just everybody couldn't sing Sacred Harp.

"The Chuck Wagon Gang put our music into the lives of the people. They had a tremendous radio audience which helped people identify with their music. They could sing it, and it lifted folks up. They had the material, they sang old hymns and certain new gospel songs that fit their style. And they had mass distribution of their records. They were in every shop in America and in hundreds overseas, maybe thousands.

"When they finally went on the road, the Chuck Wagon Gang sang at some of the big concerts, but they also played every little town they could—like Sylva and Franklin and Hendersonville in our neck of the woods. People knew what the Gang looked like. They could talk with them.

"That's how our gospel music got started in the beginning, and gospel music in the beginning sounded more like the Chuck Wagon Gang or the Inspirations than any other way. Among the first with that sound were the Old Hickory Singers, the Jordanaires, and the John Daniel Quartet. They didn't have a vibrato. The original Oak Ridge Quartet didn't have a vibrato, either.

"The Statesmen developed vibrato when Jake Hess came to sing with them. I remember the shock of the

people when they started it. To an extent, the Blackwood
Brothers had it all the time. The Statesmen changed to
vibrato from what they were with Bobby Strickland. I was
there when they changed it, and some people didn't like
it and said it's an unpleasant sound to the average
person. Now, a certain class of people thrive on it, but
the guy who drives the pickup truck will turn it off almost
every time."

"The Statesmen were my all-time favorite quartet,
back in the days of Big Chief Jim Wetherington, Rozie
Rozell, Jake Hess, Doy Ott, and, of course, Hovie Lister
at the piano.

"As far as good singing goes, take that Statesmen
album *Out West*—an album of Western songs—and listen
to it if you want to hear some real work that's the best they
ever did. On something like that is where you can find
whether they can sing or not, and they said that album sold
almost nothing. But it was the best work they ever did.

"Jack Toney is close to the best lead singer ever. I
think Smitty Gatlin was the best. Ronnie Hutchins, if he
had stayed with us or with a group like us, he might have
been the all-time, most accurate lead singer. You won't
catch him flat. You won't hear him leave out a vowel, and
you won't hide a vowel from him. Ronnie will hit the vowel
and he'll hit it right. But he's had voice problems and
sickness, and he hasn't taken good care of himself. Singing
with mixed groups and country music singers didn't help
him. He wasn't geared for it, and it wasn't natural to him.

"But, James Blackwood now. I mean it when I say
nobody's in his class in gospel music. When you see
James come into a singing, you can tell right off that he
loves those people. He comes in like a gentleman, he goes
to work, and he's always nice. As far as I know, he has
never said an ugly word to anyone, he has never been
impolite to anyone, he's never come off stage raw or
rugged, on stage he's never said anything derogatory
about anybody in politics or any individual, or anything
bad about any thing or situation.

"James is strictly professional when he goes on stage. I've never heard him criticize another singer, never heard him complain about the piano or the public address system. But the big thing with James is that he loves to see the people and he works hard for them. He loves it! Right now, he is almost eighty years old, and I watched him at the convention last fall (1998) and he was working it like he was just trying to get started, like it was his first night on the job. He's just as neat in appearance as he ever was, always courteous, and always professional. The only thing I ever thought he did wrong was to over-peddle songbooks through the audience many years ago, and after a while he stopped that."

Martin switched the conversation back to superlatives.

"The best singer I ever heard? The best gospel singer ever? You're talking about literally singing, all the way around? Not necessarily my favorite? Man or woman, either one?"

He stared at the floor a few seconds, deep in thought, running singers through his mind.

"I'd have to say Vestal Goodman," he finally answered. "She'll hit that vowel and that note like Big Chief. I don't care where it is, put it on the table over there and she'll hit it. Mom Speer was that way. Yes, I'd say Vestal is the best singer who ever walked onto a gospel stage.

"I mentioned Big Chief a minute ago. Big Chief is the best bass singer ever. Talk about being accurate, he was. Forget it, there has never been anybody who could sing bass with him. We used to go to his church at Christmas and sing, and Big Chief was just something else! J.D. Sumner was a showman. He was deep. He had the voice. Voice was first with J.D. and he was great. If he didn't hit his notes exactly when he was away down there, it didn't matter because no one could tell the difference. He was that low."

# 12

# Archie

Though Archie Watkins had never sung anywhere but in church, he was not a total stranger to music. But music was only one thing he enjoyed while growing up. His life was sports. He was an athlete whose existence centered around football, basketball, softball, track, whatever was in season. Ball, ball, ball! That's what he lived for. His desire was to go to college and become a teacher of physical education and a coach.

Prior to 1964, Archie's mother's brother, Walter Laws, sang in the Smoky Mountain Quartet with Paul Smiley, Claude Gossett, Earl Douthit, and Verna Parton at the piano. This quartet rehearsed next door to the Watkins home, so Archie was exposed to good music from the word go. Archie was still in elementary school as were Troy Burns and Ronnie Hutchins, and Jack Laws was in high school.

"I learned a lot about singing," Archie said. "Not the fundamentals of singing, but I learned how much I loved it and what music meant to the people, and probably that helped develop my ear for harmony." A deep love for gospel music was embedded in him because he heard it all the time in his formative years, and his love grew stronger as those early years passed.

"It was the same with Jack Laws," Archie said. "Jack's father, Wayne, was a brother to Walter and my mother.

Their family sang. When we talked about singing then, we were not thinking about people's thoughts and attitudes toward singing today. I'm just talking about singing at church. Except for the Smoky Mountain Quartet, singing then was just a let's-get-together-and-sing-a-little thing. We did it for a pastime."

Some other boys got together to sing and called themselves the Bryson City Quartet, but they only sang a few months, and they really were not in the Smoky Mountain Quartet's league. The Bryson City Quartet was not an organized quartet aspiring to find a place in major concert singing.

"When we started singing in what later became the Inspirations Quartet," Archie said, "it happened so fast that it was the kind of thing nobody saw coming. Nobody really knew what was happening; nobody had a vision. Martin had no thought of organizing a quartet when he began to have singing sessions in his basement in the evenings. There was a love for singing in all of us and I think the biggest thing we had, other than the Lord being on our side, was that we could harmonize.

"I don't mean just those who sang with the Inspirations could harmonize. Our people could! We didn't have a piano at Spruce Grove Baptist Church where Jack, Troy, and I went to church. We didn't have any musical accompaniment. We just had the harmony. My great uncle, Burgin Watkins, knew music. He did the pitching of the songs—and we sang the old-time harmony like 'do, do, do, me, sol. . . .' He didn't even use a tuning fork or pitch pipe, he just pitched it with his voice and everybody kind of hummed till they got the harmony and joined in. Uncle Burgin and Aunt Bonnie could sing the shaped notes both ways, backward and forward."

Jack's father, Wayne, knew harmony. He also played guitar. When Archie sang in the choir, it was Wayne who helped him learn the tenor part. "I remember on page ninety-six in the hymnal," Archie said, "was a song titled *Lord Lead Me On*. There is a tenor part in the chorus, and Wayne would show me how to hit that part and find the harmony."

In the early 1960s, the Smoky Mountain Quartet was the biggie in Bryson City. The Bryson City Quartet sang a lot for a few months and then broke up. Paul Higdon had a Second Saturday Night Singing that moved from church to church, and anyone who wanted to sing or listen and enjoy it could go. Soon after Martin and Candler Cook moved to Bryson City, the Smoky Mountain Quartet also broke up.

Archie, Jack, and Troy were reared together, and their parents took them to church where they sang with each other, realizing eventually how much they loved music, but having learned little about quartet singing.

In 1964, making the seventy-mile trip from Bryson City to Asheville and back required all day on twisting, two-lane roads. Not everyone in Swain County had an automobile, and some of those who did preferred to walk when the distance was not long, and they often walked to neighbors' homes in the evenings and picked and sang together, having a good time. That was a main force in almost all mountain communities at that time.

That afternoon in the spring of 1964, when Jack Laws stopped at Archie's house and said, "Archie, come and spend the night with me," Archie had no idea that evening would change his life's course.

Walking to Jack's house, Jack said, "Before I go home, I promised Walter I'd come by Martin's house and sing a little. Some of us get together up there and sing of an evening."

"Yeah, I'll go with you," Archie said. He had never been to Martin's house, but he knew Martin. He was a high school freshman that year and was in Martin's general science class and his homeroom. Walter Laws, the tenor singer, didn't come that evening.

"It was one of those deals the Lord had planned," Archie said. Since Archie was the only other person there, and he had sung a little first tenor at church, Martin asked him to join in.

"You know," Archie said recently, and tears came to his eyes, "that came as a result of Mom and Dad carrying me on their back, walking up an old gravel road, taking me to church, seeing that I knew right from wrong, and helping me. I happened to be in the right place at the right time that night."

Archie's father was James Clarence Watkins, whom folks called J.C. or Red, owing to the color of his hair. His mother was Edith Laws Watkins. There were five kids in the Watkins family, and their parents took them all to church.

Troy was a fourth cousin to Archie and Jack.

They didn't know too much about singing, but they could tell if they were harmonizing. "Martin is a great piano player," Archie said, "but he, like us, still had a lot to learn at that time. Let me say that Martin Cook is the best rhythm piano player I've ever heard. He can play the rhythm! I mean, he can really play it! You don't have to have a drum. When we started singing, he could follow us. If we started singing a song a certain way, he could find what we were doing. We did it more that way than us following him. Whatever we were hitting in the harmony, he'd follow us. When it came to hitting the harmony, it was a matter of whatever felt good to us. There again, that's what kept us from sounding like the Blackwood Brothers or the Statesmen and most every other group that came along. Finding how to make a song fit us instead of us trying to fit a song, that gave us our identity.

"Jack was the guy who could hear harmony. When we hit a good chord, oftentimes it was Jack who said, 'Boys, that harmonizes.' By the same token, when we hit an impure chord, Jack would cock his head sideways and say, 'Something ain't right!' He knew it instinctively. He has a great ear and he knows singing."

That was the way the Inspirations Quartet came together.

Harmony is born in the souls of some. Years later, when Archie's daughter, Melissa, was in elementary school she proved that harmony ran in the family. She could sing the melody of *Silent Night* beautifully. She could also sing the alto notes with no one singing with her, and then she could sing the other part, everything but the bass, because it was born in her to hear harmony.

Remembering when he had quit football and curtailed basketball to give full time to singing, Archie finally encountered something else that could have interfered with singing. He fell in love!

He met Cindy in 1965. Dean Robinson, still singing bass, worked in the Qualla Supermarket in Cherokee. Dean would tell all who would listen about the Inspirations' singing, and one day Jake and Earl Battle, who owned the supermarket, asked, "Why don't you all get together up at our house and practice? We like what you're doing and we'd like to hear you. We'll have some cake and coffee and sandwiches, and we'll sing."

The get-together was arranged in late January of 1965. Archie remembers that he had turned sixteen on January 6 and was getting his driver's license. Archie, Martin, Jack, Ronnie, and Dean practiced there in the Battle household.

Everyone had a good time that evening. Jake's stepdaughter, Cindy, sat on the couch, listening. They lived in the Qualla Community on U.S. 441, which goes through the Cherokee Indian Reservation and on across the Smokies to Gatlinburg. Their home was about a mile from the Gateway toward Cherokee.

"She went to Sylva to high school because Qualla was in Jackson County," Archie said, "and I went to Bryson City, but big as the rivalry was between those two schools—and it was BIG!—I discovered that I had fallen in love at first sight. That was it! I knew that as well as I knew my name.

"I thought about her all the time," he said, "and a little later on we were going to have the Kingsmen come to Bryson City for one of our promotions. I mustered up enough nerve to call Cindy and ask if she'd go to the singing with me."

When Cindy accepted the invitation, Archie borrowed his father's blue and white Rambler station wagon with a stick shift, and took her to the singing. They began to date regularly, but they never had a Saturday night date except at a singing. By that time the Inspirations sang somewhere every Saturday, and when Archie and Cindy dated, they did so at the singing, though not conspicuously.

"We in the Inspirations had already come up with our set of rules for moral conduct," Archie said, "which didn't allow any of us to spend much time with a girl at a singing, so when I took her to a singing I wouldn't let her come near the record table. I was afraid somebody would think I was flirting with a girl—which I certainly was.

"But with us, singing was strictly serious, and no one broke the rules. Cindy understood. She looked at our singing the same way we did, as a ministry, and she was happy to live by the rules, too. She still is."

Cindy's maiden name was Bumgarner. She was from pioneer mountain stock. Her father, Glenn Bumgarner, was from Wilmot on the Tuckaseegee River west of Sylva. Her mother, Lucille Reagan, was born in Smokemont, which later was taken in by the Great Smoky Mountains National Park, and her family moved away when the park was formed and their house torn down."

Archie's parents also came out of the Smoky Mountains when the park was established. "That's what makes the park so dear to us," Archie said, "our families came out of it. The government took a lot of our county to establish the park. My mom went to school on Noland's Creek within the park boundaries, where the Road to Nowhere ends."

The government treated Swain County just as it treated the American Indians, making huge promises that were never fulfilled. It promised Swain County a road to Townsend, Tennessee, and built a few miles of it, boring a large tunnel through a mountain—and then politics dead-ended the road. Today the road is known as the Road to Nowhere.

Archie and Cindy were married the year she was graduated from Sylva-Webster High School and a year after Archie finished at Swain County High.

Their wedding was set for Monday night, June 10, 1968, at Shoal Creek Baptist Church after the Inspirations had sung in Jacksonville, Florida, on Sunday night and driven all night to get home.

"Let me tell you how important singing was to us," Archie said. "We got married on Monday night so I wouldn't have to take any time off from singing. We sang every Thursday, Friday, Saturday, and Sunday, and not any of us missed singing for anything but death or hospitalization."

The wedding was to be at seven-thirty that evening, but when Archie got home Cindy told him that the church had a scheduled meeting at seven-thirty that couldn't be delayed, so the wedding was switched to seven o'clock.

"I forgot to call poor old Ronnie and tell him the wedding time had been changed," Archie said, "and when he and his mama drove up in the church yard, we were coming out of the church. Ronnie never forgave me for that. It really made him mad, and I think he thought I'd done it on purpose."

The newly-weds took an apartment in the Highlander Motel in Bryson City, the motel the Inspirations purchased in 1971 and changed its name to Inspirations Motel.

The next great moments in the lives of Archie and Cindy Watkins came in 1971 when their daughter Melissa was born, and in 1974 when their second daughter, Amy, was born. Archie was absent on both occasions, in Greensboro when Melissa came along and in Akron, Ohio, when Amy arrived.

Melissa became a great high school athlete. She went to Converse College on a full basketball scholarship, played one game and one minute of another and tore in two the ligament across her knee and never played another game. She earned a degree in math and science.

Amy, who graduated from Western Carolina University with a degree in business law, is married and, at this writing, will make Archie and Cindy grandparents in October, 1999.

Archie became a farmer who raised cattle. He and Cindy lived in Bryson City for two or three years and then moved to Qualla about 1971 and built a house on a thirty-five acre farm. He rented land also, and farmed, ran cattle, and grew hay on about seventy acres.

"Singing as much as we did," Archie said, "farming became a headache, so I sold all my cattle last year and quit farming. We still have the thirty-five acres and have built a campground on part of it and I fool around there a lot."

He and Cindy bought a motor home in which they go here and yonder, and he said if he thought he could keep up with the quartet bus, he'd just take his motor home on the road.

"But I'm not as young as I used to be," he finished, "and I can't drive that much."

Actually, there came a time a few years ago that Archie considered quitting the Inspirations and retiring from the road.

"I had seriously given it a lot of thought," he said, "and had really planned to retire. I thought twenty-five years was all I had to do, but the Lord wasn't ready for me to retire. I was ready, but He wasn't.

"The way I feel now," he added, after he put the feeling aside. "I want to sing as long as I live."

Ask Archie who his favorite gospel singer of all time is and you'll get a surprising answer.

"I'm going to let you in on a little secret that may bust the bubble of a lot of singers," he'll say, and then he will add, "My favorite singer was Jimmy Jones."

If you've followed gospel music for a long time, you will immediately think of Jimmy Jones who sang baritone and bass for the Deep South Quartet, the LeFevres, and some others, and you'll be wrong.

"No, not that one," Archie said, "although he was a good singer. The one I'm talking about sang with the Harmonizing Four, a black quartet. Jimmy Jones was a bass singer in the thirties and forties. In 1926 a bunch of boys started singing in Dunbar Elementary School in Richmond, Virginia. They called themselves the Harmonizing Four, and Jimmy Jones was one of them."

In 1964, the year the Inspirations were organized with Martin, Archie, Ronnie, Jack, and Dean Robinson, they had a recording of the Harmonizing Four, a new reproduction of a record the black quartet had made many years before, and on that record were several songs that the young Inspirations had heard other quartets sing.

"You remember the song *I Love to Call on Jesus* that Rex Nelon sang?" Archie asked. "Jimmy Jones sang it first. Remember the song that Hovie Lister sang, *You Gotta Live Like Jesus Every Day*? Came right off a Harmonizing Four record. Songs like *His Eye is on the Sparrow* that bass singers love to sing—Jimmy Jones sang it on that record. *The New Jerusalem* came off that record.

"What about *Getaway Jordan*, the song the Statesmen rode for so long? Ronnie calls it Hovie's sugar stick. It came from one of those black groups. I don't know if it was the Harmonizing Four or the Golden Gate Quartet or the Jubilaires.

"A gospel deejay in Arkansas told me that when the Harmonizing Four made a record that gospel groups would line up to buy them so they could borrow their arrangements."

Archie became interested in the Harmonizing Four. He has tapes of songs off their records that he plays all the time. "They sang like a Southern gospel quartet," Archie said, "but they had a richness in their voices that few others have.

"I got so wrapped up in their singing that that's all I listened to for several years in the late sixties. They had a quartet sound, beautiful harmony, and they were excellent on all four parts."

All the Inspirations wanted to meet Jimmy Jones. They thought they had the opportunity in 1964 when J. G. Whitfield held an International Songfest in Nashville, for which he brought in singers and groups from all over, including a quartet from Sweden. The Harmonizing Four were on that program, but unfortunately Jimmy Jones had already left the group.

Time passed until the early 1990s, and the Inspirations sang in Richmond. Archie said, "Boys, I'm going to ask around here and see if anybody ever heard of the Harmonizing Four. At dinner that evening, the Inspirations were in a restaurant in which an elderly black man was eating, and Archie asked him, "Sir, have you ever heard of the Harmonizing Four?"

The man said, "Oh, yeah, they used to sing around here."

"You know anything about them, how to get hold of them?"

"No," the man said, scratching his chin, "but there's a fellow down on Main Street at the Record Rack who knows 'em."

"I called that man," Archie related later, "and he got plumb beside himself. He said he had some records of the Harmonizing Four, some forty-fives, and a cassette or two of Jimmy Jones's solos, so I got in the bus and went down there, right in the heart of town and found the Record Rack.

"The man was so excited that someone had come in asking about the Harmonizing Four. He said that three of them were still alive, Jimmy Jones, Lonnie Smith, and Tommy Johnson, and he gave me their phone numbers, but somehow I didn't have the heart to call them."

A year later, in Richmond again to sing in a church, Archie screwed up his courage and dialed Jimmy Jones's number. A woman answered.

"Could I speak to Mr. Jones?" Archie asked, but the woman said he had passed on that year. That was in the early '90s.

"I'm really sorry," Archie said, "but let me explain who I am." She appreciated his calling and told him, "Thomas Johnson is still alive." He was the baritone.

"Do you think he'd mind me calling?"

"No," she said. "He'd be proud."

So Archie dialed Thomas Johnson's number and Johnson answered. "Boy," Archie said, "he was nice, just as nice as anyone could be. He was eighty-one years old and said he'd try his best to come to the church and hear us that night.

"I didn't figure we'd see him," Archie continued, "but as we were singing I saw a little black man, bent and frail, come in the door with a young boy. He came down the side, just grinning. He was carrying one of our *He's Our Guide* albums. He had brought it for us to sign. His grandson was a big fan of ours who had heard us sing on television, and I think the old man was getting it signed for him."

Archie did a lot of research on those black quartets and came to a conclusion that they contributed heavily to gospel music, especially to harmony patterns. "If I had to put my finger on where a lot of our gospel singing came from," Archie said, "I'd say a lot came from those great black gospel groups of yesterday.

"Back in the forties, the black groups would have the highest singer take the melody. That's inverting the harmony just as we do it today. I think that's where it came from.

"The Harmonizing Four," Archie said, "sang like the Statesmen, the Oak Ridge Boys, the Swanee River Boys, and many other quartets. That probably helped make Jimmy Jones my favorite singer."

# 13

# Physical Fitness

L ike many other quartets, the Inspirations love all sports. They while away many hours of riding by discussing sports. Unlike most other quartets, though, the Inspirations also love to play the games they talk about.

From the start of their career thirty-five years ago, when they reached a town in which they would sing but not spend the night, they did not—nor do they now—take a motel room to clean up in. At first they went to the YMCA where they spent an hour or so working with weights, walking the treadmill, running, and exercising. Now they go to health spas and do the same thing. After showering there they are ready to go sing.

"We don't belong to the YMCA anymore," Martin said. "I belong to the Franklin Fitness Center, a health club in Franklin, which is just a few miles from Bryson City and from Caney Fork.

"YMCAs have deteriorated a lot," he said. "They went downhill in most places. There are still some nice ones around the country, but they are few. Fitness centers have taken over. Most towns of five thousand people or more have a nice fitness center. Some are hospital-owned wellness centers, and they are the best ones. In Hattiesburg, Mississippi, the hospital has a tremendous wellness center. They even check your blood pressure there.

"This is the way we keep ourselves fit," Martin said, "and when we're in good physical condition we feel better and can sing better."

Martin started this routine in 1957. He had just graduated from college and was teaching in Haywood County, living in Canton. There the huge Robertson Memorial YMCA was the only place in town to work out, and Martin availed himself of it while he played piano for the Kingsmen Quartet.

After the Inspirations were formed, they traded the director of the YMCA record albums for memberships and the entire quartet worked out frequently.

"We could use those memberships to get into any YMCA in the country," Martin said. "We used them constantly, keeping our muscles toned, trying not to let all that bus-riding turn us to flab. We went into these towns and the first thing we did when we got up was go to the YMCA, and then of a night, after the singing was over, the last thing we'd do was play basketball wherever we could.

"Many times," Martin continued, "the folks who would sponsor our singing would be high school coaches, trying to raise money for a project, and after the singing they would have a team lined up to play us, and they would have the best players they could find. If we finished singing at eleven o'clock, say, we would play basketball until about one in the morning."

Archie, who had been a star basketball player in high school, remembers going to Lexington, Tennessee, to sing at a school during basketball season. Paul Smiley, who had sung with the then defunct Smoky Mountain Quartet, made that weekend trip with the Inspirations.

"We had some friends in Lexington, Kay and Nancy Wyatt," Archie said. "Kay has an insurance business there and they promoted us every year for a while. Knowing how we liked to play basketball, Kay arranged for a game in the gymnasium the afternoon of the day we sang, and he recruited coaches and physical education teachers from around the county and had a crackerjack team lined up, waiting to ambush us.

"Paul Smiley was tall and all arms and legs, and a pretty fair basketball player himself. And all of us had been playing every chance we got for a long time."

Kay's team came out in basketball uniforms, and the Inspirations who had YMCA shorts dressed in them, and the others wore jeans.

The school had brought its student body into the gym to see the game, and the place was filled.

Seeing all this, the Inspirations smelled a rat, and Kay was grinning like the Cheshire cat, knowing he was going to pull one over on the quartet.

"We'll play you and do the best we can," Archie told them. "But don't expect too much of a game."

That was one day the Inspirations were really on their game. Smiley and Mike Holcomb, who is tall, played inside; Martin, who is very strong, set screens and blocked out, and the other guys went wild. The Inspirations had plenty of firepower; remember, Archie was a high-scoring all-conference player in high school.

Suddenly, the Inspirations were ahead, and then they began widening the gap, and soon they were winning by such a wide margin that the classes began getting up one at a time and marching out of the gymnasium in single file.

"They had really prepared for this game," Archie said. "They had the scoreboard lit up and the clock running, and an official scorekeeper, and all of that, and we poured it on them so badly that the classes just left."

The Inspirations weren't rough intentionally, but they were rough enough because basketball to them was simple physical exercise. Doug Plemmons, a basketball player at Western Carolina, went with them one weekend and said later that they played so hard he had trouble getting out of bed on Monday morning. "I've never been through anything like that," he said.

In warm weather, the Inspirations played softball.

"When the Primitives traveled with us on the bus for that year and a half," Martin said, "we really had softball going. We had a pretty fair team. We could beat about any church team we played until we went up to Pastor Locklear's church in Michigan, and the best I remember they beat us something like twenty-one to two. That was our most embarrassing game. Come to find out, though, they had been beating everybody and were state champions of the church leagues. That beating was so bad we almost lost our desire to play."

Martin shook his head. "We played too hard, I guess. We had all kinds of accidents in those games. Roger Fortner hit Troy in the nose with a pitch one day and broke Troy's nose. He stayed in the hospital a couple of days. I think we had two broken noses. I remember breaking somebody's nose, but I don't remember whose. I've been trying to forget it."

The Inspirations were so sports-minded that about the only team they didn't challenge was the Atlanta Braves, and that probably crossed their minds when the Primitives rode with them.

Gluttons for punishment, they certainly didn't neglect golf and tennis.

Here is how Archie described their first golf game:

"We got into golf," Archie said, "and old Eddie was the only one who had ever played the game. We thought he was a pro. He knew all about professional golf, knew the players by name, and knew how to play the game. The rest of us didn't know up from down about golf.

"We were in Tupelo, Mississippi, and a friend, Gene Sisk from the radio station, took us out to the country club where he was a member. The course was crowded that day and there were a lot of fellows waiting to tee off, so when we went up on the first tee, we had a pretty large gallery watching.

"Not any of us knew what to do so we told Eddie to go ahead and tee off and show us how. He put his ball on a tee, backed away, and took a few practice swings. Then he stepped up to the ball and wiggled his hips, and wiggled them again. He shifted his feet and lined his driver to the ball and wiggled again. But he wasn't satisfied, so he stepped away and took a few more swings and wiggles, then approached the ball and started wiggling again.

"I believe it took him twenty minutes to tee off, and I knew then why it took so long to play a round of golf. He took so long, we started laughing and kidding him about it. Golfers were lined up behind us, watching Eddie, shaking their heads, and wondering what have we got here?

"Finally, Eddie got his feet just right and reared back and took a mighty swing and topped the ball. It dribbled off to the right. When that happened we went down on the tee, rolling and laughing, holding our sides, and I know all those who were lined up were asking the Good Lord why He had put such a bunch of idiots in front of them.

"I don't know how to account for it, but Eddie dribbled his tee shots all day and the rest of us knocked the socks off the ball. Every one of us beat him."

They did tennis the same way. Eddie and Troy dressed themselves out in fancy tennis apparel, the whole bit: shorts and racquets, sweaters, and expensive tennis shoes.

On a singing trip to Brookhaven, Mississippi, the Inspirations visited Doug Griffin and his family. Doug was going to college and playing on the tennis team and he and Eddie hatched up the idea of playing Martin and Archie. Martin had never played tennis and Archie had played very little.

"They thought they would beat us like a drum," Archie said. "They were ready to really whip up on us, especially since we'd beaten Eddie so bad in golf. But we could do nothing wrong that day, and we laid an embarrassing beating on Eddie and Doug."

Growing up in a small town like Bryson City, in an extremely rural setting bordering both Fontana Lake and the Great Smoky Mountains National Park, the

Inspirations have nursed a great love for outdoor sports and activities, which they had been accustomed to all their lives. And Martin, especially, coming off the head of Caney Fork, loved the outdoors.

All the guys are inveterate hunters, fishermen, and campers.

"My folks have always loved to hunt," Martin said, "and so have I. When I was a boy I couldn't wait till I got home from school to go squirrel hunting.

"We loved to fish, too. I remember Dad and I would get cane poles and head back in the woods to catch trout. I always looked forward to those fishing trips. So hunting and fishing were two of the big things we did."

Martin owns eight treeing Walker hounds and his boys, Myron and Michael, love to go bear hunting with their dad and the hounds.

"We often go down to the North Carolina coast in the Wilmington area," Martin said, "and bear-hunt there. I've hunted on the coast when the tide was in and water was up to my armpits. I've really had great experiences bear-hunting."

In two different hair-raising experiences, Martin killed bears within a few feet of him. "I killed both of those bears at such close range that the shotgun wadding and pellets went in the same hole."

In swamps on the coast, the undergrowth is so thick that visibility is often limited to fifteen feet, which is too close for comfort in bear country.

Martin and Michael were crawling through swamp thickets, parting the brush with gun barrels. Their fifteen dogs had treed a bear.

"The way that bear was fighting those dogs," Martin said, "it sounded like a bulldozer at work."

He could see blood on the ground from the dogs injured by the bear's great swipes.

Suddenly, looking at the blood, Martin realized the bear was close at hand and when he looked up the bear was there, on its hind paws, looking at Martin through beady eyes, not more than six feet away, maybe closer.

Martin didn't have time to aim. He pointed his shotgun toward the bear and pulled the trigger. The pellets and wadding smashed into the same hole in the bear's chest, and the brute fell dead.

"That happened so fast," Martin said, "that I didn't have much time to get scared, but the second time I shot one that close, I did have time to be scared, and there couldn't be anything more scary than a mad bear charging you."

His dogs treed a bear in the coastal swamps. Martin took a long shot at him and suddenly the bear disappeared from view. He had either fallen or jumped out of the tree.

After the shot, Martin's gun failed to eject the empty hull, and he worked the hull out and put a fresh one in, and when he looked up, the bear was charging him like a runaway freight. He was close already and moving fast, roaring angrily.

"I just shot into him," Martin said. "I didn't have time to aim that time, either."

Pellets and wadding smashed into the same hole between the bear's head and shoulders and killed him instantly.

"We have good friends all across the country that we've met while singing," Martin said, "and we visit them a lot. It helps break the monotony on the road, and many of those people will remain friends of ours for life. We have made it a point not just to sing to people, but we get to know them, and hunt and do things with them. Always have. I think that's one thing we do differently from most other quartets."

The Inspirations made friends with some hunters in West Virginia, and Jack recently went to hunt with them.

Jack is a veteran bear hunter whose kills number more than a hundred. He has killed so many that Martin introduces him as "The old bear-hunter himself, Jack Laws." He drives to West Virginia to hunt with those friends every bear season.

In the fall, the Inspirations used to go to Ethelsville, Alabama, on the Mississippi line, where a retired highway patrolman, a motorcycle officer named Henry Copeland, had an eighteen-acre farm.

Deer hunting was good on Copeland's place, and the Inspirations would spend a week there, hunting in the daytime and singing and gorging themselves on venison, gravy, and biscuits in the evenings.

"We've never hunted in the West as a group," Martin said, "but the boys go out there and hunt individually. Archie hunts out West every year."

Martin enjoys deer hunting. He bought a place in Georgia where deer hunting is excellent. The place is equipped with little hunting stations, built like outhouses, with cutouts in the sides to shoot from. The hunting stations are scattered along game trails so a hunter can sit and relax and wait for a deer to come to him.

"It's fun and a lot easier than bear-hunting," Martin said. "With those stations on the trail, we don't have to drive the deer; they just come by.

"You know," he added, and it was easy to tell that he was a lifelong student of wild game, "deer do just like cows. They go the same trail. And bear do the same thing. They don't just wander around through the woods. When they're feeding they'll feed where the food is; but if they're moving, they'll go the same path their ancestors used.

"Up on Caney Fork when they're moving, they go through those same trails they went through for my grandpa. That's amazing to me. They say rattlesnakes may travel three, four, or five miles in the summertime, but the rascals will go back to that same rock crevice, that same den that their ancestors denned in. They don't just wind up anywhere by chance. They go home."

Hunting recently in Georgia, Martin and his son Michael experienced coyotes making an attack on what they believed to be a deer.

Coyotes have been brought in from the West and stocked in some of the South's forests, and fox hunters have purchased others and put them out in the wild so their dogs could run both foxes and coyotes. Some of the coyotes escape the dogs and keep going, living in the wild. There are even some around Caney Fork.

"First," Martin said, explaining what he and Michael heard, "one coyote made a sound like a little kid, an excited, sharp sound. He was down on the creek, singing like a small dog. That went on for two or three minutes. Then another started up, and another.

"What they were doing was circling. The first one had spotted the prey and sounded off, and the others began circling around. Pretty soon, it sounded like a bear fight. The prey must have eluded them for they broke and ran back across the hill. They continued their high-pitched howling, but if it was a deer they had surrounded, it got away. Once it broke out of the circle and ran, they couldn't catch it. It was strange to hear."

"We've always jumped from one thing to another," Martin said, "from basketball to softball, to golf and tennis, and hunting and fishing. We've always had a kick—that's what my brother Candler calls it. We bounce from one thing to another."

When they got on the hunting kick, J. G. Whitfield had several stores in Pensacola, Florida, and the Inspirations armed themselves there, each buying a gun from him.

Candler said a kick is a three-sided thing: "First, it can't make any sense; second, it can't be profitable; and third, it costs you money."

So the Inspirations went through the guns and hunting stage, and came to the horseback riding stage. "That was one of our best kicks," Martin said. "Everybody bought a horse."

They loved riding into the head of Caney Fork and camping out. The head of Caney Fork, an area known as Bearwallow, is remote. It reaches up the mountains to a point under the Blue Ridge Parkway, into wild country that was once a haven for moonshiners.

When the quartet hit the horseback stage, Eddie was the neophyte. He had never been on a horse. Martin directed Eddie toward a horse named Old Champ. "That's the calmest horse you'll ever see," Martin said. "Just get on and he'll follow right along with us. He'll carry you so easy you'll think you're Gene Autry."

He wasn't spoofing. He was not visiting a cruel joke on Eddie like range riders played on each other in days of old. Old Champ really was a gentle horse. But he had a mind of his own that Eddie's couldn't match.

"When we started, I did like Martin told me," Eddie said, "and slacked the reins on the horse's neck, and Old Champ followed the others nicely. We got up the road to a church, probably a quarter of a mile from where we started, and Old Champ turned around and started back for the house, just plodding along."

Eddie had no idea what to do. He yelled, "Whoa! Whoa!" and the horse just kept walking. He walked all the way back to the house where Ora Blanche was standing. Old Champ walked up to her and stopped.

"What are you doing back, Eddie?" she asked.

"I don't know," Eddie replied.

Eddie soon got the horse turned around and the old boy plodded back to where the group waited.

Eddie bought two horses then, a mare and a stud, and soon the mare increased the size of Eddie's herd with a brand-new colt.

Archie bought a big stud horse and Mike, a beautiful palomino.

Once, the Inspirations rode to Preacher Dillard Wood's house away up Caney Fork, and Preacher Wood came out to greet them. He looked over the horses and, pointing to Archie's stud, said to Martin, "Cook, that stud horse ain't gonna work." He knew the horse.

"Why not?" Archie thought. He looked over the other horses to make sure all were not mares, and they were not. Archie's horse wanted to walk around on his hind legs all the time.

"The horse was diseased," Archie said, "and we didn't know enough about horses to realize it. One of his testicles had a cancer on it, and when he got around other animals, his body released certain chemicals. When those chemicals hit the cancer they set him on fire. He was really in bad shape."

So Preacher Wood was right. The horse didn't work out. Archie sold him, telling the buyers of the problem, and they put the horse under surgery and he regained his health.

On one of their frequent excursions into the woods, Jack became a rodeo rider. The group rode up Deep Creek near Bryson City to the Bryson place, where they camped. Jack had to work and planned to go in later in the day or the following morning.

He borrowed a beautiful mare from a fellow named Joe Thomas, and riding up Deep Creek came to a wooden bridge. Looking through the cracks between the boards of the bridge floor, the horse could see water rushing below. Frightened by the water, the horse tried to jump off the bridge, but somehow Jack coaxed it back to normal and got it across the bridge.

Farther up the road, a grouse flew up ahead, shattering the air with its wing beats, the horse went nuts again, crow-hopping and sunfishing like a rodeo pony.

"That was a scary horse," Jack said as he told the Inspirations about his ride.

Archie grinned, and not wanting to miss an opportunity to chide Jack for sleeping so much on the bus, said. "Probably what had that horse spooked was the rolled-up mattress Jack tied behind the saddle. That mattress is six inches thick."

"Whatever it was," Jack replied, "that was still the scariest horse I ever saw."

The most hilarious horse stunt any of the singers pulled came the day Troy tried to mount his horse and couldn't.

Troy is short, and he couldn't get a foot high enough to put in the stirrup.

"He took the horse over by a picnic table," Mike said, "and climbed on the table so he could mount the horse from above. We were all riding out of the place when someone missed Troy and we looked around and saw that horse going round and round the picnic table with Troy hopping around on the table on one leg, trying to get aboard."

Roger Fortner borrowed his father's work horse for one of the rides. The horse was a monster, about 1,800 pounds, with big hooves. Going down the road, the rest of the Inspirations broke into a gallop, racing to a certain point, and Roger whacked that work horse in the ribs with his heels, and the horse leapt forward and dashed down the road, running on pavement. Suddenly, the horse slipped and spreadeagled there in the road.

"It looked like it just splattered all over the road," Mike said, "and then it slid in a ditch. That was some horse wreck!"

They went on to the Bryson place and put the work horse in a stall. She went in all right but wouldn't come out. Roger tried to back her out and she'd put her back hooves on the ground and brake herself.

"Finally," Mike said, "we had to turn her around inside that stall, and it busted the sides of the stall to pieces."

Most of the fellows were happy when they moved on to their next kick.

# 14

# Ronnie

The most traumatic thing ever to strike an Inspiration knocked Ronnie Hutchins for a loop in November of 1997. A doctor told him he had lymphoma, a tumor of lymphoid tissue in his neck, and that his death was imminent, probably within nine months.

This was crushing news for one who was only three months shy of his forty-ninth birthday.

When the tumor finally grew to such size that everyone noticed it, Ronnie left the Inspirations and was replaced by Matt Dibler. For some time, he had been watching a growth on his neck, but he attributed it to singing.

The growth never pained him, he never had a sore throat from it, and it interfered with his swallowing only a tiny bit now and then.

When the doctor told him that his tumor was malignant, Ronnie felt his world caving in. For a while he went around and around with himself, alternating between abject fear and a peace of mind that he couldn't explain.

Finally he decided that if he had to die in nine months, he would bypass radiation and all else and let death come as it willed.

"I thought if heaven is real," he said, "what am I doing here?"

That didn't lessen the weight he felt in his chest. His heart was heavy. He spent time reviewing his life and determined that he could have done better. "I never did anything drastically wrong," he said, "but I know I haven't lived the life I should have. I haven't lived up to the expectations of the Inspirations."

Ronnie's mother, Faye Shook Hutchins, turned eighty-three on June 29, 1999, during the Singing in the Smokies. His father, Clinton Roosevelt Hutchins, passed away December 13, 1993, after spending a lifetime telling folks he was named for Teddy Roosevelt. He didn't particularly like Franklin D.

Mrs. Hutchins worried gravely about her son.

Ronnie worried, too, and one day the thought crossed his mind to get a second opinion, and he telephoned the office of Dr. William E. Mitchell, a trusted Bryson City physician, and scheduled an appointment.

After a thorough checkup, Ron waited anxiously for the physician to give him the news, and when Dr. Mitchell came in, he was smiling.

"They said you're going to die in nine months, did they?" he said. "I say Bull! Son, you don't have a thing to worry about. You don't have lymphoma; you've got something wrong in your neck here, some kind of infection. You're going to be around a lot longer than nine months."

Having felt a month before as if the Empire State Building had collapsed on him, Ronnie began to feel that the debris had been cleared away and he was going to be all right. He was jubilant.

But Dr. Mitchell slowed his celebration down. "We still have a bit of surgery to do," the doctor said. "I'm going in there and see what the infection is and remove it."

A year and a half later, Ronnie had only a scar on his neck to show for his fright-of-a-lifetime.

But removal of the growth didn't bring him out of the woods. Recuperating nicely for a couple of days, he suddenly began feeling ill again. He became worse, and worse, and worse still, and Dr. Mitchell ran tests and couldn't figure what the trouble was.

He had Ronnie transferred to St. Joseph's Hospital in Asheville where dozens of tests were run, and finally, early one morning, a team of skilled medical personnel, wearing masks and shields, rushed into his room and loaded him onto a gurney.

"What's the matter?" Ronnie asked. "What's going on?"

"Tuberculosis," a nurse replied, and the team rolled Ronnie rapidly out of the room and down to another floor and put him in an isolation room.

Lying there wondering what would happen to him next, Ronnie felt the fears and anxieties returning. He remembered that his grandfather had died from tuberculosis.

He was in and out of the hospital for eleven weeks, and finally his physicians reported to him that they thought he had licked the disease. What a joyous day that was! The trip back to Bryson City was perhaps the best drive he ever made.

After spending all of 1998 in recuperation, he was declared cured.

He did not go back to singing immediately. His place with the Inspirations had been filled.

"I'm not a dummy," he said. "We have always had a rule that if a guy left the group he couldn't come back and pick up where he left off unless there was an opening. I have left several times and have never come back and imposed myself on the group. Martin wouldn't have let me, and I wouldn't have expected him to. I know Martin too well. He plays by the rules and we all respect him for it.

"Besides," Ronnie added, "with Matt they've almost got the old Inspirations sound back. Matt is the ideal person to be there singing."

At this writing, Ronnie goes out with the Inspirations one weekend a month, filling in for whoever needs or would like to be off.

Possibly the greatest good to come out of all of Ronnie's travail, he summed up in a simple statement.

"I love the Lord," he said, "and I'm probably the straightest I've ever been."

Ronnie's dad was one of ten children. He worked for the WPA in the depression and during World War II on the construction of Fontana Dam. Much of his life was spent working in lumber mills and furniture factories.

His mom was a waitress and Avon lady who was one of fourteen children. She and Ronnie live on the place where he was born, but in a newer house.

Ronnie's singing career with the Inspirations has been up and down. Probably a better way to express it would be to say in and out. For various reasons, not any of which had anything detrimental to do with the quartet or its personnel, Ronnie left the Inspirations four times.

He was one of the original members, starting when he was fifteen after that narration of Little Red Riding Hood that Martin Cook saw him do in chapel one day.

Most of the quartet guys date the beginning of the Inspirations to 1964, but they didn't really hit full stride until 1966 when they made their first recording with Martin playing piano, Archie singing tenor, Ronnie on the lead, Jack at baritone, and Troy singing bass. But Ronnie's perception of the beginning of the quartet goes a bit farther back than that.

"Actually, Troy wasn't a member of the original Inspirations Quartet," Ronnie said. "He was only fourteen and he came along after we were singing as the Inspirations. I have always thought the Inspirations really began with Dean Robinson singing bass. It's probably more realistic to date the quartet's beginning from that first recording, but Dean was with us a good while after we called ourselves the Inspirations. Not that it really matters; it's just that I have always thought that way. . . ."

Unlike some of the other original members, Ronnie had never sung with any of them before. He didn't know Troy until Troy joined the group.

Ronnie remembers these details in the formation of the Inspirations:

Jack sang with the Bryson City Quartet until he joined the Inspirations in 1964. In that Bryson City Quartet, Donald Watkins, Archie's brother who has been the Inspirations' bus driver for many years, sang first tenor, Jerry Bowers lead, Dean Robinson bass, and Margaret Ashe played piano. They sang like that at Paul Higdon's Second Saturday night singings before 1964.

"In school," Ronnie continued, "we'd go to chapel and Martin would play specials on the piano. He liked to play *Keep on the Firing Line.* He had that wide-open style, still does. He hasn't changed except he's better at it now. Martin would play at the drop of a hat, and he would wear his own hat and wear it kinda loose."

Soon after Martin began playing with the Bryson City Quartet, school let out and he went to Kentucky to work for the National Park Service.

Archie started tagging along with his big brother, Donald, who didn't really like to sing. Donald was the outdoors type who liked construction, big trucks, and playing in the dirt. That made him happy.

Soon the Bryson City Quartet discovered that Archie could sing, too. "Not only could he sing," Ronnie said, "he could sing on pitch and sky high. Back then he could sing through the roof. He used to hurt me when we first started out. It aggravated me. I'm a natural baritone, not a natural lead, but I can stretch my voice out and pull it off. I've done it all these years singing lead."

"After Dean Robinson, Ray Dean Reese sang bass with us for a few weeks. I call him the Inspiration That Never Was. The funniest thing Ray Dean ever said was that he thought he'd just go somewhere and find himself a job because he didn't think we were going to make it. We still jab at each other. Ray Dean is good at dishing it out, but he's good at taking it, too. He can take anything you give him and over the years we've given him some good ones."

Ronnie continued: "What memories we all have of that van. We learned to sing in that old van. We slept on top of each other in it—we were all little then. The only one who couldn't crawl on top of the speakers and sleep was Martin, and whoever could get to the van the fastest after the singing was over, and crawled on top of the speakers, got to sleep there. They were big wooden speakers, and I believe I remember Archie having something to do with building them.

"We shined our shoes in that old van," Ronnie continued. "Later, when we had a bus, I remember times when Martin would tell us our shoes weren't shiny enough. He told us so often it became second nature with me to tell when I had shined my shoes enough. We spit-shined them. Martin was just a few years removed from the army in Korea, and he learned to spit-shine his boots in the Army. He taught us to use a pair of thick panty hose. We could either use ice water or spit on them. Wet the shoes and then work in the polish until the shoes had a nice, hazy coating, and then we would shine it off. People wouldn't believe it now, what with patent leather and stuff like that, and I guess we got a little lazy somewhere along the way, but it's a lot easier to wear patent leather than to spit-shine shoes."

Ronnie rubbed a finger across the whiskers growing on his upper lip and chuckled. "I remember we had a left-handed, upside-down guitar player for a while. Eddie something. I can't remember his name. He lived in Clarksville, Georgia, and he had a mustache—so the Inspirations for a few minutes had a mustache.

"Even now," he added, "when I go singing, I shave my mustache. I grow it for three weeks and then shave it off."

Ronnie is thankful for the discipline the Inspirations have maintained over the years. "Not many boys were disciplined as much as we were," he said, "and we liked it. It helped us grow to manhood and helped us become better people."

Discipline and self-policing. Helping each other out. Pulling each other from difficult situations. The Inspirations have always policed themselves, and will go to the ends of the earth to right any wrong to any member of the quartet.

Once in the early years word circulated in a small Alabama town where the Inspirations sang that Jack and Ronnie had been seen outside a singing drinking beer. A preacher spread the story.

It was not true, but today's gossip becomes tomorrow's news. When Martin heard the tale the preacher had told, the Inspirations were driving home after singing up north. They were supposed to be home to Bryson City the next day for the Fall Color Festival at Inspirations Park. But Martin was so aggravated and worried about the rumor that he directed Donald Watkins to head for Alabama.

The bus arrived in the Alabama town during the night and Martin got a policeman to go with the quartet to the preacher's house in the middle of the night. They woke the preacher and Martin "straightened him out," according to Ronnie, and nothing more was ever heard of that rumor.

Ronnie Hutchins' career with the Inspirations has been fragmented into four different parts. He was the quartet's original rolling stone, rolling from one thing to another, trying to find his place.

He sang with the quartet five years from 1964 till 1969. He admits part of his reason for leaving was being young and foolish.

"I went to California," he said. "My big brother Norman was on a construction job out there, and I thought I wanted to get into that work. But when I got there, I saw that construction work was not what I was cut out for."

He got a job with a brokerage firm called Sutro and Company.

"I was a broker trainee," he said, "which, I discovered, was a fancy term for a gofer."

He returned to sing with the Inspirations in September of 1971 and stayed until May, 1973, when wanderlust struck again and for thirteen years he was something of a drifting gypsy, sowing his oats.

The LeFevres, one of the long-time favorite groups on the gospel circuit, had reached the end of the trail and some members retired. Their bass singer, Rex Nelon, who grew up in Asheville, had purchased the group and took on some new singers. He hired Ronnie to sing the lead.

Almost the first thing Rex did was make a recording. He told Ronnie that he wanted a song from him that could be recorded immediately. Ronnie chose one of the Inspirations' older songs, *He'll Hold My Hand.* He had been singing the song for years and could record it next day if necessary.

"I'd always loved that song," Ronnie said, "and we had always featured Jack on it. So I cut it and it took off. We had a good combination of the old LeFevres and the new LeFevres, and everything clicked. Apparently I had chosen the right song, for we got a Top Five Grammy nomination for the album *Stepping on the Clouds.*"

Ronnie sang with the LeFevres, who later changed their name to the Rex Nelon Singers, for three and a half years, and left in November of 1976 to sing with a group trying to break into country music, Willie Wynn and the Tennesseans. Less than a year later, Ronnie and Willie and the Tennesseans became a backup quartet for country singer Crash Craddock. Later, Ronnie put together a quartet called the Southern Knights and backed Craddock for another eight years. Country and some rock stars like to get gospel singers to back them on stage because the gospel boys generate great harmony.

"Crash Craddock is still one of my heroes," Ronnie said. "He treated me well. The bus was clean and he did not allow drugs or drinking on the bus. We even took off our shoes before going into the back of the bus."

After the country bug wore off, Ronnie came back to the Inspirations in 1986, during their days in Gatlinburg. "It was pretty obvious that Gatlinburg was going to die out," Ronnie said. "We had great songs but nobody really cared, so we gave up the Gatlinburg thing and went back on the road."

Ronnie left the Inspirations in 1988 after two years, worked as an accountant, and returned again in 1992. He sang with the Inspirations then for six years until illness struck him down. Since his recovery from tuberculosis, he has enjoyed singing one weekend a month.

Ronnie was the only Inspiration who went through college. The other guys had enrolled at Western Carolina, but when they hit Atlanta with such force and found themselves in the big-time, they no longer had time to attend classes.

Ronnie enrolled at Western Carolina College in the fall of 1967 after finishing high school that spring. By the time he went to college, the Inspirations were becoming big business. He had difficulty working his studies into his singing schedule, and at the end of that first quarter he flunked out of college and put his full time to singing.

As the years rolled by, his regrets for failing to get a college degree grew deeper, so in 1981 he enrolled again at Western Carolina, which by that time had become a university.

"I was determined to get my degree," Ronnie said. "I'm not the sort of person who likes the idea that something beats him. I got to the point where I said I'm going back and do this, and when I enrolled again at Western Carolina in 1981, I deliberately chose accounting as a major because I'd been told it was the hardest subject in school.

"There again, the days of discipline as a kid with the Inspirations really helped," he said. "Most kids don't have the discipline we had, and that had a lot to do with my education."

Ronnie received his college degree in 1985. His final grade-point average was a healthy 3.8 out of a possible 4.0.

"I wouldn't take anything for my time with the Inspirations," Ronnie concluded. "We saw America through the windshield of a bus. We watched the interstates grow up. When we started, we traveled two-lanes, sometimes even the back roads. There were no interstates  then."

Ronnie thought it interesting that, in the early days, everybody wanted a piece of the Inspirations, wanted to buy into the group. "There were so many," he said, "that we thought they might be coming out of the woodwork. Even Mr. Whitfield. We talked about it, and I know we made the right decision. We agreed that money was not what we were after. If we were going ahead it was going to happen, and if it didn't, money was not going to buy it."

That may have been the soundest business decision the Inspirations ever made. They continued to sing as they always had, owing nothing to anyone but their fans.

Ronnie's all-time heroes in gospel music were Uncle Alphus LeFevre first, Smitty Gatlin second, and Jake Hess third. All were lead singers.  "Uncle Alphus knew more music theory and technique than most of us will ever learn," Ronnie said. "He wrote out charts on every song the LeFevres sang.  He was quiet, unassuming, a perfect gentleman, and a scholarly mentor."

Ronnie has been song leader at his church, Arlington Baptist in Bryson City, for quite a long time. "I'm not music director," he laughed. "That's too fancy a term for a small church. I am the song leader."

He grew up in that church, was saved there at the age of eight, and has always loved it.

"The only thing different about the church since I was a boy," he said, "is there is no longer a picture of Jesus on the cross at the church. We took it down because our pastor, the Reverend Ed Kilgore, said that Jesus is not on the cross now, and most of all, I think, because picturing Jesus on the cross is glorifying the killing rather than the resurrection."

The young Inspirations, above, put all their energy, heart, and soul into a 1960s rehearsal. L-R: Archie, Jack, Ronnie, Troy, and Martin—playing piano.

With a 35-year track record, Martin Cook, left, is regarded as one of the best quartet managers and pianists in gospel music.

The Inspirations were regulars on the nationwide Gospel Singing Jubilee, 1968-1981. Shown below, around 1970, are L-R: Martin (at piano), Ronnie, Archie, Jack, and Troy.

Through the 1970s and into the '80s, the Inspirations, above, were the hottest quartet in the business. L-R, front, Jack, Martin, Roger, Dale, and rear, Archie, Troy, Eddie, and Mike.

Right: Looking professorial in horn-rims, Archie and Ronnie sit in front of Martin, Jack, and Dean Robinson in one of the quartet's first formal poses.

Singing their hit song, Thank You, Lord, at the 1997 Singing News Fan Awards program at the National Quartet Convention in Louisville, Ky., the Inspirations, below, include L-R: Archie, Ronnie, Eddie, Myron, Mike, and Martin. In black suit is emcee Ken Davis.

Letting 'er rip on a taping of the Gospel Singing Jubilee, above, are L-R: Martin, Roger, Jack, Archie, Troy, Eddie, and Mike.

Below, Archie puts a high top to the Inspirations sound with his first tenor vocals. He sings with great feeling and expression.

One of the Inspirations' most cherished moments, above, was in 1971 when they visited Dr. Billy Graham and his wife, Ruth, in their mountaintop home in Montreat, NC. L-R: Archie, Troy, Jack, Martin, Ronnie, Eddie, Mrs. Graham, Billy, and Marlin.

In the Grahams' living room, below, the Inspirations sang several songs, after which Billy and Ruth, gave them a standing ovation. L-R, seated, Martin, Ronnie, Marlin, Eddie, and Billy, and standing, Archie, Troy, and Jack.

Doing the "Holcomb shuffle," top, Mike puts everything he has into a song. Behind him are Matt, Jack, and Archie.

Center left, Myron in a rare singing moment. Center right, Ronnie is still a favorite lead or baritone.

At right, evangelist and gospel disc jockey Moris Andrews, second from left, never played any other quartet but the Inspirations on his radiocasts. Here with Moris, L-R: Archie, Marlin, Martin, and Ronnie at Maranatha Baptist Church in Atlanta February 14, 1971.

An early shot of the quartet, above, made at a log cabin in the Great Smoky Mountains, included L-R: Troy, Martin, Ronnie, Jack, and Archie.

Below: For most of the 1990s, the Inspirations, with Martin in center, were, clockwise from lower left, Eddie, Myron, Mike, Archie, and Ronnie.

The Inspirations have traveled in style in three motorcoaches through the years, first (below) in a brown General Motors bus, next in the Big I (center), a gold and white Silver Eagle in which they traveled almost three million miles, and presently (above) in a new multi-colored Silver Eagle, with driver Donald Watkins at the door.

Once an Inspiration, always an Inspiration. Singing in a reunion concert, top photo, are Archie, Troy, Ronnie, Eddie, Chris Smith, Marlin, and Mike. Center, Martin accepts one of the many Favorite Gospel Group awards the Inspirations have received at the National

Quartet Convention. With him, L-R: Mike, Eddie, Troy, Archie, Jack, and Roger. At one time, below, the Inspirations featured the Smoky Mountain Trio from their quartet. Here in Hawaii, on an excursion the quartet made many times, are L-R: Archie, Troy, Eddie, and Martin.

The Inspirations turned it all loose, above, on a song in the early 1970s. L-R: Archie, Ronnie, Eddie, Martin, Marlin, Jack, and Troy.

Left, Martin Cook walks away from the Church of the Nativity in Bethlehem on a trip to the Holy Land.

Below, Wes Gilmer, in light-colored jacket, of WGUN Radio in Atlanta, presents the Inspirations with a framed citation during an Atlanta concert. The Inspirations were featured many times on Gilmer's "Suppertime" program. At left is Promoter J. G. Whitfield, and beyond Martin are Ronnie, Eddie, and Troy.

Above, practicing in Martin's basement in Bryson City in the 1960s are Ronnie, Archie, Jack, Troy, and Martin.

Left, Mike accepts one of his Favorite Bass Singer awards, voted to him by readers of the Singing News.

Below, in a promotional picture pose for their recording of The Country Needs The Cross, L-R: Archie, Eddie, Mike, Troy, Martin, and Myron.

Above, full of Christmas spirit, L-R, front row: Troy, Martin, and Ronnie, and in rear, Myron, Archie, and Mike.

Right, On stage at an outdoor sing are, L-R: Mike, Jack, Martin, and Myron.

Below, Archie and Troy hit some high notes.

Above, finishing up a song, L-R: Troy, Archie, Eddie, and Mike.

Right, Jack Laws departs a jet in Hawaii. The Inspirations sang many times on these excursions.

Below, as part of the Singing in the Smokies, Archie climbs a ladder in a special promotion, singing a favorite Inspiration hit, They're Holding Up The Ladder.

Matt, Mike, Ronnie, Archie, and Jack, above, are singing in the Smokies.

Right, Jack and Troy harmonize.
Below, Archie, Troy, Eddie, Mike, and Martin in a happy mood.

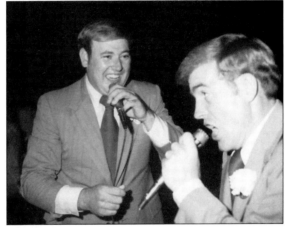

Mike, left, digs low as Jack, Archie, Matt, and Ronnie harmonize behind him. Myron and Martin play at right.

Martin and Ora Blanche sit in swing in front of their three children, Myron, Marcia, and Michael.

Below, Getting with the people, Martin urges the crowd on at the Singing in the Smokies.

A funny moment during a reunion singing, above, Ronnie, Eddie, and Marlin share a laugh.

Left, Matt and wife, Paulette, pose with daughters Lindsay, left, and Sabrina.

Below left, Jack takes the lead.

Below right, Troy strikes a handsome pose.

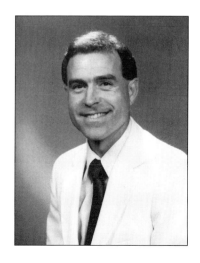

Singing down among the spectators, above, Matt shakes hands with a fan at the Singing in the Smokies.

Right, Archie's family relaxes on the patio, L-R: Amy, Cindy, Archie, and Melissa.

Below left, Jack hands microphone to Martin. Dale Jones and Mike are in background.

Below right, Mike, singing a low note, listens to himself to make sure he is on target. Matt and Eddie sing to Mike's right.

# 15

# Troy

Troy Burns and Abraham Lincoln shared identical beginnings. Both were born in log cabins, Lincoln on February 12, 1809, in the backwoods three miles south of Hodgenville, Kentucky, and Troy on February 10, 1952, on Lands Creek just north of Bryson City. Some folks in Troy's neck of the woods still believe Lincoln was born to Nancy Hanks in a log house in the woods outside Cherokee, on a site just a few miles from the cabin in which Troy first saw daylight. If the latter story of Lincoln's birth is true, then both the sixteenth president and Troy Burns were born in the Great Smoky Mountains, and Troy came along two days shy of 143 years after Lincoln's birth.

Add to those the fact that both Lincoln and Burns were born into poverty, and you'll see the parallel. The greatest difference was that Troy's ambitions and chosen career stopped somewhat short of the White House.

On such grounds are great stories written, but Troy needed no such link with a past giant of American freedom to be classified with the successful in life. He earned his own spurs so swiftly and so solidly that at the ripe old age of forty-one, after living the nomadic road life of a professional singer for twenty-seven years, Troy Burns hung up his tuning fork and retired from singing with the Inspirations.

"That may not sound like a long time," Troy said, "but when you stop and think that I had been singing that way since I was thirteen, and figure I've seen two million miles roll by the window of our bus, you'll see how I fit such early retirement into the picture of my life."

Indeed, he had spent his early life working on the go, and he had reaped a bushel and a half of rewards, not the least of which was a good living. His accomplishments included a Singing News Fan Award as the best lead singer in gospel music for the year 1977 when he was twenty-five, and he also shared in the six fan awards the Inspirations won as the favorite gospel group in the nation in the 1970s. In some of those award-winning years he played the bass and in others he sang lead.

On the day of his birth, Troy's mother, Mildred Fox Burns, married to Richard Burns, was only fifteen years old. The log cabin belonged to her parents, and she had gone there to give birth to her baby because they couldn't afford a hospital bill.

Dr. William E. Mitchell, who was just starting a lifelong medical practice in Bryson City, attended the birth. He had driven out the gravel road from Bryson City and remained with Mildred Burns until she had her baby. While she was in labor, she rememberd the doctor sitting in a straight-backed, cane-bottomed chair, propped against a wall, reading a magazine.

The cabin contained only a kitchen and a combination living room-bedroom, where the family sat around the fire on cold winter days and slept during the nights. The partition between the kitchen and living room was the only one in the house.

Troy sums up his early life easily. "We lived in that cabin two or three years until Daddy left to work in the mines and Mom went to Gastonia and took a job in a cotton mill. She took me with her. In the late 1950s, Mom and Dad moved back to Bryson City where he got a job and she stayed home with me.

"We were in poverty growing up," he said. "I didn't know what poverty was. I never went hungry. We had our own chickens, raised a big garden, and if we were fortunate we had a hog to kill in the fall, and a milk cow. Moneywise, we lived in poverty. I read a report that said if your family income is not $3,300, you are considered to be in poverty. I remember thinking, My Goodness! We *are* living in poverty!"

Church was a major part of Troy's young life. He attended Spruce Grove Baptist Church with Archie and Jack, and he and Archie were both saved at an old-fashioned altar on the same night.

By the sixth grade at the age of twelve, Troy's voice had not yet changed. Archie and Jack, with whom Troy hung around, were already singing in local churches as the Inspirations, spending their evenings in Martin's basement, hammering out what they considered to be the best arrangements of the songs they sang. On weekends, even before the Inspirations were formed, Troy, who picked the guitar, sang a lot with Archie and Jack. They all sang at church.

Troy was trying to sing with the Inspirations, but his voice was changing and he couldn't quite cut the mustard, and that's when Ronnie joined the quartet. When Troy's voice changed and deepened and he started singing bass, the Inspirations brought him in after Dean Robinson left and found that he sang a very good bass, although still just thirteen.

He had been singing with the Inspirations just a week or two when they cut their first record at Mark V and sang those weekend dates in north Georgia churches, which gave them their start toward professionalism.

Even then, the Inspirations had no idea what road they were traveling. "We just liked to sing," Troy said. "We cut that record because we thought we might make a little money selling it. We were traveling in that white Greenbriar van, and I remember the first time we tried to sell that record, we put out five copies for sale at a church in North Wilkesboro, and when the singing was over and everyone had gone home, we had sold one record. We put the other four back to try to sell somewhere else. I think we ordered either two hundred or five hundred of those records to sell at our concerts. The album was titled *Our Pioneer Heritage.*"

At about that time, the Swain County school system disposed of its small, worn out record players for 78 rpm records. Archie's dad, who was school janitor, got three of them and gave one to Troy. "I put the records of different groups," he said, "like the old Oak Ridge Quartet, the old Kingsmen, and the Chuck Wagon Gang, on that player and picked and sang along with them. That's one way I improved my singing.

"We didn't make any money for a few years," Troy said. "If we got a PA system and we didn't have the money in the treasury to pay for it, we individual members put up the money. To pay for the first suit I ever had, I did carpentry work and mowed lawns. When something had to be done to the van, we put up the money.

"If young groups starting out today would take what we did as a rule of thumb and say, 'Look, we know for the first five years we're in this just to sing and try to make a go,' I think more would survive. We never had a dream, none of us gave a thought to things turning out like they did, but we did work at it. That was an every night thing for us. I mean, every night for years.

"When Archie and Jack and I sang together, even before the Inspirations were started, we could feel the harmony. We knew exactly which way it should go, even on brand new songs."

Troy sang bass for his first five or six years with the Inspirations. They were having a good time until *Jesus Is Coming Soon* came along. "We recorded it," Troy said, "had albums made, and got a radio list from somebody. We hand-addressed the envelopes and sent the whole album and a letter to five hundred stations, and overnight they started playing that song. After that, we realized that if we worked hard and stayed at it, we might amount to something."

Troy sang bass until 1970 and left the quartet. "I left so I could make some money," he said. "I was eighteen then and we were singing four nights a week and still weren't making but a hundred dollars a week, maybe a hundred and fifty in a good week." He went to Greensboro and took a job with J. P. Stevens Company in the teletype department. That was before computers when things were done with punch cards and such.

While Troy was gone, the Inspirations hired Marlin Shubert to sing bass. They were doing a concert in Greensboro and Martin called Troy. "We need a bass player," he said. "Would you be interested?"

"I don't know," Troy said. "I might be."

He got a bass and played with them in the Greensboro engagement. He enjoyed it so much that he moved back to Bryson City and rejoined the quartet as bass player, and that's what he did for several years, singing an occasional song

"When I came back," Troy said, "the momentum was building much stronger than when I left. They had done that special for CBS, and that gave them recognition. The Vietnam war was going on, and more people were looking to the spiritual, and they had grown in popularity by leaps and bounds."

So great was the Inspirations' appeal that they soon bought and sold records by the bus load. "That sounds made up," Troy said, "but it's true. We would take the bus out to Canaan Records in Waco, Texas, and load it with thousands of albums. We might get ten thousand at a time, and the bus would be loaded down.

Once, the Inspirations brought home a busload of records titled *I'm Taking A Flight,* and stacked them in their storage rooms. They sold hundreds of the records before the letters and telephone calls began coming in, complaining about the album.

It turned out that Canaan had packaged the wrong album with the Inspirations' cover on it. "I don't remember whose album it was," Troy said. "It was some old guy in a hat—that's all I remember—who sang country songs. Canaan finally got the mess straightened out and we refunded or replaced as many albums as we could. That was a major mixup!"

When the Inspirations recorded at Mark V in Greenville, South Carolina, they made a record called *Just As Long As Eternity Rolls*, and had only five hundred records pressed. A fire burned part of Mark V and destroyed the master tape for that album, which quickly became a collector's item, going in flea market sales for up to two hundred dollars each.

When Ronnie left in the mid '70s, the quartet got together and asked where we were going to find a lead singer, and Troy said, "Let me give it a try."

"They didn't know it," he said, "but I'd been standing back there singing lead the whole time I was playing that bass. So I tried, and we made it work, and I sang lead until I retired in 1993. It wasn't always easy. I had sung bass so long that it wasn't as easy as I thought to change over. I sang lead but thought bass. It was only after a couple of years that I was comfortable with it."

People wondered why one so young should retire from a job that was paying so well, and Troy explained:

"I had been on the road thirty years. I started when I was thirteen and here I was forty-two, and during the last two or three years, the job quit being fun. I was burned out. Ask my wife, when we were going to leave on Thursday, I would get depressed on Wednesday night. It was just like I was going to go to somebody's funeral. I said, 'I can't figure out what's wrong. Why am I feeling this way?' And it boiled down that I was sick of traveling, sick of getting on that bus and taking off."

One of the things that may have spurred him on toward retirement was an innocent incident of realization that occurred a couple of years before Troy left the quartet.

A woman came to him at a concert one evening and said, "Troy, I just wanted you to know that I used to watch you on the Gospel Singing Jubilee when I was in kindergarten, and now I'm a registered nurse."

"That kind of hit me," Troy said. "I realized how much of my life I had spent on the road singing—actually two-thirds of it—and that made me begin to think of settling down."

"I have a teen-aged son, Trey, who was small then," Troy said, "and when I left the road I had the opportunity to coach him in Little Leagues and see him play other sports. I play golf with him, and I get to do so many things with my family that I hadn't been able to do, that I enjoy it tremendously.

"You miss too much when you're on the road that much. My heart goes out to people who have spent their entire lives singing—like J. D. Sumner, James Blackwood, Glen Payne, and George Younce. My heart goes out to their families. Singing was their total life, being away from home.

"Don't get me wrong. I'm thankful I had the opportunity to experience life with the Inspirations, and to enjoy it so much, but the time came when I knew I had to leave the road. I feel I'm doing exactly what God wants me to do. I am with my family, and I have a singing ministry. I sing every once in a while. I emcee certain programs, like gospel music weekends, and I'm really, really active in our church. My wife teaches Sunday school and I sing in church. So, as for singing, I'm still able to do it when I want to, but I don't have to hit the road like I did."

He had to curtail his solo ministry three years after he retired. "All of a sudden," he said, "I was doing a hundred dates a year on the road. I woke up one Sunday morning in a motel in Florida, got up, got ready, and got in my truck to go set up at the church where I was singing, and suddenly I said, 'Lord, why am I doing this? I'm retired.' My family was back home getting ready to go to church and I was in Florida doing exactly what I had retired from. So I cut back, and life has become more regulated."

Four or five years before Troy left the road, he and his wife, the former Tammy Odom, an all-Smoky Mountain Conference basketball player at Robbinsville High in the late 1970s, went into the pizza business. They opened Papa's Pizza To Go stores in Bryson City and Cherokee and a video store in Bryson City. Before Troy retired, they had three more pizza places, in Loudon, Tennessee, and in Raeford and Columbus, North Carolina. They eventually sold the latter three pizza stores, but still own the other three businesses.

In 1998 Troy bought an apartment building on the east side of the campus of Western Carolina University and is remodeling it. In June of 1999, he bought the 66-unit Laurel Oaks Apartments on Little Savannah Road west of the campus and has all units filled, mostly with college students, and has a waiting list of many names.

Troy has a twenty-eight-year-old son, Chris, who flies the Air Care helicopter for a large hospital in Charlotte. Chris has two children, Drew, nine, and Shannon, five, who give their grandpa a fit every chance they get.

Troy and Tammy's son, Trey, was a freshman point guard on the Swain County High School varsity basketball team. At this writing he is going into his sophomore year.

Troy has a lot of hobbies that he enjoys when he can: hunting, fishing, camping, weight lifting, running, skiing, flying model airplanes, taxidermy, and he frequently writes songs and sings his own compositions.

Troy likes to write parodies. He wrote a parody on Eric Rudolph, wanted for the Alabama abortion clinic bombing and the Atlanta Olympics bombing, who ran the FBI ragged trying to catch him.

"They'd been looking for him for about a year," Troy said, "and I woke up one morning and wondered why Ray Stevens hadn't written a song about this. I took a pad and walked up Deep Creek and sat down at the falls, thinking about the FBI's involvement and what some of the people in Andrews (where the search was concentrated) said about Rudolph, and about the guy who supposedly helped him with food and the truck and all that, so I put it all together and in about ten minutes I had a song."

He called the song *The Eric Rudolph Song* and wrote it to part of the tune of *Rudolph, the Red-Nosed Reindeer.*

Back home, Troy went into his little studio in the basement, in which he has a digital player, and recorded a digital track for the fun of it. As he worked, Tammy was banging the wall with a hammer, hanging pictures, and Troy could record only between hammerings.

"I called Chuck and Mickey, a couple of disc jockeys on KISS-FM in Asheville, and played it for them. They liked it and asked me to bring it to them as soon as I could. They downloaded it on their computer and played it over and over and over again on the air."

Troy then called musicians in Nashville and set up a session to record the song correctly, but something came up that prevented him from going, so in his truck he called the musicians on his cell phone and played the demo he'd done. The musicians, who were all listening over the phone, wrote down all their chord sheets and went into the studio to put it together. In a couple of hours, they called Troy back and played the track over the phone.

"That sounds good," Troy said, so they overnighted the track to him and he took it to Knoxville and recorded the vocal professionally and put it on a CD. He mailed the CD to John Boy and Billy, who have a syndicated rock show out of Charlotte, and they played it two mornings in a row and gave Troy's 800 number.

"My phone rang off the hook," Troy said. "People like Randy and Spiff from Fox 97 in Atlanta called and wanted to hear it, and I sent them a copy. Large market country stations in the midwest played it, and its success astounded me."

Soon after that, when President Clinton and Monica Lewinsky made the news, Troy penned another parody called *Blue Pill Bill* that had about the same success across the country as the Rudolph song.

"In my apartments," Troy said, "when a new tenant moves in, I give him a couple of my CDs. On them I have the Rudolph song, *Blue Pill Bill,* a song about Maggie McGee, and another one I wrote about a couple in love in the Smoky Mountains. On the end of each CD I record my version *of How Great Thou Art.* The people who move in listen to the songs and almost die laughing, and then they will come to me and say, 'That's the best I ever heard *How Great Thou Art'.*"

The Inspirations love to rib each other and no one ever lets the others know when they're coming to grief. Once Archie had a terrible case of allergies for a month and Chris Smith went along to fill in if Archie needed help. He stood on stage behind the quartet and doubled Archie's part, and the Inspirations thought no one suspected.

At intermission a woman came to the record table and asked, "What's that boy doing back there?"

"He's just singing along," Archie said. "He's a new singer who can sing all four parts, and he's helping us out."

"Something's wrong, isn't it?" she asked with the excitement of discovery, keeping her voice low. "And I know what it is. Somebody's having trouble singing, and I believe it's Troy."

# 16

# Center Stage

Jack Laws is a big, stout man. As the foremost bear hunter of the Inspirations, he has the strength of a lion. He is a gentle man who makes friends easily and keeps them.

No one knows whether his strength had anything to do with what happened to his doghouse bass in the big auditorium in Chattanooga one evening. A doghouse bass is an upright bass fiddle, often called a bull bass or acoustical bass. He treated the instrument roughly all the time, slapping as much bass out of it as possible.

The Inspirations had just hit their stride in their first stand and were going well when suddenly, without warning, Jack's bass exploded.

"It had a wooden bridge," Jack said, "and I had it leaning with too much tilt. All of a sudden, I heard a loud POW! It sounded like a shotgun and for a second I thought I'd been shot."

The bass was miked to amplify its sound for the audience, and the amplification caused the explosion to sound like a stick of dynamite.

"It was hilarious," Eddie Deitz said. "And while Jack stood there in wonderment, the crowd went crazy. They were still laughing about the bass when they left the auditorium that evening."

As soon as Jack figured out what had happened, he ran off stage, set the bridge back up, and came back grinning, and played the remainder of the program with gusto, grinning ear to ear.

Nothing like that ever happened to Eddie, but he had his crazy nights, too. The Inspirations drove to Jackson, Tennessee, to sing in a high school auditorium.

On the way, they stopped to eat, and Eddie realized he wasn't feeling well. He ate very little, got back on the bus, and the farther they went down the road, the worse he felt.

"I could feel a virus welling up in my stomach," he said, "but I wasn't the first Inspiration to go to a singing sick. If any of us was sick, we still had to go. If we weren't too sick to sing, we had to sing. If we were too sick to sing, we stayed on the bus and sweated it out.

"Martin was sharp. He knew if we ever got to stay home sick, there would always be somebody wanting to stay home."

Eddie thought he could make it through the performance that evening, but after a couple of songs the other guys were looking at him strangely. His face was green! He made it through three-fourths of the program and suddenly left the stage. He barely got behind the curtains when everything inside him came up.

The others made him stay on the bus for the second round.

Troy pulled many a laugh in practice sessions by making up funny words to songs. On the bus, the guys would sing a song, and Troy would come up with cute words and phrases to draw a laugh.

In the song *Stepping on the Clouds*, Troy would ham up the second verse. At the point where he would sing, "Going past the moon and the stars and the planets; I'm gonna walk on the Milky White Way," and on the bus he would sing, "Going past the moon, in a baallllooooooonnnn . . . ." and the other guys would break up. Only in practice, mind you. But practice makes perfect, and on stage in Birmingham one evening, Martin hit the intro to *Stepping on the Clouds*, and when they reached the second verse, Troy sang, "Going past the moon . . . ." and that was all he could think of, but without missing a beat he sang, "Going past the moon. . . doodle do do de do," and the quartet almost came unglued. It was all the Inspirations could do to keep their faces straight for the remainder of the program.

Folks often wonder, if the Inspirations never know what they're going to sing next until Martin hits the introductory chords, how do they keep from starting off on the wrong tune?

They don't. At least some don't, and when one starts on the wrong song, the whole quartet is suddenly fouled up.

Once, shortly after Eddie started singing the first time with the group in 1969, singing in a large church, Martin struck a quick intro and Ronnie, thinking it was another song, started singing the wrong tune. By the time he reached the end of the first line, he was three steps too high and singing the wrong words.

The rest of the fellows came to an abrupt halt, but Ronnie kept going, and Eddie, still a little new and green, said directly into the mike, "Martin, that's the wrong key!" His words echoed all over the church, and he was as embarrassed as Ronnie.

Perhaps the most embarrassing incident that ever happened to an Inspiration, happened to Eddie backstage in Winston-Salem's Reynolds Auditorium. The Inspirations had driven all night to get there and were excessively tired when they arrived.

All of them wanted to take a shower, so they trooped to the shower rooms, and Eddie got into the wrong stall. He was in the Ladies room. When he finished his bath he stepped out to towel off and was drying his hair when Connie Hopper came in and stopped face to face with Eddie.

The accident so embarrassed Connie that instead of turning and walking out, she just stood there and screamed. And then she fled.

Neither Connie nor Eddie ever mentioned the incident to each other.

Eddie also had what was perhaps the most unusual thing happen to him. In 1971 the Inspirations were singing in the City Auditorium in Jacksonville, Florida. Before the quartet went on stage, Sandy called Eddie and said she was having labor pains and was going to the hospital to give birth to their first baby.

Eddie tried to get an airplane reservation to return home, but not any were available, so he called Sandy and said he would have to come home on the bus.

No one told the baby of the delay, however, and a beautiful daughter, whom they named April, was born before the quartet left Jacksonville.

Four years later, the Inspirations were singing in the same auditorium in Jacksonville when Eddie called home and Sandy told him she was having labor pains. "I think I'm going to have to go to the hospital," she said.

At intermission, he telephoned home again and was told that he was the father of a fine baby boy, Brandon by name.

Ask Eddie and he'll tell you he hasn't been to Jacksonville since.

Paul Smiley was once the Inspirations' business manager. One day Martin told Paul to do something, and Paul forgot to do it. In a business meeting later, Martin asked Paul, "Did you do so and so?"

"Yeah," Paul said, "I got it right here on my list." He pulled a piece of paper out of his pocket and read it. "Uh . . . well. . . hum. . . It's not on there," but to save face, he quickly added, "Tell you what, I've got two lists!"

Once, when the Inspirations were still in high school and Richard Nixon was running for president, they were singing in Lenoir and the church was packed. People sat everywhere. If they couldn't find a seat, they found a perch, or simply an open spot on the floor where they could stand and listen.

Martin and the church's preacher made an altar call just as a man walked in the door of the church. The man came down the aisle, got on his knees, someone dealt with him, and he got up.

The preacher asked him, "Do you have anything you'd like to say?" and he answered "yes."

He faced the audience and said, "I thought the Lord called me to preach, but I found out today he didn't. He called me to umpire ball games. And I want you people to know I'm campaigning for Nixon and want to get all the votes I can for him."

Martin and the preacher stared open-mouthed at each other, wondering what to do next. All of the Inspirations were dying to laugh. The preacher recovered first and said to Martin, "Brother Martin, why don't you close the service with prayer?" and Martin, as tickled as the rest, replied, "No, you go right ahead, preacher."

The preacher quickly dismissed with a prayer and the Inspirations hurried to their laughing place.

When Chris Smith sang with the Inspirations, a snowstorm prompted cancellation of a date in Georgia, and the singers sat in Martin's house talking. Chris commented that he had been to all the Inspirations' singings he could get to before he joined the quartet.

"Ever been to the Singing in the Smokies?" asked Martin's wife, Ora Blanche.

"Yes," Chris answered, "last summer. I bought my ticket from you."

"You did?" she exclaimed. "What did I say?"

"You said 'How many?'" Chris replied. "And then that guy in the red coat who took up tickets at the gate said, 'Keep on truckin'.'"

That would have been Mac McBrayer, who took up tickets for many years and acted as the Inspirations' official greeter at all their singings on the mountain. He advised almost everyone who came in to "keep on truckin'."

Ronnie recalls that the Statesmen were the reason the Inspirations, when they were kids, would jump off stage while singing and make contact with the audience, shaking hands while they sang.

"Hovie was the person to watch," Ronnie said. "If anyone was going to do something to get your attention, Hovie Lister was the one.

"I think we were all a little reluctant to jump off stage," Ronnie said. "I know I was. I remember when Derrell Stewart of the Florida Boys jumped off stage once and landed with a loud crash in the orchestra pit."

Jumping was hard to do. The stage and spot lights shining into the singers' eyes blinded them so they couldn't see the floor below the stage.

One evening the quartet had a song going great and the audience responded with round after round of applause. Finally, Archie jumped off the stage and Jack and Troy followed. Ronnie, standing next to Martin, who was playing the piano, hesitated, and Martin reached out and pushed him off stage without missing a note.

"Martin pushed me off several times," Ronnie said. "It was like bailing out of an airplane in the dark, but I guess it was good because it got us over any fear we might have had of crowds. I think my problem was that I am more comfortable with people one on one. I may make friends with everyone in the house, but I'll do it one at a time."

Martin laughed about it. "I pushed Ronnie off the stage several times. I'm very capable of doing that. When I thought they ought to get out in the audience and shake hands, I'd start pushing. I guess at one time or another I pushed every one of them off stage."

J. Bazzel Mull, the preacher from Knoxville who has produced and emceed thousands of gospel singing programs on television, listened to the Inspirations one autumn evening and after the concert he said to Martin, "I want you and the boys to sing at my funeral."

Martin thought that was quite an honor, and he knew J. Bazzel was sincere in his request when he telephoned the Cook home several times and told Ora Blanche he didn't want the Inspirations to forget that he wanted them to sing at his funeral.

One Thanksgiving Preacher Mull, in his gravelly voice, called and Martin answered the phone. The preacher said, "Doc, now I don't care what you're doing, I want you to plan to be there and sing at my funeral."

"Well, preacher," Martin answered, "the only way we can do that for sure, because of our schedule, is to go ahead and schedule it right now. Let's set it for January the fifteenth."

Preacher Mull laughed uproariously, and he still laughs about it when he is around Martin.

The Inspirations pride themselves in the fact that they have never made a record pitch from stage, but once they wished they had.

In Nashville, they were on a program with the Blackwood Brothers, and James Blackwood, either feeling generous or needing money, announced a special: They were selling ten record albums for twenty dollars that night.

"The crowd made a mad rush for the Blackwood Brothers' table," Eddie said, "and almost knocked our table over getting to James. We stood up on our little boxes all night watching the Blackwood Brothers sell, and we sold fifty-eight dollars worth of records that night. Everybody went home with ten Blackwood Brothers albums tucked under their arms."

# 17

# Eddie

Except for the presence of one little two-letter word in the English language, Eddie Deitz could have been one of the original Inspirations. The word was "no."

One evening in 1964 when Eddie was seventeen, he and his dad and mom, Coy Deitz and Dorothy, whom everyone called Dot, were sitting at home when the telephone rang and Martin Cook wanted to speak with Eddie.

"Eddie," said Martin, "I've got a bunch of boys down here in Bryson City and we're singing around once in a while. We're looking for a lead singer and wondered if you'd be interested."

At the time, Eddie was singing with his mom and dad, both of whom came from singing families, he from the Deitzes and she from the Jamisons. When he got off the phone, Eddie told them of Martin's invitation and asked what they thought about it.

"Well, it's a long way to Bryson City," Coy said, "and the roads aren't as good as they should be. It'll be a lot of traveling for you." Bryson City was twenty miles west of Old Savannah where the Deitzes lived in Jackson County, and the road was a curvy, two-lane highway that might pose driving problems for one of Eddie's age, so he decided it would be best if he didn't take Martin up on his offer.

"I called Martin back," Eddie said, "and told him I didn't think I should do it, and I missed becoming an original Inspiration right there. So Martin got Jerry Bowers to sing the lead. That was before Martin found Ronnie Hutchins."

Two or three times later that year, Eddie and his family sang where the Inspirations were also on the program, and on a couple of occasions Jerry couldn't come and the Inspirations got Eddie to fill in that day.

"I would sing with them occasionally after that," Eddie said. "I remember filling in at the Ritz Theater in Sylva one Sunday afternoon, and another time up in Cashiers, south of Sylva. After singing with them several times, I began thinking, Hey, I wish I'd said yes when Martin called me."

Two incidents in the next three years were major in Eddie's life. The first came during a revival in July of 1965 at East Fork Baptist, Eddie's home church on U.S. 441 between Sylva and Franklin, when he yielded to an irresistible call to preach the gospel. The second incident was two years later, in 1967, when nineteen-year-old Eddie married seventeen-year-old Sandra Dillard. Sandra and Cindy Bumgarner were best friends at Sylva-Webster High School. Cindy later married Archie Watkins, but at that time Eddie and Sandra began double-dating with Archie and Cindy, and Archie soon realized that Eddie would like to sing with the Inspirations. He told Eddie to start learning all the Inspirations' songs and that his chance might come.

Sandy came from Dillardtown, a Jackson County community settled by the Dillard family. For years there were only about four houses in that community where her father, Ralph Dillard, and his three brothers lived, so the place became known as Dillardtown.

For Eddie, the opportunity to sing with the Inspirations came in 1969 the first time Ronnie Hutchins left the Inspirations. Eddie quickly came aboard to sing with

Archie, Jack, and Troy and he knew the quartet's songs so well they didn't skip a beat.

Soon after Eddie was graduated from high school in June of 1965, he enrolled for the summer session at Western Carolina College with the thought of becoming an elementary school teacher.

He was singing with the Jamisons, but since he had turned down the opportunity to sing with the original Inspirations, he no longer thought he would get a chance to sing with a top group.

"I sang with the Jamisons," he said, "and all they did was local stuff. I begged them to go on out—they were certainly good enough—but they didn't want to. There would have been too much involved for them to become full-time singers, so I had pretty well given up the thought of singing and was going to be a teacher."

That July of '65, Kenneth Crawford, the pastor of Eddie's church, East Fork Baptist, began a revival which he preached himself. He started on Sunday morning and talked about missions and outreach and how there was a need in their church for someone who would go out and minister. He made a call, asking if someone carried a burden for what he was talking about, but no one responded.

He made the same call for four nights. "He must have had it on his mind and heart," Eddie said, "but no one came forward."

On Thursday morning, Eddie couldn't get the preacher's call off his mind. He was quite concerned and began to pray about it in his car. Suddenly, Eddie said aloud, "Well, maybe it's me!"

He prayed, "Lord, I don't understand. I have a lot of respect for our pastor and for what he's asking, but nobody is coming forward. If it's me, Lord, that you want to be a minister, just let him talk plainer about it tonight and I promise you, I'll step out."

In the revival that evening, Rev. Crawford preached from Isaiah 6 where the Lord said, "Whom shall I send, and who will go for us?" His sermon was so clear on the subject that Eddie discovered his heart was down in the pit of his stomach.

"I walked forward and surrendered," he said, "and looking back, I can see that I made the right decision. I believe I really have gone out from that church and ministered. Mine was a very distinct call!"

Eddie did several months of interim pastoral work, and in 1967 accepted a call to his first regular pastorate at the small Big Ridge Baptist Church in Glenville, beyond Caney Fork where Martin lived. Dave Pruitt, driver's education teacher at Sylva, who lived on Big Ridge, was instrumental in getting Eddie to come to the Big Ridge Church. The church had only nine enrolled in Sunday school. In the summer, however, when people escaped the heat of the southern lowlands and came to the coolness of the mountains for two or three months, attendance at Eddie's church swelled to thirty-five or forty.

The agreement was that Eddie would keep the Sunday morning offering as a salary. For months, his salary was $20, the amount that Dave Pruitt and his wife placed in the collection plate each week as a tithe! No one else contributed. It was there that Eddie had his first three converts. He baptized two little girls and an eighty-five-year-old man.

From there, Eddie moved back down toward East Fork to the New Savannah Baptist Church, where he preached part time for four months until called full time by Crabtree Baptist in nearby Haywood County, and there his ministry began to thrive. Enrollment and attendance increased steadily until the church was filled on Sunday and ushers had to put out extra chairs for the overflow. Eddie baptized forty converts in a short time and *The Waynesville Mountaineer* published a story on his rapidly-growing ministry.

"I've often wondered what might have happened there if I hadn't left," Eddie said, "but Ronnie quit the Inspirations and Martin asked me to join them in July of 1969. I was twenty-two years old and had a distinct call from the Lord to go singing."

Here's how it was: Going home on a Wednesday night from church, Eddie suddenly suggested to Sandy, "Let's go to Charlie's Place and get a hot dog."

Charlie's Place was a drive-in restaurant in East Waynesville, owned and operated by Charlie Woodard, Sandy's mother's brother, who had grown up in Pumpkintown in Jackson County. Charlie's hot dogs were the best west of Cape Hatteras. Ben Woodard, known as Wolf, was Charlie's brother, a man who prided himself in memory. He could wait on a dozen cars, record every order in his memory, and as the orders came up he would serve each car correctly. He did that many times.

Headed for Charlie's Place, Eddie and Sandy approached Lake Junaluska, outside Waynesville, and a huge bus rounded a bend and ran them off the road.

"That was the Inspirations!" Eddie exclaimed. The only place they could be going was to Eddie's house, so he turned and drove quickly home. The bus was parked there, waiting for them.

Martin didn't beat around the bush. "Ronnie's leaving," he said, "going to California. His last date's Saturday night.

"That's too bad," Eddie said.

"Are you interested?" Martin asked. "If you are, let's go in the house and sing a few songs."

The quartet trooped into Eddie's house and Martin sat at the piano and began pounding out the intro to *Jesus Is Coming Soon.* Eddie sang it clearly without missing a note. He had taken Archie's advice and learned all of the Inspirations' songs.

Martin hit another intro and Eddie sang that song. Then he sang another, and his voice blended with Archie, Jack, and Troy's. He knew all of the songs and could identify each song by its intro.

"Sounds like you know them as good as we do," Martin said. "I'll tell you what: If you can decide by tomorrow, we're going to Homer, Georgia, and I want you to go and listen. That'll be Ronnie's last stand. Then we're singing again Sunday and I want you to sing that one with us."

Eddie didn't wait until tomorrow to make up his mind. He decided that night that he would go.

"Now, here I was," he said. "It was 1969, I was twenty-two years old and my wife was nineteen. We were being paid eighty-five dollars a week and living in a rock house, and Martin had said, 'I'll give you a hundred dollars a week if I have to give it to you out of my pocket.' He was true to his word. In fact, the money doubled, tripled, and quadrupled in just a month."

Going south with the Inspirations that weekend, it was obvious that Eddie couldn't be in church Sunday, so he wrote his resignation and Sandy took it to church on Sunday morning and read it to the congregation.

"I was totally knocked away to leave that place," Eddie said, "and yet they've asked me to come back and preach twice. Some of the dearest friends I have are there in Crabtree, and if I sing anywhere around, they come to hear me. So, I know it was a right decision. If it hadn't been right, it would have cost us terribly."

For seven years, Eddie's ministry lay in song, and the Inspirations matched his enthusiasm. Never has there been a more enthusiastic quartet in gospel music. They sang and rode the bus and sang again and rode the bus and sang again, and everywhere they went the crowds cheered and encouraged them and realized what good work these young men were doing.

"During that time," Eddie said, "I preached when I could, but we were so busy from 1969 until the middle '70s that I didn't have a chance to preach much."

In 1976, Eddie's home church, East Fork Baptist, called him to a full-time pastorate, but Eddie did not feel at the time that he could leave the Inspirations. He felt, indeed, that he and the Inspirations did the work of the Lord among thousands of people, and he felt a call to continue. But at the same time, this was East Fork Baptist, this was his home, and these were his people, amongst whom he had grown up.

"We worked out an agreement between the Inspirations and the church," he said. "I agreed to accept the call to the church but would split my time between the two. I promised I would be at church at least twenty-six Sundays a year and would sing with the Inspirations twenty-six. Because the quartet came home most Sundays, I was present every week for the Sunday night and Wednesday night services, and the medium we struck was a happy one."

He sang three years that way, and then resigned from the quartet the last of September, 1979, to go into evangelistic work. He had sung with the Inspirations for a little more than ten years. At the start of this new vocation, Eddie remained at East Fork Baptist until 1981, the church's 100th anniversary, and resigned to pursue revival work. For six years he did nothing but preach revivals wherever the Lord directed him.

He returned to the Inspirations again in 1991. His mother died of cancer April 29, 1991, and he had sung with the Inspirations in a reunion performance two evenings before. He came back full time on May 4, 1991, the weekend following his mother's burial. His father died, also of cancer, on December 19 of that year.

Eddie sang with the Inspirations then until October of 1998 when he resigned to sing with his family, which had a desire to form a gospel group.

No one who knew the story of Eddie's birth was surprised that night in 1965 when he walked down the aisle in East Fork Baptist Church and dedicated himself to the work of God. At his birth, he had been foreordained for the ministry.

His mother, Dot Jamison, was a beautiful singer who sang locally with her sisters. They sang all the time and were quite accomplished at it. Reg Moody, a

Sylva funeral director, called upon them sometimes three times a week to sing at funerals.

Eddie was born September 11, 1947, in C. J. Harris Community Hospital in Sylva. He arrived prematurely and weighed a bit under five pounds. The doctor told his parents that their baby was "really sick," that he was a blue baby, and to prepare them for the worst he said the baby probably wouldn't make it.

Coy and Dot Deitz were distraught, but they had a strong faith in God. Coy went behind the hospital and put his knees on the bare ground and prayed:

"Lord, you made our baby and if we could have him, we really want him, but we want your will to be done. If it is not your will that our baby lives, we will accept it, but if you will let our baby live we will make a covenant with you. I promise that I will live right, that we will take him to church and teach him how to live right and how to pray. I dedicate him to you right now as your servant."

A half-century later, Eddie said, "You see, I didn't have a lot of choice. My daddy marked my path."

Coy went back into the hospital and sat with his wife for a couple of hours, and the doctor came in. "I have good news," he said, "the baby is doing a lot better."

Coy thought a miracle had been wrought. Eddie's condition improved daily. At that time, it was usual for a new mother to remain in the hospital with her baby for five days, and on the fifth day Dot went home—and Eddie went with her!

"Until I was thirty-four years old," Eddie said, "other than having a little cold, I was never really sick. In 1981 I got pneumonia because I had been traveling too much, but since that time I have been well. Looking back, I feel that my daddy and the Lord touched me with a mighty anointing."

The Deitzes had one other child, a daughter named Lisa who came along sixteen years after Eddie. Lisa married Terry Wilson and they live in Pumpkintown, not far from the old home place, with their two children, Kristopher and Sheridan. Eddie and Lisa have been very close all their lives.

Before he returned to the Inspirations in 1991, Eddie had accepted the pastorate of Franklin Grove Baptist Church in Bryson City. He preached his first sermon as the church's pastor on February 2, 1986, and has been there since. The church has about five hundred members and on Sunday about a hundred come to Sunday school and an average of three hundred for the worship service.

Eddie and Sandy moved to Bryson City in 1992. Their children are now grown. At this writing, April is twenty-eight, married to Eric Lambert of Albemarle, a brother of gospel singer Amy Lambert Templeton. They live in Eddie's mom and dad's house on East Fork and Eric manages a carpet house in Sylva. He sings in the family group.

Brandon is twenty-four. He loves children and is involved in youth activities in Swain County. He coaches a Little League baseball team and a Junior High team and is always involved in those community activities.

The family singing group, which came together in 1998, was the reason for Eddie leaving the Inspirations later that year.

"Every now and then," Eddie said, "Eric would bring home a sound track and sing a solo, and one day April, Brandon, and I sang with him and folks thought it was good. We put some tracks together and sang one Sunday night at Scotts Creek Baptist Church not far from Sylva and the people seemed to like us.

"To be honest," Eddie said, "I didn't want to leave the Inspirations, but I saw that my family needed me more. April and Eric had a real desire to sing and after a lot of deep consideration, I decided they could never make it without someone who knew the business. Gospel Music is a business. There is so much more to operating a successful group than just standing up singing, and I thought I could help them do it, so I made that sacrifice. I knew they had potential and a unique sound, and I realized we could be a family group. I was fifty then and thought if I'm going to do it, I should do it now. So in October of 1998 we went into it."

Perhaps the most difficult thing about running a singing group is the booking of dates. "Booking and managing a group is a really big job," Eddie confessed. "Before it's all over I may have to go up on Caney Fork and shake Martin's hand for all the hard work he has done over the years that we didn't realize he was doing.

"You call someone and say we're passing through, how about booking us to sing in your church?" Eddie said. "They'll say, well, let me get in touch with whoever it is that can okay it and I'll get back to you. A month goes by and they don't return the call, and you call again and get an answering machine. It takes a lot of hard work."

Through all this, Eddie still pastors his church. "I feel I get pulled from every side," he said, "and sometimes I get a bit scattered, but otherwise it's going well."

The Inspirations have been good to Eddie, and vice versa.

"The Inspirations have been a special group for a special time," Eddie said. "I think we all just happened to be together when the Lord wanted us, not by accident but by ordination of God. There was a feeling about it that it was meant to be.

"I was singing with the Jamison Family the first time I heard the Inspirations, and I thought: They don't sing so well; I'm not sure they'll make it. But the reason I thought that was because they were so different, and I didn't realize it at the time. Less than three years later I was singing with them.

"Archie has always said, 'We don't sing the best; it's not

that. It's an unseen X-factor that the Lord has blessed.'

"And I want to say something about Martin," Eddie continued. "Although he has had to be the boss over the years, there were times when we didn't agree with him, times when we thought he was stubborn, times when we didn't want to go along with him, but I'm going to say that Martin Cook has been a man of integrity and has insisted on doing things in certain ways that sometimes young boys don't like to do. He has been a good leader, and he was a good role model. He was certainly a good businessman, and I believe God anointed him for these things.

"Archie has been a real trooper. He has kept himself clean and has always been faithful to the group. He has always been respectful of Martin. I think, for all of that, the Lord has blessed Archie in a very unusual way."

Eddie came up with the slogan the Inspirations use: "Originating in the heart of God, developed in the word of God, these are the Inspirations."

"That's the way I feel about them," he said.

Eddie has been a writer and hopes to write more. He has written several songs and one book, *What Does Prayer Enable God to Do?* The book was inspired in a strange way.

"A lady, Debi Wilson, came to my office one Valentine day," Eddie explained. "She said she had a question that she felt God wanted her to ask, but she didn't know why. Her question was: What does prayer enable God to do?

"I had been raised in a family of prayer," Eddie said, "but at that moment I could not give a concise answer to her question, so I began to do what all preachers do: I began to say preacher things. I knew what I said hadn't answered her question, but she was very gracious. She made me feel that I had said some profound things, but when she left I knew I hadn't said anything. I had fumbled the ball."

Eddie went home and sat on the sofa with Bible in hand. He said, "Lord, I feel like a fool. My life was because of prayer. I was dying when I was little and my dad prayed so hard you healed me. I felt that I lived because of prayer, but I didn't have a clue what to say to Debi Wilson about prayer."

He thought long about it and began to search the Scriptures, feeling that the answer was there. "It was as though the Lord spoke to me," he said, "and said if I really wanted to know about prayer I should ask Jesus because He knows more about it than anybody."

Eddie thought the idea was good, so through a concordance he looked up every scriptural reference to Jesus praying or about something Jesus said about prayer. Jotting these things down, he concentrated on those principles that would teach what prayer constituted.

"I preached for twenty weeks on the subject," he said. "and it really made a difference in our church and in my life. After I finished, I realized that God wanted me to write these things in a book. So I began to write. . . and that's how the book came about."

Eddie has also written ten or fifteen songs. Songwriting isn't the easiest form of writing. A person cannot say, I'm going to sit down and write a song, for songs don't come that way. If the inspiration to write a song hits you, you must write it down while it's clear. Inspiration can strike anywhere.

Eddie wrote a song while mowing the yard one day. "It had been raining for days," he said, "and my yard had gotten terribly high. I got up one morning and the sun was shining so beautifully. I started mowing and got to thinking about how for days it had been raining and how clouds had built up in the sky, but then I thought the sunshine is bright today. I began thinking about the day Jesus died; the Bible said it was dark and cloudy. I could imagine lightning and thunder and thought it had been then like it had been around our house for a few days, but on the third day he arose and the sun was shining. I would stop mowing now and then and write my thoughts down, and before I finished mowing, I had written the basis for a song called *The Son Rose This Morning.*"

He wrote a song titled *Bells of Joy* that the Inspirations recorded and another called *Longing for Home* that was also recorded.

"I found it incredibly hard to pitch a song to the group I was singing with," he said. "It was much easier for Squire Parsons to come over and pitch a song to us. It made no difference what he wrote, we had an open mind to it, but we closed our minds to whatever one of us wrote. I think it was because we were all together so much, we didn't think any of us had sense enough to write a song. I finally quit pitching songs to the Inspirations, and when I stopped pitching I stopped writing."

Eddie's favorite singer is Jake Hess. "He and the Statesmen are the ones who created a desire in me to sing. When I was three or four, Daddy and Mama would take me every month to Asheville for the All-Night sings in City Auditorium. I liked all the groups, the Blackwood Brothers and Statesmen and the Harmoneers, the Homeland Harmony, the Sunshine Boys, the Speer Family, the Chuck Wagon Gang, and the LeFevres. I loved the Bill Cobb Trio and the Sons of Song, and I loved Lee Roy Abernathy and Shorty Bradford. But I sat with bated breath waiting for the Statesmen. I loved J. D. Sumner and though the Blackwood Brothers weren't my favorite group, James Blackwood is my favorite person in the whole world.

"Jake Hess is the only person I ever asked for an autograph. He patted me on the head. Later on when we were pretty hot I reminded him of that. He was no longer with the Statesmen, who were on the decline then, but I told Jake that he was my inspiration. I told Hovie Lister, too, and it pleased them both."

Outfitted in overalls in the early days as if they are ready to hoe the corn, the Inspirations, above, pause for a few songs. L-R: Martin at piano, Eddie, Jack, Troy, Ronnie, Marlin, and Archie.

Mike, left, is one of the lowest bass singers in the world. Nicknamed "Six-four, Ninety-four" by Martin because of his height and slender build, Mike can sing as low as anybody in the business.

Below, you'll find some of gospel music's most enthusiastic fans at the Singing in the Smokies.

Practicing in Martin's home in the early days, above, are Martin, Ronnie, Troy, Archie, and Jack.

On one of their cruises to overseas ports, center left, the Inspirations line up on deck. L-R: Myron, Martin, Troy, Mike, Eddie, and Archie. Is that really a halo over Martin's head?

Left, dynamic Martin Cook gets happy playing for the Inspirations.

The early 1990s cast of Inspirations, right, included Myron in center, and clockwise from left, Mike, Eddie, Archie, Troy, and Martin.

Below, in 1986-88 the Inspirations included L-R: Ronnie, Myron, Martin, Troy, Mike, and Archie.

The Inspirations of the early 70s, above, included Martin at left, and across the table from left, Jack, Eddie, Marlin, and Archie.

Left, Mike and Matt are great friends and fellow Baptist preachers.

Right, Archie accepts one of his numerous Singing News Fan Awards.

Below are the "original" Inspirations, Jack and Martin in front, and behind them Archie, Ronnie, and Troy.

Right, rehearsing the instrumentation for a song, Myron plays the bass and Martin the piano in the Cook home. There are pictures of the family on the piano.

Center left, with nothing behind them but mountains, sky, and water, the Inspirations sang into two microphones in their early years, but here, in 1964, they use three on the shore of Watauga Lake in East Tennessee. L-R: Martin at piano, Ronnie, Jack, Archie, and Dean Robinson.

Center right, the late R. L. (Mac) McBrayer, ticket taker and greeter at the Singing in the Smokies, passed people through the gates with a friendly "Keep on Truckin." That's Marian Fortner, the Inspirations' office manager, with him.

Bottom, these early 1970s Inspirations consisted of, L-R: Troy, Ronnie, Archie, Martin, Eddie, Marlin, and Jack.

Morris Carlton, who has helped run the Inspirations' booth at the Singing in the Smokies for many years, chats with a fan.

Fans mob the Inspirations' booth at intermission during the Singing in the Smokies.

Mountain and forest frame Inspiration Park where, in this picture, Martin holds forth with the audience.

Posing at the Singing in the Smokies are Martin, Troy, Ronnie, and Myron.

Above, Archie really puts himself into a song. The others are Matt, Jack, and Mike.

Right, Mike's wife, Boo, runs the concession stand with a friendly word and smile. No, she is not singing.

Below: Inspiration Park, Hyatt Creek Road between Bryson City and Cherokee, North Carolina.

Top, getting an enthusiastic okay from Martin, far right, are Mike, Ronnie, Troy, and Archie.

Center, Jack takes a baritone lead with Matt, Mike, and Archie harmonizing behind him.

Left, Donald Watkins, Archie's brother, has driven the Inspirations for many years.

Above, Eddie gets his teeth into a song, and almost into the mike.

Right, Fort Wilderness is Archie's campground in the Smokies.

Below left, Mike and Jack.

Right, Troy loves to sing and can do either the lead, baritone, or the bass with feeling.

Top left, Mike with his family, Nathan, Bavaria, and Niccole.

Above, Marcia Cook, Martin and Ora's daughter, is an efficient secretary for the Inspirations.

Left, Archie greets a fan.

Below, Marian Fortner laughs in the ticket booth at the Singing in the Smokies as her granddaughter, Kelsy, gives change. At the Inspirations' behest, Marian baby sat Kelsy for months in the Inspirations' office.

On a children's celebration at the Singing in the Smokies, above, Jack and Matt kid with the kids.

Left, Martin is the group's patriarch and emcee.

Below, Jack and his wife Brenda.

Above, on Martin's 63rd birthday at the 1999 Singing in the Smokies, Ora Blanche is at his side and children from the audience gather around to wish him "Happy Birthday!"

Left, Ronnie with his mom and dad, Clint and Faye Blanch.

Below, a happy Martin strolls through the crowd as the Inspirations sing a cappella on stage.

Above, a lot of hardware is required to put on a gospel sing as this shot from behind the Inspirations shows.

Left, Archie has had more chart songs than any other singer.

Below, Mike, Ronnie, Eddie, and Archie, with Martin playing, sing during a worldwide telecast on the Gospel Music Television Network, July 4, 1996.

Above, Martin walks the hills above his home, shown at left, and the church he has attended all his life, behind him.

Right, Matt points toward heaven as he hits a solo run.

Below, Eddie in his office at Franklin Grove Baptist Church.

Above, Jack's smooth baritone is featured on many songs. Backing the Old Bear Hunter are L-R: Archie, Eddie, Marlin, Troy, Ronnie, and Martin.

Below, Archie and friends relax around the concession stand at the Singing in the Smokies.

Above, Matt, off stage, ends a song and the Inspirations on stage give it a rousing windup.

Below, Archie, Ronnie, Jack, and Troy filming the Gospel Singing Jubilee in the 1960s.

*(Photos by, or from the collections of the Singing News, Teddy Greene, Heather Payne Sannooke, Tim Gardner, Ewart Ball, The Asheville Citizen-Times, and the Inspirations.)*

# 18

# Let it Happen

Ranging widely across the nation, especially the South and Midwest, the Inspirations are popular for their sincerity, their tunefulness, the content of their songs, and their good humor and friendliness.

No matter where they sing, be it in Geraldine, Alabama; Vossburg, Mississippi; Winston-Salem, North Carolina; or Louisville, Kentucky, they usually manage to fill the house.

After thirty-five years of traveling and singing, the Inspirations have changed their basic outreach from large city gospel sings to smaller towns, singing in high school auditoriums and gymnasiums, churches, and community buildings, and feeling they are taking music to the people.

"Take our situation at home," Martin said. "It used to be that when anyone in Bryson City wanted to go to a gospel concert, he had to go to Asheville, Knoxville, or Chattanooga, but this pattern has changed in the last several years. When anyone in Asheville wants to hear the music, he has to come to Bryson City, or Candler, or some other small place. That's where most singings are held now."

Unlike most quartets, the Inspirations do not go on stage with a fixed program. Martin dictates what will be sung, and he puts the songs in order, you might say, by the seat of his pants.

Like Hovie Lister used to do with his Statesmen Quartet, Martin hits the audience with several quick songs before anyone on stage says a word, and all the while he is gauging the crowd to see what songs it might be in tune for.

"I don't even know what I'm going to play when I get on stage," he said. "I know that I will follow a certain pattern that we have found to be effective over the years, and I may have one song in mind that we'll open with, but I don't even tell that to the boys.

"We have sung so much together," he added, "that they know the intro to everything we sing, and when I hit that first intro on the piano, they come right in. And until we finish that opening song, I don't know what we're going to sing next.

"The Inspirations may be the only quartet in America that has never known what it would sing until it gets on stage. Certainly, there aren't many more.

"That may sound as if it's coming from a screwball, but we've found that it works best for us," Martin said.

A typical program? It doesn't exist in Martin's mind. But a typical skeleton of a program is fixed firmly in his brain.

Some singing folks think the risk of repetition is too great that way, but Martin cannot recall a night when the Inspirations sang the same song twice. "Maybe a time or two in thirty-five years," he said, "have I called for the same song twice on one program. I'm not saying I've never done it; I'm saying I don't remember ever having done it."

He does not tell the boys what song is coming next, not at any point in a stand. They hear the intro, recognize it, and come in on cue.

"I don't force anything," Martin said, "just let it happen. If I feel people want to hear fast songs, we give them a lot of fast ones. If I feel they want to hear *Beulahland*, we give 'em *Beulahland*. It's important to gauge the mood of a crowd. . . no, I'll say it's imperative to gauge their mood, because then we can sing what they are in a mood to hear."

At the start of a program, Martin will often call for *Beulahland* and *Amazing Grace* back to back.

"I'm not locked in on any sound track," he said. "I can do it any way I want to, and I don't worry about throwing the boys a curve. They're too smart for that. They know the intros, and they instantly know what we're going to sing."

This is not leaving anything to chance; it is instant organization of a program Martin tailors to suit the crowd as the Inspirations go along.

The pattern the Inspirations weave as they move through a program is not just a jumbled group of songs. The songs extend a thought or message from one to the other. They might begin with *Beulahland* and come right back with *It'll Be Worth It All*. Folks get the message. They know the quartet is telling them that Beulahland will be worth it all.

"Our basic pattern," Martin said, "is to do three songs in rapid succession, and then say a welcome to the people. If the crowd is a little lethargic, we'll do a fast number, like *Footsteps*, to wake up the people. *Footsteps* has become more or less our theme song. It wakes 'em up every time. We don't have anything else that will get a crowd's attention like *Footsteps*.

"Our second song will usually be a slower, lighter song, like Ronnie might sing *Lord, I Want to be a Blessing* or *He'll Hold My Hand*, and Jack will follow with *Jesus Savior Pilot Me*. Now we've got their attention and we can start letting our steam off.

"We don't form the pattern by accident. On the second song, after a hard-charging opener, we relax and get our harmony together. *He Made a Way* is a good second song; so is *The Unseen Hand*. If you don't have someplace early in the program to pull your harmony together, you'll likely run loose all night.

"The third song, then, is usually somewhere in between, not as exciting as the first, nor as slow as the second, but still a good, solid song, such as *Jesus Is Coming Soon* or *What's That I Hear*, which are good tempo songs with a solid ring to them."

What is the reasoning for fashioning a program in this way, which is contrary to the way most other groups sing? "That's one reason we go back to a place for the thirtieth time and find the building filled," Martin explained. "I try to use my head in the song selection to keep the program running smoothly. And all the guys do their parts. They get the harmony established, and a lot of their tones really excite a crowd. That's not by accident, either. We work on tones and breathing and harmony and blend. We try not to leave the quality of the singing to chance."

Some songs, of course, are just songs. But others are great quartet songs. One of the best is *Glad Reunion Day*, which has been around forever, and another is *Beautiful Star of Bethlehem*.

"Those songs are in the same key and same range," Martin said. "One year we did a Christmas tape, put five new songs and five old ones on it. We worked hours and hours. Word produced it, and I guess they spent twenty thousand dollars on it. That was fifteen years ago when twenty thousand was a wheelbarrow load of money.

"And, do you know the song that sold the tape? It was *Beautiful Star of Bethlehem*. A fellow in Charleston, West Virginia, who owns four music stores, played that song in all his stores and said, 'Man, they just couldn't buy it fast enough!' We sang it through the first verse and then inverted and let Archie do the melody through the second verse to the end of the song. Now, that's gospel music down the middle.

"One more thing while we're on the subject," Martin added. "With songs like *Glad Reunion Day, Beautiful Star of Bethlehem*, and *Amazing Grace*, you can tell a good quartet from a bad one and a great quartet from a good one."

Martin changed the subject.

"Let's talk about contact with the audience," he said. "I think it's necessary to make stage contact and keep contact with those who have come to hear us sing.

"Some in the business talk about our doing things that are not gospel music, and they're away off base. They are the ones who got out in left field and almost buried gospel music, trying to be professional like Elvis, or somebody.

"Not that we don't need professionalism like that, we do, but we need to do it right. Our job is not just to entertain, but to uplift people as well. That's getting to the border of the ministry in gospel music.

"Now, from the standpoint of theater, we need to face the people in the audience. They need to see our faces, our facial expressions. We don't need to turn our backs to them and look at the floor. There are certain basic things we need to do, and we do them.

"You don't see any of our boys hunting night crawlers on the floor with their clothes half on. I had dramatics under Mrs. Winnie Killian at Western Carolina and you don't do that; you face your audience, and you don't lose eye contact with the people. It's the same with public speaking: You can't fiddle around, you have to keep eye and facial contact. A lot of groups don't realize that, because they haven't been trained in stagemanship.

"And that's not all of it. Spirituality has to be there. Now, here is the professional side: Your chords have to be right, all the guys have to say the words and syllables exactly alike or you're never going to have harmony. If I say 'I' and you say 'Illiii,' it won't harmonize. Listen to some of the major groups and pay attention to the words. They're not even singing the syllables alike. They're singing just like you'd pick four people off the street and say, 'All right, now, we've got us a quartet,' and they really don't know the difference. That's one thing about Hovie Lister: He *trained* the Statesmen. They didn't leave much to chance."

An example was a conversation Martin had with one of the nation's top five gospel piano players. The man approached Martin at a slack time at a singing, and asked, "How do I work with a new tenor singer, with his pitches and his part, and so on?"

Martin answered, "Now, Archie's top note is an A-flat. You have to find out what your new tenor's top note is and work with him from there."

"I've got to tell you, Martin: I don't know what they're singing. I don't know music. I don't know the notes; I just play."

"That's one of gospel music's biggest problems. When the pianist 'just plays,' the singers can only 'just sing,' and the quality of gospel music slides a little farther downhill."

Two quartet pianists Martin likes are Wally Varner and Hovie Lister. "Wally is a good showman, a good entertainer. I like him and I like his music. Hovie may not be as good a piano player as Wally, I don't know, but he's as good a quartet pianist. He says he isn't a pianist, but an accompanist. Whatever, they are the best.

"The Statesmen were great, but I think they could have done even better with the talent and ability they had if they'd had a greater variety of pitches. I'm not suggesting they should have changed their style; I'm suggesting they should have sung in different ranges with each guy doing what he could do best, and it's hard to imagine, but they might have been an even greater quartet.

"I look at that like a coach. A football coach has eleven players. He knows this guy is good throwing the ball, and this other guy is better running the ball. When he wants somebody to run the ball, he'll not give it to the one who throws. And then he has another guy who can block, just knock people out of their socks. He doesn't have him throwing the ball. That's like the Statesmen: Although they were at the top, and they were great, I think they might have been greater still, and that's saying a lot.

"When we walk on stage Thursday night, or Saturday night, or whenever," he said, "the first thing I'll do is figure who is really singing tonight, and if somebody is hoarse and not singing well, I'm not going to have him trying to do things he can't do.

"There have been times when the Inspirations only had two singers doing an average job. I'm not talking about a superior job, just an average job. Sickness enters into that, and so do other things. You have to work around adversities like that. Your voice will not be at its best every year, I don't care who you are or what you can do. There will be a year or two when your voice just won't do the job. Well, I don't go out and hunt a new singer. I let the other guys run with the ball that year. You'll find that for a couple of years everything a certain singer sings will be hot as a pistol, but the year will come when it will be somebody else stepping up front. It'll shift around like that. Or maybe you'll have two people, and any song they sing will be hot. You've got to push them, let them run, make the most of them while they're cooking."

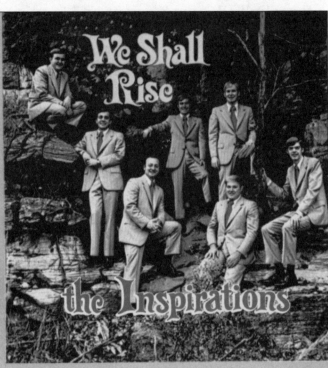

We Shall Rise • I've Come Too Far • I've Got That Ole Time Religion • Walk And Talk In The New Jerusalem Way • When I Inherit My Mansion • There Is A Fountain • It's Worth It All • Heaven Must Be A Wonderful Place • What A Morning • Jesus Will Outshine Them All • Never Failing God • After While

Ⓟ 1972 WORD, INCORPORATED
COMPATIBLE CASSETTE CC-9725

# 19

# The Old Bear Hunter

Although he worked at odd jobs at times around Bryson City, all Jack Laws ever wanted to do was sing.

And go bear hunting.

"Bear hunting was my second life," he said. "Singing came first."

He learned a great love of music in his early years, and it wasn't long until he felt a deep desire to sing, wherever and whenever he could.

Every day he listened to Radio WNOX in Knoxville to hear great gospel quartets like the Blackwood Brothers and Harmoneers. He once told his parents, "Right there's what I'm going to do one of these days." He knew it and began to prepare himself for singing.

Born December 17, 1944, Jack felt he had music in him from the start, especially harmony, and the only training he ever had before joining the Inspirations was one ten-night singing school during his teen years. But he came from a musical family. His father, Wayne Laws, and his uncles sang beautifully, and he was around gospel music all his life. Jack's uncle, Walter Laws, was a mainstay in the Smoky Mountain Quartet, one of the most popular quartets in the western end of North Carolina.

Archie sang with the Bryson City Quartet now and then, and once, when Tony Bowers didn't show up for a session, the others went by Archie's house to get him to sing that evening. However, Archie was busy and couldn't go, but Jack was there and he went. He sang so well that the quartet soon had him singing all the time. He started singing with that group in the very early sixties, perhaps '61 or '62.

Archie's brother Donald, Dean Robinson, and Jerry and Tony Bowers sang in that quartet, with Margaret Ashe playing the piano. Jack sometimes sang with it. The quartet was simply one in which the guys sang for the love of singing. They seldom made public appearances, being satisfied just to sing at someone's home.

When Jack began singing with the Inspirations in Martin Cook's basement, Martin quickly saw that he knew harmony and could sing it.

"Jack was solid as a rock," Martin said. "Singing baritone, he put great support to the Inspirations' singing."

"I love harmony," Jack said. "I love to sing it or hear it, but if it gets under three parts, then I'm no longer interested. It has to be a trio or quartet before it's real harmony. Two-part harmony is not harmony, it's a blend. It takes three parts for harmony, and my part, the baritone, is to blend those other two parts, the one below me and the one above me."

But singing was costly for Jack. "He paid a bigger price than any of us because he wanted to sing," Archie said.

Jack lost his job at a grocery store because he wanted to sing, and he was married and working full time when he lost it. He was young and strong and did all the heavy lifting at the store. He stocked shelves, swept the floor, carried groceries, and performed other chores.

The weekend the Inspirations made their first singing venture to Goshen Baptist Church in Wilkesboro, he hired the store owner's brother-in-law to work in his place for five dollars.

When he returned to work on Monday, the owner was stocking merchandise, and he was mad.

"We don't need you around here any more," he told Jack. "You might as well go to the house."

Jack replied, "Well, that's all right. I'm going to be singing for a living."

"Naw," the owner said, "that'll never happen."

"Watch what happens," Jack said. "I'm going to sing."

He worked odd jobs around Bryson City before he began making enough money with the Inspirations to live on. That was when the others were still in school. In those early days, Martin, Troy, Archie, and Ronnie could sometimes take Friday afternoon off from school if they had a singing date that night. Then they sang Saturday and Sunday, and went back to school on Monday. If they had to make a long trip on Friday, Martin would hire a substitute teacher for the day, and the others would make up the work they missed.

Jack was paddling a different canoe. He couldn't take off anytime he wanted to, but his desire to sing was so strong that he took off anyway.

Later, Jack quit the Inspirations a couple of times, but he always came back, and the quartet was glad to see him coming. The first time he quit, he drove a mail truck for a while, did a couple of weeks of construction work, picked up odd jobs here and there, and when he really needed money he sold off pieces of property he owned near the Great Smoky Mountains National Park.

"The second time I left," he said, "I did about the same thing . . . nothing!"

"I don't know of anybody in gospel singing," Martin said, "then or now, who can sing better than Jack Laws on baritone."

Jack didn't finish high school. He quit and took a job in the grocery store in Bryson City.

Jack's wife is named Brenda. They had a son in 1987 whom Brenda named Baron after her favorite cologne. Jack also has a thirty-three-year-old son, Barry, and a twenty-three-year-old daughter, Melea, from a previous marriage.

Until he suddenly became disabled in 1987, Jack waited almost breathlessly each year for bear-hunting season in the fall. Bear hunting was a tradition with the Laws family. Autumn in the mountains is a beautiful time. Nothing compares with walking in the woods when leaves have changed color, or breathing crisp air that promises frost and precedes winter. Bear or no bear, gun or no gun, fall is a great time to spend in the woods. For the Lawses, hunting bear only added to the excitement and enjoyment of life—and to the family larder, for bear, correctly cooked, is a delicious meat.

The first bear hunt Jack went on with his father hooked him for life. Swain County has always been filled with good bear hunters, eagle-eyed men who could shoot a gnat in the rear across the river, and Wayne Laws was one of them.

"We found a bear up on Wiggins Creek west of Bryson City," Jack said, "right up next to the Great Smokies park, and we ran him out of the mountains into a settlement. There was a field, a branch, a garden, and a road on the other side of the small valley. That bear climbed the bank onto the road, and Daddy shot him from so far away it would have been a good shot with a scope. He had an open-sighted, eight millimeter, high-powered rifle made in Czechoslovakia and used in World War Two.

"He only had four shells," Jack continued, his eyes alight with remembered excitement. "He shot a second time and missed, shot a third time and hit it, and then one of his dogs rushed the bear and just knotted up on his chest. The bear started down the road with the dog hanging on him, and Daddy shot him with his last shell. The bear fell in the branch and landed on top of the dog, which came out from under him hollering. We thought Daddy had shot the dog, but when he fell the bear mashed him and broke a rib."

It is no wonder that hunt made such an impression on Jack. The bear was a monster, weighing 550 pounds.

That same year, Jack began breeding and raising his own stock of bear dogs, Redbone, Blue Tick, white, black, and tan, a little Airedale, crossbreeding to get the best blood mixture possible.

Oftentimes, it is hard to tell where the boundary of the Great Smokies park lies, which now and then causes problems for bear hunters.

"I never knowingly hunted in the park," Jack said, "and I never could teach my dogs to read boundary signs. Only thing I taught them to read was bear sign. If they ever ran a bear out of the park, I never knew it."

Jack does not remember the first bear he killed, and he doesn't know how many bears he has killed. "If I had to make a hard guess," he mused, "I'd say a hundred or so. I know it's been a lot."

The last bear Jack killed was in October of 1998 in West Virginia. "My youngest son and my uncle and I went to West Virginia," he said, "and bought our licenses. I rode everywhere I went there because I can't walk hardly any distance any more. All the hunting land there is very accessible."

Jack once killed a bear in Canada that weighed more than 600 pounds. He shot a second one of about that size on his own property bordering the park.

"That was a big bear for here," he said. "I never did have any trouble getting bears up. I guess more bears cross my property than any place I've ever seen except West Virginia."

Jack usually armed himself with a .357 Magnum pistol when he went bear hunting. "Yeah," he said, "I've used it a lot hunting. With a pistol, I've killed several bears, a deer, a bobcat, the last wild boar I killed, and I've shot a lot of snakes' heads off with a pistol." He killed the wild boar with a snub-nosed .38 caliber pistol.

He has had only a couple of close calls with bears. Once he was so near a live bear in the wilderness that it took a swipe at him and fortunately missed. Another time, he hunkered down to shoot a picture of a bear at an overlook, and when the flash went off, that bear also took a swing at him. Jack bristled and instead of the bear running him off, he wound up running the bear off.

"With my rifle and dogs I was never afraid of a bear," he said.

He used to go all over the country hunting. He was bear-hunting in Canada with Dolly Parton's double first cousin, Coy Parton, of Sevierville, Tennessee, when Coy killed a bear that weighed more than six hundred pounds.

Because of his disabilities, Jack is unable to roam the mountains hunting as he once did, but he still enjoys nature. He and Archie own a hunter's paradise that borders the park. Not long ago Jack went up there alone, camouflaged himself, and began using a turkey-caller.

"I was behind a big tree," he said, "and three old gobblers came within spitting distance without seeing me. I was right at the park line, and suddenly turkeys were coming up to my back, clucking and gobbling, and soon there were so many I never saw or heard of anything like that in my life. And I never even had a gun."

Jack doesn't own a gun now. When he became disabled twelve years ago and had to quit hunting, he sold all of his hunting guns.

"Whatever it was that caused my disability," Jack said, "affected everything about me but my voice. It left me with the full ability to sing."

He has had back surgery twice and needs more, perhaps a result of his years of running through rough woods trailing bears. One of his hips has been replaced twice and doctors have told him he should have the other replaced. He has arthritis and a few other ailments.

But he still cannot resist doing things in the Great Outdoors. Now, however, he farms. He loves to watch things grow. "I've got two hundred and nineteen tomato plants," he said.

Will he sell the tomatoes? "No," he chuckled, "I'm going to eat them. We put 'em up, can 'em, and I give all the boys things out of my garden. They can hardly wait for my garden to come in. I've got three different patches, about an acre altogether, I guess, filled with beans, corn, okra. You name it, I've got it in my garden."

When he had his first hip replacement, he gardened on crutches. Now he works his garden from a chair, dragging it with him as he progresses along a row.

He is in constant pain, but you'd never know it; the smile seldom leaves his face.

Jack loves children, and is well fortified with grandchildren. He has six of his own doing and two step-grandchildren. They range in age from five months to twelve years.

He feels that hundreds of children across the country are grandkids. Jack is probably the favorite Inspiration with kids, because he picks at them and seeks them out, and remembers them from town to town.

"There's one that I've been picking at since she was a little girl," he said, "and the other day she sent me a picture of herself in her wedding dress. As she was growing up, every time we were anywhere around, her parents would bring her to the singing and she'd be right under my arm at the record table. She'd stand there looking up at me with her big ole eyes, and my heart would just melt.

"Kids are special to me," he said. "I love 'em all."

Once when the Inspirations were singing in Gatlinburg, a little girl came to the record table and said she had come to see the old bear-hunter, and because he wasn't there she cried through the singing.

Jack has a great sense of humor and uses it often. Once, Ronnie and his family had a calf they intended to kill for beef. Somehow the calf got loose and headed for tall timber.

Knowing Jack's expertise in the woods, Ronnie asked Jack if he would help locate the calf, and, of course, he was happy to do it.

Because of his lifetime of hunting and his great voice, Jack could duplicate the sound of any animal.

He would go up one ridge and Ronnie and his family up the other, and as soon as he got out of sight, Jack would bawl like a calf. Ronnie and his folks would run to that ridge, and by the time they got there, Jack was on another. He would bawl again, and here they came again. Then Jack would slip behind them and bawl again.

He ran them through the woods until their tongues hung out and then he caught the calf.

# 20

# Organization

The quartet that handles its business in a slipshod way, out of its shirt pockets, so to speak, doesn't last long. In this day of complex tax laws and business arrangements, a sound structure must support the singers on stage.

Actually, stage work is only a small part of a quartet's operation. No quartet keeps singing by accident or by rote. There must be a sound link between the singing on stage and a business structure.

"We have a regular corporation," Martin said, "and when we set it up in 1971, we stipulated certain things to protect those members who are presently singing."

Ownership of the quartet is determined by the number of years members have spent with the Inspirations. When a man drops out, he forfeits his part of the ownership. It must be owned by persons active in the quartet.

But the papers of incorporation protect the name of the Inspirations and extend it beyond the present ownership of Martin, Archie, and Mike.

"Anyone who sings in the quartet," Martin said, "has the right and privilege to continue singing, using the name Inspirations at no charge. The name itself can be continued. If Archie and Mike and I quit today, the other boys would have the right to continue using that name. They could buy and sell material just as we do, but they couldn't do wholesale or royalties or anything like that. We want the guys to have the right to continue the name without having to pay somebody who's not singing any more. That's the only way we can keep young people coming in and continuing on."

About half of the quartet's income is derived from the sale of records and tapes. "We buy them and sell them at a profit," Martin explained. "Basically, we make about as much off sales as we do singing concerts."

Each singer has assigned duties, and if all keep their work up to date, the quartet's operation runs smoothly.

For example, Martin does the booking and handles all financial matters. He is responsible for knowing the group's financial status, and for management of the group in general. He is also responsible for personnel—hiring, firing, planning, all of that.

Mike is in charge of inventory, seeing that the quartet is stocked with merchandise. His responsibilities include overseeing the loading of the bus at the beginning of a concert tour. He makes sure that the material that should be on the bus is on it. And every other month, Mike writes the quartet's newsletter, which is an important link between the group and its followers.

Archie is responsible for the bus and PA system.

"We have a mechanic named Colen Jenkins," he said. "He lives in Bryson City; in fact, he went to school with us. He checks the bus every week, gives it a good going-over, and does whatever needs to be done to it."

That's one reason the bus the Inspirations finished with in 1998 ran for two to three million miles, carrying the quartet to the ends of America and beyond.

"Colen is a lifesaver," Archie said, "or maybe I ought to say he's a bus-saver. He worked on Eagle buses for Trailways for twelve years and is very knowledgeable as a mechanic. He saves us a fortune."

Archie's brother, Donald, who drives the bus, said, "Colen found things on the old bus that we didn't know were going wrong, and if he hadn't checked them we would have been down somewhere. We've only broken down twice on the road in all the time Colen has been checking our bus."

Matt Dibler, the present lead singer, has no duties at the moment. He has not been with the group long enough to learn its operation to the point that he can accept responsibility.

Each person has certain duties when the Inspirations arrive anywhere for a concert, and these responsibilities are cut and dried.

Whoever is singing baritone has to take the speaker boxes in. That is Jack's duty at this writing. Archie and Myron carry the sound system in and put it in place. They set up the control board and make it operational, then connect wires and microphones, and test the system to make sure the sound is right.

While this is going on on stage, Mike and the lead singer set up the quartet's record table and displays and get ready for business.

Sometimes the Inspirations sing a 45-minute first stand, which saps strength and energy, but at intermission they gather at the record table to take care of business.

When they finish there, it's back to the stage again for the second round, and then tear down, load the bus, stop somewhere to eat, and hit the sack, bound for another place to go through the same setting up and knocking down routines, and sing the same songs. But the work is not boring, primarily because they are working with people, many of whom they know, and all of whom they consider to be friends.

Tough as life is on the road, it's just as busy back home. At this writing, the Inspirations office is located in the old Skylite Motel east of Bryson City. The offices occupy considerable space, much of which is for storage of their products.

Marian Fortner is the Inspirations' secretary. Recalling the old adage, "A woman's work is never done," she stands as a shining example to womanhood. Truly, her work is never done. And neither is Marcia Cook's. Marcia is the daughter of Martin and Ora Blanche, and she works in the Inspirations' office, too, busy as a bee.

On occasion, others are called in to help with the workload. No one complains, however; such a workload as these women have is testimony to the fact that business is good and growing.

Twenty-four years ago, the Inspirations' secretary was Pat Fortner, who now operates a thriving Bryson City real estate business.

At the time, Marian was employed by the Swain County School System. She had been secretary for Alarka School for six years. She had worked as a tutor and as a teacher's assistant. She made out the county's lunchroom reports, and had various other duties.

The workload became too much for her, and one day she prayed, "Lord, please get me out of here. Please send me a job. I'll take it even if it's less money."

A dedicated Christian woman who keeps a Bible on her desk and reads it every day before she begins work, Marian prayed that prayer often.

One day Marian increased the fervor of her prayers. "Lord, please send me a job," she prayed especially hard that evening as she cooked supper.

That night, her telephone rang. Martin Cook was on the line.

"Marian," he said, "I understand you're looking for a job."

"When can I start?" she blurted.

He said, "Tomorrow."

"No," she said, "I have to give two weeks' notice."

"Well, go ahead and give it," Martin said, and the next morning she turned in her notice to the school board and two weeks later went to work for the Inspirations. She and Pat worked together the next ten years.

"I am sure that my connection with the Inspirations through Pat didn't hurt," she said. "I took the job for about thirty-five dollars less money and in about two months the schools tried to hire me back at more money, but Martin told me that I was not going to go back, and he gave me a nice raise."

The work she does now is not all that easy, but it is very pleasant. She loves the quartet and all the people connected with it, and she plunges into her work with enthusiasm.

"The business has grown tremendously," she said. "We have tripled in size since I came. We do the promotions, advertising, newsletters, mailing, mail orders, handle the music companies—we do everything but drive the bus and sing."

She is in charge of the Inspirations' promotions. "We promote in a lot of towns," she said. "Some of our best dates are the ones we promote. We work as partners with promoters in these towns. We do the work on our end, the promoter does it on his end, we pay all bills at the singings, then take that money back off the top and divide what is left on a percentage basis with the promoter.

"We have huge mailing lists of people in these towns and we mail information to them about the next singing. When we send a mailing, we include the latest newsletter. Marcia does all of this. I do the financial stuff, write the checks, and make sure that all pertinent figures and information goes to the accountant who does the quartet's taxes."

Marian maintains telephone contact with promoters and checks on everything. She mails promo packages for road promotions, and sees that promoters get whatever they need. Together, Marcia and Marian pack mail orders.

In 1998 the Inspirations paid more than a hundred thousand dollars to people other than those who work for the quartet.

"Most of those checks were for royalties," Marian said, "money paid to those who write our songs. That made up the bulk of the eighty-eight 1090s we issued last year.

We pay royalties twice a year and we are very meticulous about paying our writers all the money they have earned. We pay many people who work at the Singing in the Smokies each summer."

It is Marian's job to handle the financial end of the Singing in the Smokies. She pays those who work at the singing, ticket takers and all, and counts the money and makes deposits at the bank.

Marian started the Inspirations' three music companies and tends to all copyrighting. The quartet makes its own recordings, renting studio time and jobbing out the work of manufacturing tapes. Marian handles all of that.

She says the Inspirations have never encountered a major problem in these areas, but there have been minor ones.

"When the quartet recorded *Jesus Is Mine*," she said, "three people claimed to have written the song. Marvin Norcross of Word Publishing Company in Waco, Texas, and I were going back and forth from here to Texas with this problem. Everything had to be up front with Marvin. He was a meticulous man. And one day when it appeared we might never know for sure who wrote the song, Marvin said in disgust, 'Marian, I think I wrote that song.' We finally found who wrote it and paid the royalties."

Marian talked enthusiastically, happy with her job.

"It's exciting," she said. "We work hard, but there is a lot of excitement about it. I have had a good time here. The Inspirations are good people to work for. My son was raised with them. He came by the office after school and stayed with me, and I didn't have to hire a baby-sitter.

"When my granddaughter was ten months old," she continued, "she was in a day care and a baby almost bit her jaw off. I had her here with me the next day and was going to take her to a sitter, but Martin and Archie dropped in and nixed that. They said, 'You're gonna keep that baby here,' and that was final. For two and a half years I kept my grandbaby here and did the office work.

It was great having her here. The guys would come in and oftentimes they would feed a bottle, and Marcia learned to diaper when she stayed here. It isn't on every job you could do that."

Marian had never had a job like this one. "All this is new to me," she said. "It wasn't hard for me, because I started most of the things we do. We didn't have a music company; now we have three, which have grown into hundreds of songs. I had to start that from the beginning. I set up the promotions myself. The quartet hadn't started that when I came. The singing on the mountain was already going on.

"I keep up with all three music companies now. We have the Praise Music Company, the Inspirations Quartet Music Company, and Tuckaseigee Publishing Company. We pay our royalties through them. There is a lot of music in Praise that the Inspirations haven't sung. We bought that company after it was established. Most of the songs in our companies, though, are songs from our albums, songs the Inspirations sing.

"We have our own independent recording company, the Inspirations Record Company, and I take care of all the business in that. I get everything together, see that all of it is properly copyrighted, and when the quartet goes to the studio to make a record, Mike brings a big package to me and I have to get everything together on the songs they're going to record. I do the layouts the way they want the album to look, and then I get someone to design it. There is a company in Atlanta, American Sound and Video Company, that manufactures tapes and CDs for us.

"We have good relations with that company and get anything we want from them at any time. Our credit is good. We're listed with Dun and Bradstreet. We have a good relationship with all the people we work with."

Marian keeps a date book and records all the dates Martin contracts for. "He schedules sometimes a year ahead," she said, "and I call all the promoters and find out what they want, what they need to promote."

For the Inspirations, Marian keeps files on everything. "If we have a problem, we can usually lick it through the files," she said.

She is proud that the Inspirations have never had a check to bounce, although that has not always worked the other way around.

The quartet pays its bills regardless of anything. Once the Florida Boys had a bus accident outside their home base in Pensacola, Florida, and were late arriving for the Singing in the Smokies. The crowd was going down the mountain when the Florida Boys pulled in and realized they had missed the singing.

"We paid them anyway," she said.

Any time the Inspirations schedule a new town, Marian makes a file on the town and puts in it everything pertaining not only to the singing but to the town. The quartet believes in not leaving anything to chance.

The Inspirations do about sixteen dates a year for the Harper and Sons booking agency in Nashville, and a few with Becky Simmons and some with Sonny Simmons. But the quartet promotes most of its own big dates.

One of the things both Marian and Marcia look forward to each day is answering the mail. Every letter the Inspirations receive gets answered.

"We have a lot of people tell us how touched they were by the Inspirations," Marian said. "Got one the other day saying they were glad Jack was back, because his song, *God's Last Altar Call*, had something to do with their son getting saved. They said they didn't especially like gospel music and had gone to the singing because they had to for some reason. They liked that song, bought a tape, and it touched their son.

"We've gotten hundreds of letters like that. We don't have room to keep them because over the years we have received hundreds of thousands of letters. We have only had a couple of negative letters ever, and we've had no hate mail or anything like that."

When Marian answers a letter, if the person who wrote asks for something to be done personally by one of the singers, Marian sees that the letter is passed to that singer.

"We got a letter from a fellow on a ship stationed off the coast of Bosnia," she said. "He asked for some literature on the Inspirations, and I sent some tapes along with the literature and told him how we appreciated him being there, and I signed the letter, 'The Inspirations.' I wrote to him on and off for about a year.

"When he came home, he brought his wife and baby down here and went to Jack's house. He asked Jack, 'I want to know which lady wrote me all those letters. I know the Inspirations didn't do it.' So he came by the office and when he found that I had written the letters, he said, 'I just wanted to meet you and say thanks.' I believe that's the most embarrassed I've ever been. But it really thrilled my heart."

Letters come to the Inspirations from all over the world. They have received recent mail from Ireland, Uganda, Australia, England, Hawaii, Canada, Mexico, Thailand, Germany, and even one from Russia.

"A fellow in England calls," Marian said, "and orders tapes and pays eighty dollars postage to get them airmailed over there."

Once, some people came from Canada and said they knew the Inspirations well. They had a white Cadillac. They bounced checks all around Waynesville and even one or two with the Inspirations.

"We have people from all over the world come to the Singing in the Smokies," she said. "June Willy comes from West Virginia and helps. She keeps the office when Marian has to be on the mountain. The Willys were good friends, and when Mr. Willy died, the Inspirations drove to West Virginia and sang at his funeral. Robert and Opal Hice came every year to help, but he recently died of a heart attack. A couple from Mississippi, David and Gloria Hartfield, and some from Pennsylvania often come and help us."

"It's nice," Martin said, "to have someone working for us who is as loyal and interested in her job as Marian. We don't have to worry about things at the office when we're away; we know Marian will take care of them. She will go the extra mile to do things right."

That, of course, works both ways.

"Martin tells me," Marian said, "when I need to be off just to close the door and leave. I don't have to do that often, but when I really need to, I do it. That's a privilege I wouldn't have anywhere else."

The Inspirations have a great love and respect for Marian.

"Marian Fortner is in a class all her own," Martin said. "I'd have to hire two or three to replace her. She knows the office and the mechanics of it far better than I do, and she loves her work.

"I trained her like I wanted her trained, and now I don't have to tell her what to do. We've got a structure that's hard to explain. People have freedom to do their thing. Marian knows she's expected to get the mailout down to the post office, and it's her business how she gets it done. If she's going to spend money to buy this or do that, she'll ask me first, and I appreciate that, but I know she isn't going to spend money frivolously. The office is her problem and I don't tell her how to run it. I just tell her what I want done, and I know it'll be done.

"A lot of people might take advantage of a situation like that, but Marian wouldn't. We have full trust in her, and she has never let us down."

Even with proper office help like the Inspirations have had, managing the quartet put a strain on Martin for many years.

"One of the things I didn't realize for years," he said, "was the responsibility involved in keeping things going. I don't feel that responsibility now because we've all got the kids raised and our lives planned out, and we've got thirty-five years behind us, which makes my job easier, because we are known and it isn't hard to book all the dates we want.

"But through the years I know now that I had a tremendous amount of pressure because we all had to pay enormous bills—we had to raise the kids, keep our homes going, some went into businesses on the side, and we never really knew where our next payday was coming from. We didn't know whether the next date was going to be good enough for us to meet those obligations.

"The strange thing is, the pressure was there but I didn't realize it till those years had passed, and it was like you'd moved a mountain off of me. Now we've reached the point of success, I suppose you could say, where we don't have to worry so much about keeping things going, and we can enjoy it more.

"I think I was bonded so closely to the other fellows for all those years that I didn't even realize all that pressure was there until it was gone. The bond was so strong that for my part it was just like breathing. We take breathing for granted. I was bonded so closely to the quartet and what we were doing that I don't think I could have changed my part of it. God could have changed it, but there was never a choice with me.

"Some months the Inspirations have had $30,000 worth of bills to pay before anyone, secretary or singer, drew a penny. One month of 1999 we had to have $28,000 for things like making tapes and CDs, buying a stock of records, whatever, before anyone got paid. That's a responsibility that all quartet managers face until they get enough corporation money in the bank to meet all their obligations.

"In gospel music," Martin said, "you've got no guarantee that you're going to have a crowd tomorrow night, and you sure don't know what's going to happen next year. All of these quartets that travel full time are no small-time operation. The manager or whoever is responsible for finance, has a great responsibility. It's no smalltime operation. Les Beasley has probably done the best job of any of us in keeping things going. The Florida Boys have been together fifty years, so they're ahead of us. They've kept the thing going, paid their bills, raised their kids, and done well. But it's not an easy thing."

More pressure comes when managers have to make personnel changes in their quartets. Archie said it was like having to say goodbye to your brother after being with him for years.

Archie added: "It's true that down through the years, we've had a real bond. We made rules, it was understood how we did things, there was no question about procedure when someone left. We had rules about all that, and everybody observed them.

"I think the whole thing boils down to one point: We've really just been spoiled."

Possibly the most unusual thing that ever happened in the Inspirations' office occurred in 1990 when a new record containing a single song came out.

The Inspirations made a new cassette tape entitled *What's That I Hear?* From the tape, they chose a song, *Eye of the Storm*, to put on a single for distribution to radio stations across the country. Before long, the single had everyone asking, "What's that I hear?"

Air play has a lot to do with successful sales of recordings and tapes in music stores and places other than at the record table at concerts. The quartet wanted a song for this single that was well done, had a good rhythm and tune, and had a strong content and message. They felt *Eye of the Storm*, featuring Archie, had all of that.

Fifteen hundred copies of the single arrived at the Inspirations' office in Bryson City, and a crew of five assembled to get the records in the mail as fast as possible. At best, they knew the job would take the best part of two days.

Marian and Marcia did all the preparatory work for the mailout, and then Ora Blanche and Robert and Opal Hice, who did a lot of work for the Inspirations, gathered in the office and went to work.

They worked hard all day. First, they printed out mailing labels for fifteen hundred radio stations, then they fixed labels to fifteen hundred mailers. Each packet had to be stamped twice, once with a first class mailing stamp and next with a "Record" stamp that told postal authorities what the packets contained.

The mailers had to be folded a certain way to receive the records, and the records had to be inserted in the mailers. Then they had to fold and tape the mailers, and finally fix postage on each mailer.

At the end of an exhausting all-day effort, eight hundred records were ready for mailing.

Ora Blanche was preparing to take the ready records to the post office for mailing when Tom Harris came in the office. Pastor of Victory Baptist Church in Bryson City, Tom also had a radio show on WBHN, Bryson City, on which he played gospel music.

"Is that a new tape?" Tom asked, and Ora Blanche replied, "This is just a single."

"Well, let me have one," Tom said, "and I'll play it on the air in the morning."

He took the record and left.

The five weary workers laughed about what a fun day it had been. They'd worked hard, but they had also spent a lot of time talking and laughing, and they'd gone to lunch together.

At half past four Ora and Marcia took the eight hundred records to the post office and turned them in, and then drove home.

The five laborers gathered in the office the following morning to complete the job. Being on a roll from the previous afternoon, they figured to have the final seven hundred ready for mailing by noon.

A short time later, Tom Harris put the record on the air, announcing it as Archie Watkins singing *Eye of the*

*Storm.* The record spun and suddenly Mike Holcomb's deep bass voice filled the studio, singing *That Same God.* Tom blinked and let the record play on through.

He then checked the label which had *Eye of the Storm* written on it.

He dialed the Inspirations office and Ora answered.

"Ora," Tom said, "I played that record on the air."

"How did you like it?"

"I liked it fine, but it's not *Eye of the Storm.*"

"What?" Ora's voice contained a bit of alarm.

"It's *That Same God,*" Tom said, "and Mike's singing it."

All work ceased when Ora told the work force what Tom had said. Silence reigned and they looked dumbly at each other and then at the remaining records.

"You'd better get in touch with Martin," Robert Hice said, but Martin was away on a bear hunt.

They figured out what happened. *Eye of the Storm* was the fourth cut on side two of the tape, and *That Same God* was the fourth cut on side one. The engineer took the song off the wrong side of the tape when he cut the record.

"We'll have to wait till Martin comes to see what to do," Ora told the others. "Meanwhile, we won't do any more work till he gets back."

On an errand downtown, Ora stopped at the post office to pick up the postage meter. "By the way," she asked the postal clerk, "are all those records I brought in yesterday still here?"

"No, ma'am," the clerk said, beaming. "We sent them right out. You didn't want them back, did you?"

"Well..." She hedged, not wanting to say anything further.

"You're going to have more this afternoon, aren't you?"

"No," she said, "I don't think so. We've sort of had a change of plans."

Archie was in nearby Sylva that afternoon and had his radio tuned to WGRC, the Sylva station. The announcer said, "Here's a brand new release from the Inspirations. It's titled *Eye of the Storm* and features Archie Watkins."

Archie settled back to listen, and suddenly Mike Holcomb's voice rumbled from the radio, singing *That Same God.*

"That's not me!" Archie said aloud, as if trying to convince himself.

No doubt there were many surprised DJs around the country when they announced that record and listened to it.

When Martin returned home and heard what happened, he said thoughtfully, "Chances of this happening are very, very slim—but it happened."

It cost $680 to mail the eight hundred records. That was money down the drain.

The record company did the batch of records over. The engineer who made the record had listened to the tune, but only for quality. He didn't even notice the words of the song.

"It never entered our minds to play the record to make sure it was the right song," Ora said.

But they play every single before fixing eight hundred for mailing now.

Considering all this, you can see that there is more to operating a quartet than singing, shaking hands, and selling records.

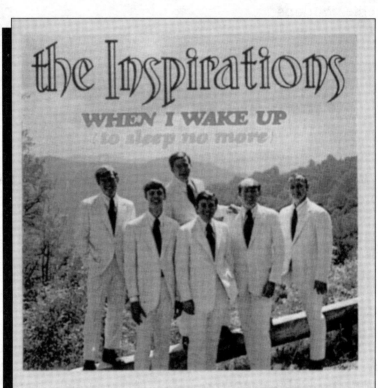

When I Wake Up (to sleep no more) • One Day I will
• There Is a River • I'm Winging My Way Back Home
• The First Look • Longing for Home • When I Got
Saved • When I Step Off on the Beautiful Shore •
Long, Long Journey • Revival Days • God's Last
Altar Call • He Brought Me Out

CC-9747

# 21

# Solid Foundation

There have been few personnel changes for the Inspirations in their thirty-five years of existence, fewer than almost any other quartet. Martin and Archie have been with the quartet all the way, Martin as pianist, of course, and Archie singing high tenor. There have been a few changes in the lead and baritone spots but not so many that they couldn't be counted on ten fingers, and they've been kept mostly in the family with Ronnie Hutchins, Eddie Dietz, Jack Laws, and Troy Burns doing most of the swapping, and Chris Smith, Marlin Shubert, and Matt Dibler singing short stints.

Eight men have logged ninety-seven percent of all time recorded by all members of the Inspirations: Martin and Archie, thirty-five years each; Troy and Mike, twenty-seven each; Jack, twenty-three years; Eddie and Myron Cook, eighteen years each; and Ronnie fifteen years in four different stints with the group. Chris Smith, Marlin Shubert, and Matt Dibler have totaled one to three years each.

"I doubt that any other quartet that's been singing as long as we have," Martin said, "could make a statement like that in truth."

Since those days when Martin was hosting singers in the basement of his home, only three men have sung bass for the quartet, Troy at the beginning, Marlin Shubert for a while, and Mike Holcomb for the last twenty-seven years, as of 1999. Oddly enough, two of them are from Jasper—Marlin from Jasper, Alabama, and Mike from Jasper, Georgia.

That record for longevity is phenomenal. The Cathedrals, for example, have made so many changes over the years that George Younce and Glen Payne joked that they had to call the roll every morning to see who was on the bus.

All three of the Inspirations' bass singers started with the quartet when they were extremely young, Troy at fourteen and Marlin and Mike at eighteen. The demands that bass singing make on a person usually call for experience, for bass is the foundation of a quartet. At times, it seems that the rest of the group stands on the shoulders of the bass because his voice supports the harmony. Other parts generate harmony, but the bass must be strong in a male quartet to carry the harmony.

Despite this youth, the Inspirations have never suffered because of the age of bass singers.

"Let me tell you," Martin said, "we have had three exceptional basses. Marlin Shubert had a clear tone and good pitch. He knew exactly where every tone was. If he was standing here right now and I said, 'Marlin, what does that low B flat sound like?' he knew where it was and he could hit it without help from a piano or another singer. He was uncanny in that respect.

"Now, all singers, I suppose, have shortcomings. Marlin's was that he had no sense of rhythm, and a lot of songs we did were handicapped in a way because of that. Oh, most in the audience never noticed the deficiency, but we on stage could tell.

"When it came to hitting hard tones, though, Marlin could hit them just like that." He snapped his fingers.

"Marlin had one peculiarity I have never seen in another singer. Sometimes he would go down for a low note, open his mouth, and not a sound would come out. He either hit it right or no sound at all came from his mouth. But if the sound came out, it would be right on pitch. He never shaded a note."

Marlin sang bass for the Inspirations for two years.

"Troy," Martin said, "could slide and blow notes right off the piano. Jack Laws is that way. He can blow notes right on down there, but Jack was better singing baritone because he could bring a harmony together.

"Troy was the smoothest bass singer we ever had. He was low enough. He could sing a low A flat when he was sixteen, and if he had stayed with bass singing, he probably would have been by far the best bass singer I've ever had any association with. He had rhythm, and he could tone it down and smooth it and harmonize right in there as well as anyone I ever heard."

He paused a moment in thought, then continued, "Mike is exceptionally good in rhythm. His rhythm is what goes. He has it in his voice. I don't know that I've ever heard another professional bass singer who could put as much rhythm into his voice. Big Chief had tremendous rhythm and accuracy and J. D. was the lowest a bass has ever been. Mike has a lot of both. He sings with great rhythm and is very accurate, and he sings down to a double low C. He has the rhythm, voice, and range. That was evident in two of our songs that he introduced, *Wake Up to Sleep No More* and *Footsteps*, and both songs became best-sellers. I'm not saying others can't sing in time with music. What I'm talking about is perfect rhythm.

"After he had been with us a few years, Mike could sing well down to a low F. Now he goes on down to a double low C. He can say his words intelligibly and go to any low note without sliding to it. He can go and hit it without blowing the note."

The Inspirations
say
**Sing Me a GOSPEL Song**

THE INSPIRATIONS say
Sing Me a Gospel Song

**Produced by Martin Cook**

Sing Me a Gospel Song • I Love to Tell • A Million Years Or More • When My Feet Touch Down at Home • Crown Him King • Love Gift from Jesus • When I Step Beyond the Clouds • Mary Cried • Waiting for the Call • He Sent Him for Me • Moving Time • Something Happened on that Mountain

CC-9881

CC-9881

# 22

## Mike

Mike joined the Inspirations in an unusual way. He didn't apply for a job; Martin sought him out. Labor Day, 1972, was a rainy day in Cumming, Georgia. The Inspirations had a singing engagement there that afternoon, along with several other groups like Bob Wills and the Inspirationals, the Kingsmen, and the Hopper Brothers and Connie.

The singing had been scheduled outside, but rain had driven it into the high school gymnasium.

Chig Cagle, a Ford dealer from Sylva, had come onto the Inspirations' bus and said, "You guys gotta go listen to that guy sing bass in there."

Martin recalls the incident clearly. "I had my little girl, Marcia, with me that day. She was five and we were outside, walking around the back of the gymnasium, under cover of its awning, when I heard this bass voice from the stage inside. It was Mike Holcomb, and his singing stopped me in my tracks."

Martin listened to the rest of the song and later looked Mike up. "He told me," Martin recalled, "that he had wanted to sing with the Inspirations for years and that he knew all of our songs."

At the time, the Inspirations were not looking for a bass singer, but Martin was keen for keeping someone in mind that he could call if one of the guys quit. Marlin

Shubert, the Inspirations' bass, had left a few weeks before, and Troy was singing bass again.

Looking back, Martin later said, "It wasn't something we planned; it just turned out that way. So many things will do that: you wonder how they're working, and all the time they're working out right for you while you're trying to figure out something else."

Later that day, Martin sent for Mike to join the Inspirations on their bus, and when Mike came aboard, Martin, Archie, Troy, Eddie, Ronnie, and Jack were waiting for him.

"Martin wanted us to sing a song together," Mike said, "just to see what we sounded like. We sang *Roll on Jordan*, and he apparently liked it."

Martin invited Mike to Bryson City two days later—on Wednesday—to audition with the Inspirations, and told him to bring enough clothes to stay a while.

"We want you to rehearse with us Wednesday, and if you fit in, and you like us and we like you, you can start singing immediately," Martin told him.

Mike was in his second year of studying computer programming and diagramming and accounting at a community college, but when Martin asked him to come to Bryson City, he knew he would leave his studies on the spur of the moment if Martin offered him the job.

In Bryson City that Wednesday, Mike practiced with the quartet. Martin pulled out some of their older songs like *What a Wonderful Time* and *Just As Long As Eternity Rolls*, songs the Inspirations had not done in so long they had almost forgotten the intricate harmonies in them, and Mike knew the songs better than the other guys.

After that Wednesday audition, Martin hired Mike and took him on tour with the Inspirations the next day. Troy became a picker.

Archie learned that Mike had been to his house near Bryson City and bought a P.A. set from him just a year before that. "I didn't remember him," Archie said. "I didn't know him from Adam."

At that time, when the Inspirations lost a man, they needed to replace him in a hurry. They were doing a lot of big singings like Atlanta, Bonifay, Birmingham, Nashville. J. G. Whitfield promoted the big dates and used the Inspirations everywhere.

All through boyhood, Mike Holcomb's favorite singing group was the Inspirations. He attended their singings, bought their records, and learned all their songs. Singing with the Inspirations was a lifelong dream.

His parents had always sung. "They were singing when I was born," Mike said. "I sang in public when I was four. Mama played the piano and Daddy and an uncle and aunt sang together. I stood on the piano stool beside Mama and sang."

He sang with a Future Farmers of America group and with the Glee Club in high school in his hometown of Jasper, Georgia, and when he was sixteen he sang with a church quartet called the Happy Harmony Quartet, and then with two sisters, Diane and Mildred Parker, and a tenor-pianist named Bobby Hales, in a group called Deliverance, with whom he was singing on that Labor Day when the Inspirations heard him.

Over his first twenty years with the Inspirations, Mike's voice matured but did not deepen. "My voice has gotten thicker and heavier," he said, "and maybe it's a little easier to sing low, but from the time I was sixteen I could hit a double low C, and when I get up early in the morning, I can sometimes go off the end of the piano."

Singing regularly does not necessarily deepen a voice. "Singing regularly makes it easier to sing," Mike said, "easier to learn voice control, and it certainly helps a singer gain the confidence he needs. If I had to hit a double low C tonight, I wouldn't sweat it. At the age of sixteen, I could hit that note, but I wouldn't try it on stage. I felt I was doing good to hit a low B flat then. That was about the lowest note I could hit well. My voice was still popping and cracking a little. But if Martin wants a double low C tonight, I'll give it to him."

"The man can sing," Martin said. "He can do pretty well what Big Chief could do, and he can do pretty well what J. D. did on low notes. He can take the lead on a song and run with it. Chief had tremendous quality and didn't miss a note. I'm sure he could have sung lower notes had he wanted to. I pray Mike will continue to work and combine the outstanding qualities of both those great bass singers."

Mike never tries to push his voice below its limits. If he can deliver a double low C, why try to go deeper? He might be able to do it, but even at that depth it is hard for the human ear to ascertain its depth.

The most unusual thing that happened to Mike on that Labor Day singing in 1972 wasn't the Inspirations offering him a chance for a job, but the fact that four different quartets on that program tried to hire him.

Bob Wills of the Inspirationals told Mike if he couldn't work things out with the Inspirations that he would hire him. Wills's bass, Ray Burdette, was leaving.

Claude Hopper's older brother, Monroe, bass singer for the Hopper Brothers and Connie, had just left, and Claude offered Mike the job.

And Tilford Salyer, a perfect stranger to Mike, offered him a job singing backup in his studio in Kingsport, Tennessee.

But when Martin made the offer, Mike needed no time to make up his mind. He had decided years before. He already knew every song the Inspirations sang, and he knew he was ready to sing with them.

He was only eighteen years old, but he was making big decisions, and today, looking in retrospect, he knows he made the right decision about singing with the Inspirations.

His parents took him to a singing in Atlanta when he was thirteen or fourteen, and that was the night he first heard the Inspirations. From that moment on, they were his favorite quartet.

From the time he was eleven until he reached mid-thirteen, he went through every young man's voice-changing process.

"That was the most miserable time of my life," Mike said. "I loved to sing, and I couldn't. My voice popped and cracked like an out-of-tune Ford, and I couldn't control it."

Then, when he regained at least partial control of his vocal cords, he began singing lead because his choir needed a lead singer. "My dad was a bass," he said, "and after I heard Troy singing bass, I started singing bass. I was fourteen years old, exactly as old as Troy when he began singing bass with the Inspirations."

The day that the Inspirations hired Mike was a banner day for all concerned. Mike has spent his last twenty-seven years singing with the quartet, and Martin hasn't had to look for a bass singer since.

"Not only that," Martin said, "Mike is one of the most conscientious Christian men I've ever seen. He reads his Bible and prays more, and is more serious about it than any individual I've known. That includes preachers and all. He is a spiritual asset to us."

Mike was saved at the age of ten, and six years into his Christian life, God called him to preach the gospel.

"I said no," Mike said, "and I fought it tooth and nail. I told the Lord He was making a terrible mistake. I didn't even like to give book reports."

He worked out a temporary compromise with the Lord. "I'll sing as long as you want me to," he prayed, "and I'll go anywhere, but I just can't preach."

He said it was as if God didn't press the subject for a while. "He let me sing, and I believe God feels the way I do, that singing with the Inspirations is the biggest ministry I could ever hope for."

But after eight years, God insisted that he take the pulpit, and Mike answered the call.

But first he got married.

He married Bavaria Lynn Mitchell of Bryson City April 25, 1976. He met her in a most unusual way.

She was standing on her head.

Bavaria was an athlete at Swain County High School. Mike had a duplex at the Inspirations' motel on Schoolhouse Hill.

"I looked out one day," Mike said, "and there was Archie's sister, Jody, talking to a girl who was standing on her head. I went out and asked Jody, 'What is that?' and Jody introduced us. Soon I asked her to go to a concert in Asheville and on that date I discovered that she went to church at Victory where the Watkins family were members. So I started going to church there."

After a two-and-a-half-year courtship, they were married at Victory. Sixteen months later, their son, Nathan, was born. His birthdate was August 10, 1977, and nineteen months later, March 27, 1979, their daughter, Niccole, was born.

Nathan grew to the height of six-feet-nine and set a passel of rebounding records for the Swain High basketball team, but his heart was in baseball. He was a pitcher and sometimes first baseman. At this writing, Nathan is a junior at Elon College in downstate North Carolina. In the summers, he plays for the Front Royal Cardinals in a collegiate-level league, the Valley League in Virginia.

"He has been clocked at pitching ninety-four miles an hour," Mike said, "and he is a tough competitor."

Niccole is studying at the University of South Carolina at Spartanburg. She is a volleyball player and in her sophomore season at Mars Hill College, near Asheville, from which she transferred to Spartanburg, her team won all eighteen of its matches.

When they were married, Bavaria, whom everyone calls Boo, and Mike built a home in Bryson City on land her parents gave them for a wedding present. They moved into the house just before Christmas of 1977 when

Nathan was four months old, and the house burned to the ground a day or two after Christmas.

They rebuilt near her mom and dad's house and have lived there now for twenty-two years.

Mount Carmel Baptist Church, to which Mike was called in 1992, was the only pastorate he has held. He resigned the church in May of 1999 because, he said, "it was time to go."

"I realized I hadn't done everything God wanted me to do in the seven years I was there, at least I didn't think I had, but He had completed His work with me there and it was time to go."

At this writing, Mike is preaching revivals when he can. "My preaching schedule," he said, "and the Inspirations' singing schedule are hard to coordinate. Singing takes precedence and I go by whatever Martin schedules for the quartet."

After twenty-seven years with the Inspirations, Mike admits that the travel schedule is rough. "It didn't used to bother us," he said, "but now it's a little strenuous. I guess that has something to do with age.

"I remember once when LeeRoy Abernathy and Shorty Bradford sang as LeeRoy and Shorty, Shorty had a problem with one of his legs. He went to the doctor who told him, 'Shorty, that leg has just been too many miles,' and Shorty answered, 'Doc, that ain't got a thing to do with it. My other leg has been just as far and I ain't had any problem with it.' We've all been a lot of miles and it seems to bother all of us a bit." But not enough, he admitted, to make him think of retiring.

Mike's parents, Alfred Carl Sr. and Sarah Piccola Holcomb, still live in Jasper. They are not in the best of health. "Dad's now seventy-three and Mom is sixty-nine," Mike said, "and their health is failing. They used to come to the Singing in the Smokies every year and stay with us, but now they're just not able to."

Singing for the Inspirations is something special for Mike. "This is not just a job to us," he said. "It's the only full-time employment any of us have ever had, except Martin. The Lord has blessed us beyond measure. We've made our living at it, and it has had a great purpose. Our purpose has always been to uplift the Lord, to magnify him, and then to be a blessing to someone else.

"If we had to approach this as just another job," he said, "it would probably get awfully boring, singing the same songs over and over every night. There is a verse in the Bible that reads, 'Many are called but few are chosen.' I really feel that we were chosen together, not just called, but chosen and given this great opportunity.

"Every person has a talent," Mike added. "Everyone in this quartet has a talent to sing. I've never understood why I was given the voice I have, but I'm thankful for the talent God has given me."

The Inspirations are also collectively happy that God saw fit to give that voice to Mike.

# 23

# Singing in the Smokies

L ike big-eyed boys at a picnic, when the Inspirations started singing in 1964, they were impressed by the established quartets and wanted to rub elbows with some of them to see how life was in the big-time.

They weren't singing much, filling a church date here and there, and they had little or no contact with other groups.

Someone among the Inspirations came up with the idea of promoting singings in the auditorium of Swain County High School, which would enable them to meet some big-time singers, and would give Bryson Citians an opportunity to hear these groups in person. Too, they might make some money to help defray their driving and eating expenses on the few singing trips they made.

It was at one of those singings that Roy Carter of the Chuck Wagon Gang gave part of his group's money back to the Inspirations because he thought they could use it, which, indeed, they could.

Besides the Chuck Wagon Gang, the Inspirations chose some of their other favorite groups to promote in the high school auditorium, including the Florida Boys and Oak Ridge Boys, whom they especially liked. They were disappointed, though, when the Oak Ridge Boys came without Smitty Gatlin, one of their favorite singers, who had left to form the Smitty Gatlin Trio. Instead, the Bryson City date was one of the first for Duane Allen and Bill Golden, two of the revamped Oak Ridge Boys.

They had good crowds for the Florida Boys and Oak Ridge, but when the Chuck Wagon Gang came in, they filled the house.

"Some of those singings in the high school were very successful," Martin said, "and gave us the idea of a festival-type singing that would run for more than one day."

There were two reasons for starting the Singing in the Smokies. First was when the Inspirations realized that as their friends came into the mountains to vacation, the quartet was going out to sing elsewhere.

"While I was with the Park Service," Martin said, "I knew that six million people came down Highway 441 across the Smokies and over the Blue Ridge Parkway into our area. By leaving, we were missing the opportunity to sing for some of them on our home grounds."

The second reason was that Martin's home county of Jackson scheduled a vote on legal liquor and he heard a county commissioner say that voting liquor in would help the schools.

"I thought we had to fight evil with good," Martin said. "We knew liquor was evil, and we thought a singing like the Singing in the Smokies has turned out, would be a good force. That's how we overcome evil, fighting it with good. We can't fight it on its own terms because the same rules don't apply."

So they rented the football field at Sylva High School, twenty miles up the road from Bryson City, and in 1967 started the Singing in the Smokies there.

They brought in groups like the Speer Family when Mom Speer was with them, the Singing Rambos, the Happy Goodman Family, the Kingsmen Quartet, and the Hopper Brothers and Connie. Their first crowd in Sylva was about five hundred people. The gate improved a little the next two years, but they didn't break even until they moved the singing to Bryson City the fourth year.

"We didn't do much that first year to help good prevail," Martin said. "Whiskey won the vote and Jackson County became wet. But we had planted a seed, and we've done a lot of good in the last thirty years at the Singing in the Smokies. I believe the scales are balanced a long way on our side now.

"We were learning," he continued, "and thought we were onto something good. After those three years, we began to see a glimmer of light at the end of the tunnel."

Indeed, the light was there, and the Inspirations began edging nearer to it.

"We left Sylva because we wanted our own place," Martin said. "It was hard to depend on other people, and we wanted to go someplace closer to Bryson City so we could run it."

They leased the old Bryson City Airport, the Sossamon Airport, on top of a hill across town from where the present Inspiration Park is, but they could only work out a one-year lease that could be renewed annually if feasible for the owner.

They stayed there four years and each year as the Inspirations' popularity on the road increased, the crowds grew larger and the Singing in the Smokies became reasonably profitable.

But the airport wasn't exactly what the quartet wanted. Martin still lived in a house he had bought on the hill above the high school in Bryson City. In the back of his mind he was looking for a place large enough that he could built a home adjacent to the singing grounds.

"I didn't want to raise my family on a town lot," he said. "I had fenced the property but I didn't want my kids to have to play inside a fence. Children need open spaces to run in."

In 1974, through his young son, Myron, Martin met an elderly bachelor named Theron Hyatt, who owned the old Ela Airport across town from the one the quartet had leased. Theron had a donkey and loved children. Nothing pleased him more than to put a kid astraddle his donkey and ride him around a bit. He began taking Myron for rides, and through that acquaintance, Martin got to know him.

When Martin told Theron what he was looking for, Theron agreed to sell him the property. They set a date to see a lawyer and sign the papers, but when the date arrived, some problems had arisen and Theron backed out.

Martin liked the place, and he remembered it the four years the Inspirations held their singing at the old airport.

During this interval, Martin sold his Bryson City home and moved back to Caney Fork where he turned the home place into a cattle farm.

He remembered the property on the mountainside just east of Bryson City, and thought it was the best place he'd seen for what the Inspirations wanted.

Theron passed away before the Inspirations found a place for their singings and left the land to Mrs. Newell Martin, whose husband had been sheriff of Swain County. Martin approached Mrs. Martin and offered to lease the land on a long-term contract.

She thought over the proposition and told Martin, "All I'm doing now is buying fertilizer for that place and paying taxes. If you can help me out, I'll let you have the place." Martin knew the Inspirations could ease her financial burden by leasing the place and said so.

They had a contract drawn up, the Inspirations leased the mountainside, and on it they built their singing ground. In the early 1970s they moved the Singing in the Smokies to its new location, where it remains today.

The Inspirations leased the land all these years but recently bought it from Mrs. Martin's heirs and at this writing have plans to build their own offices there.

The Inspirations were a recognizable group by that time, having sung in many big singings in places like

Atlanta, Birmingham, Nashville, and elsewhere, and their fame had spread widely by the 1970 segment on CBS Weekend News.

"We couldn't have bought that kind of exposure," Martin said. "It would be hard to describe what it did for us. All of a sudden, people knew who we were. We had telephone calls from many places from people who knew nothing of gospel music. Some asked if we were a barbershop quartet."

In Sylva, the Singing in the Smokies had been held one night only the first time, then two nights, and finally three nights. As soon as the event moved onto the Bryson City Airport, crowds grew tremendously, and the Inspirations spread the singing to six nights, drawing well each night.

Still, those who came from faraway places had trouble finding lodging in the tourist-oriented section where the Great Smokies and the Cherokee Indian Reservation drew millions of tourists each year. Some who came to the singings had to take motel rooms seventy miles away in Asheville.

Until enough new motels and campgrounds were constructed around Bryson City and Cherokee, many of the visitors to the singings were quartered in the dormitories at Western Carolina College, just twenty-seven miles up the road. The college was very cooperative until its summer school sessions for teachers reached such proportions that the dorms were being filled with teacher-students.

The only way the Inspirations could partially lick this problem was to extend the Singing in the Smokies to nine or ten nights, which reduced the size of the nightly crowds to manageable proportions.

In this land of tall mountains and rainy days, the Inspirations—and their fans—expect wet weather to interrupt the Singing in the Smokies at times.

"By the time we moved on the mountain," Martin said, "our crowds were big, and those early singings produced some good times. We didn't have much of a stage, just a makeshift job, and no shelter for the crowds, and when it rained, people would run to their cars till it stopped raining, then come back and listen to some more singing, and if it rained again, they'd run back to their cars."

They have weathered all sorts of drizzles and some downpours and have always come back for more. Not often did the Inspirations worry about a little rain, but lightning was something else, and there was little shelter on the mountain during the early days. Now, there is plenty.

Undoubtedly the wettest Singing in the Smokies was in 1989. That year the singing was eight days, and rain fell every day, but it did not deter the crowds at night. They came and they stayed, except for an occasional dash to their cars when the rain became more intense, and their spirits were never dampened.

"I never saw anything like it," Martin Cook said. "It was unbelievable the way people came in downpours of rain, smiling and laughing and joking and telling how they love gospel music. They waded through mud and laughed about it."

The parking lot resembled a section of the Great Smoky Mountains after a herd of wild boar rooted it for weeks—like a freshly plowed and wet field.

"I believe that's the wettest it's been in the mountains since Noah's flood," Martin said. "It didn't rain that much on the singing at night, but it rained every day. Still, except for three nights when it rained hard in the afternoon and threatened at night, the crowds were as large or larger than ever before."

One day during that singing, Thursday, July 6, two inches of rain fell in thirty minutes. Water flowed four inches deep through the record table area under its shed. That was about 6:30 p.m. and people still waded in to the singing grounds and enjoyed a great singing.

The night after that heavy rain, 3,000 people were on hand, and the Inspirations probably set a record on stage.

They sang eleven songs in twenty-six minutes before anyone spoke a word. Martin explained why. "We're here to sing to the people," he said, "and that's exactly what we do."

Quartet members who were there believe that the evening of the Fourth of July, 1976, at the Singing in the Smokies, was perhaps "the greatest event in the history of the Inspirations.

"That was the Bicentennial year," Archie said, "and we had promoted the God and Country theme. We had a lot of preachers there—we always do, because they come to the Singing in the Smokies and bring their wives and children and have a great vacation.

"We had centered a lot of emphasis on putting God first in our country, and we put the Spirit into that Fourth of July celebration.

"It was one of those times," Archie continued, "when everything was just right. Everybody was ready to have a good time. We had a great service. It didn't matter what group was on stage, the people were continually doing something—shouting, moving about, praying.

"Most nights are not like that, but I remember that Fourth of July as a great spiritual night. There was a good crowd and a good spirit at that singing, and it seems like the bigger the crowd the more excitement there is."

Martin added: "The crowd was monstrous—maybe six to eight thousand, and everybody had little flags. It was drizzling rain but no one paid attention to it. The people were so excited about what God had done and what they had and where they were that they just marched around most of the night, praising God.

"I'm talking about literally praising God in their hearts. The ones who were not walking around were sitting there crying. Many didn't even move, just sat— but they were involved. God touched that evening. I have never before or since seen it for that long a period of time. It didn't matter who was singing on stage—the Inspirations, the Florida Boys, Dixie Echoes, the Goodmans—the celebration of God and country continued through the evening. When one quartet left the stage and another came on, the crowd didn't even slow down.

"You see people get emotionally excited at ball games," he said. "You see them get excited when something good happens, but this was not that way. It was just that the people, in their hearts, were overwhelmed for their country's two hundredth birthday and what it meant to them, and that they were Americans, and that God had blessed them so, that they were thanking God and appreciating their country.

"I've had hundreds of people tell me they were there and that they had never seen anything like it."

# 24

## Myron

When Myron Cook was born to Martin and Ora Blanche on July 11, 1963, Martin was already hosting singing sessions in his basement, but had no idea that what he was doing was leading toward establishment of one of America's leading gospel quartets. Formation of the Inspirations Quartet was still a year away.

In his early boyhood, Myron didn't like the idea of his father being gone for periods of four or five days at a time. He wanted Daddy around the house.

Myron can remember once when his dad was gone on a two-weeks' singing trip that he missed him so much he wandered in the kitchen where his mother was preparing dinner, and he broke out crying.

"I want my daddy home," Myron blubbered, and Ora, comforting him, took him in her arms and gently said, "He'll be home in another day or two. Just think about him coming home and look forward to it."

"When he got home," Myron said, "everything was all right."

Undoubtedly, all, or certainly most, quartet men who have families can recall similar scenes in their own homes.

Gospel singing is not a homebound business. Those who can't bear to be away from home for days or who don't like to travel usually wind up making a living in another field.

Myron grew into his teens wishing his dad was home more, but by that time he realized that his father was doing *his* father's work. "I knew that God had called him to do this," he said, "and I knew that it was what Daddy wanted to do, so I felt better about it."

Myron had no idea that he would soon be playing bass for the Inspirations. The thought had never occurred to him. His music education at Bryson City, where he spent his first several years, and at Cullowhee High, after his family moved back to Caney Fork in July of 1972, was not such that it made him yearn for a career on the stage. Myron played football, basketball, and baseball at Cullowhee High.

When his high school graduation class filed across the stage to receive diplomas in June of 1981, Myron was not present. He was in Canada with the Inspirations for a week of singing.

He wanted to make the trip, but he had a minor dilemma because he wanted to be present at graduation also. His principal at Cullowhee High resolved the problem for him. "Take him on," he said to Martin. "There's not much to graduation. I'll mail him his piece of paper."

So Myron boarded the Inspirations' bus and rode with them through Canada.

Just after the Singing in the Smokies in 1981, Roger Fortner resigned from the Inspirations to follow his own star. He and Dale Jones were the two musicians who helped Martin make music for the quartet.

Two or three days later, Martin, needing a bass player to replace Roger for the quartet's heavy fall schedule, came home one afternoon, sought Myron out, and asked if he had ever thought of playing an instrument with the quartet.

"No," Myron answered, "not really."

"Would you like to?"

Myron was momentarily stunned at this apparent offer to join the Inspirations, which prompted him to answer in the affirmative.

"Yeah," he said, "I'd like to."

"Then you'll have to learn quickly," Martin said, "because we've got a busy schedule coming up, and we're doing the Singing in the Smokies up on the mountain the end of this month."

Myron, who had studied piano a few years under Barbara Dooley at Western Carolina, admitted being able to chord the piano a little, "but not much." He launched himself seriously into this new endeavor.

Stacking the record player with recent Inspirations records, Martin taught Myron to listen to the beat of the song and coached him along for a while until he learned the basics. Then, for hours each day, Myron played the bass to the records.

"I learned by ear," Myron said, "and I guess I learned enough, because I've been at it eighteen years now."

His first official playing was Labor Day weekend in the Inspirations' annual singing in Inspirations Park.

As the years have passed, Myron has become proficient in slapping out a good rhythm on the bass guitar.

For the last ten years, Myron has been taking courses at Southwestern Community College in Sylva, studying for an associate in general education degree.

"Then," he said, "if anything happens in this crazy business, I'll have something to fall back on."

Myron, who is the deeply loyal type, would fight anyone who made a disparaging remark about any of his friends in gospel music. That could keep him busy for weeks because everyone in the business is his friend.

"The best thing that's happened to me in music," he said, "has been the people I've met and the friendships I've made. I've found a lot of role models in gospel music, like George Younce, Glen Payne, Ed O'Neal, Connie and Claude Hopper, Bill Gaither, and most of all, I guess, my dad. I've really gotten to know my dad these years I've been playing, and he'd be a good number one role model for any boy."

The other two of Martin and Ora's children, Michael and Marcia, are out of school and gainfully employed. Marcia, born in 1966, works in the Inspirations office with Marian Fortner, the quartet's secretary.

Michael, who came along May 28, 1968, is the cattleman of the family. He runs purebred Herefords and some mixed Charolais and Beef Master breeds. He supervises the operation on the Cooks' two farms, a 110-acre farm on Caney Fork, where the Cooks live, and a 128-acre farm near Washington, Georgia, about forty-five minutes from Athens.

Ora has spent her time being a housewife for the family and mother for the three kids, except during the Singing in the Smokies, when she helps operate the ticket booth each night.

"She's usually a very calm person," Myron said, "except during the Singing in the Smokies. She goes kinda crazy then. We all go crazy then."

# 25

# Gatlinburg

By the mid-1980s, the Inspirations had been on the road more than twenty years, riding the bus, setting up the sound system and record table, singing, selling, knocking down, reloading, and riding to the next location.

All the guys were so wrapped up in their mission, however, that the miles didn't seem as long as they were—at least, not at first.

But the day came when all had youngsters at home, and the road became longer and more arduous. Gone four days a week didn't do a lot to cultivate family life. All were blessed, of course, with wives who understood and who fully supported them in their work, and that helped, but it didn't erase the drudgery of an existence on the road.

Retirement had even crossed Archie's mind, and Archie was the stalwart. He was the only singer who had sung with the Inspirations continuously for those twenty years. Even he began to feel the drag of the road, the occasional loneliness when he yearned for home and family.

They all did. Take four days out of a week and a man misses a lot of his children's growing-up time. That was no pleasure. That they were doing the work they honestly believed God meant for them to do helped them through rough days.

But the time came when they truly grew tired of the road and tired of the way concerts were conducted.

So in 1984 they did something about it.

They worked a lease agreement with Ogle's Restaurant in Gatlinburg, Tennessee, one of the area's leading tourist towns, a lively place in the summertime. They leased a five hundred-seat auditorium over the restaurant, came off the road the first of June, and promoted nightly singings themselves. They parked the bus in Gatlinburg and left it, and went home to mama and the kids.

Riding back and forth across the Smokies daily, they sang five nights a week in Gatlinburg, sometimes six. Their singing was well received, and they made thousands of new friends from all over the world, folks from Australia, England, Canada, Africa, Haiti, and elsewhere, who had come to Gatlinburg to vacation.

"We met people that nobody would ever have sung the gospel to," Martin said, "and we still get letters from a lot of them, even after ten years."

Singing in Gatlinburg was like working a mission field. But they discovered that, as good as their work was, they grew as tired of singing in the same place all the time as they had grown of the road.

"It was actually good for us," Martin said, "because it gave us an annual beginning and end to the road. We looked forward each year to the first of June because we knew we were finished on the road for a while and could anchor in Gatlinburg. But by October we were looking forward to going back on the road."

Singing in Gatlinburg took the Inspirations away from many of the people they had sung to in concert for twenty years.

"When we went back on the road in November," Archie said, "a lot of people would come to us and ask, 'Are you boys singing again?' They thought we had retired.

"But we sure didn't slow down when we spent those summers in Gatlinburg. Instead of singing four nights a week, like we did on the circuit, we sang five and sometimes six in Gatlinburg. That was a lot of singing. But all of our singing was nearer home. We didn't have to travel a thousand miles to a concert.

"We also missed too many of the good singings that we really enjoyed, and we knew our fans missed us. One time we couldn't go to the convention because we were tied up in Gatlinburg. We really got to wanting to go to those singings again. We missed the big ones."

The only variation to their schedule of singing nightly in Gatlinburg was the Singing in the Smokies, which they continued all the while they did the Tennessee shows.

"Singing in one place all the time got boring," Martin said. "We stayed there five years, and that was a year too long. I don't think I ever got bored going anywhere but to Gatlinburg, but I got to the point that I'd almost grit my teeth to go into the place over there."

The opening of nearby Dollywood hurt the Inspirations' crowds that last year, and all the guys were ready to quit and go back on the road on a lesser schedule than before.

So by 1989 the time to leave had come. The Inspirations ended their summer schedule in Gatlinburg and jumped back into the mainstream with both feet.

They reduced their schedule from what it had been five years before and began to enjoy singing more. They renewed acquaintances and made new friends. They sang in small towns they had never visited before.

"Gatlinburg served a purpose," Martin said. "It was our anchor for those five years—an anchor in the storm, you might say.

"But most of the big singings are in the summer and we enjoyed getting back to them. Now we usually leave home on Thursday and return Saturday night after the singing so we can go to church on Sunday morning. We sing something like a hundred twenty dates a year now, and that's not a back-breaking schedule."

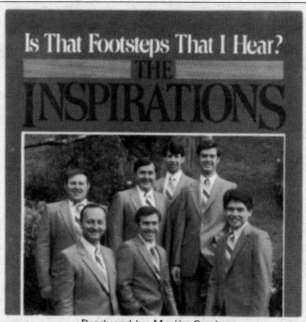

THE INSPIRATIONS
Is That Footsteps That I Hear?

Produced by Martin Cook

I Firmly Promise You • Is that Footsteps that I Hear? • Hold On • Count Me In • Jesus Rescued Me • Let Us Sing • Thank God I've Made It • Let's Restore the Family Altar • Touch Me Again, Lord • My Soul Is Satisfied • I'm the Reason • I've Got My Foot on the Rock

CC-9883

CC-9883

# 26

# Matt

It is strange, indeed, how paths run parallel for a time and finally converge. Matt Dibler was born two years after the Inspirations began singing professionally, and all his life he wanted to sing with them. When the opportunity came, he made the most of it.

Matt's first fill-in experience with the Inspirations came in 1992, subbing for Eddie, who had a funeral to preach that weekend.

Matt and Mike were already good friends, both being Baptist preachers. They preached in each other's churches at times. Matt was pastor of the Open Door Baptist Church in Easley, South Carolina, for twelve years until 1999, but a part of his heart has always been devoted to singing. One day, Matt told Mike that he would like the opportunity to fill in for someone when a member had to be absent.

Mike sent him several tapes and a list of about thirty songs and wrote, "Be ready to sing lead, baritone, or tenor on any of them." It was noticeable, Matt thought, that Mike, the bass singer, didn't say anything about learning the bass parts.

For a couple of months after receiving the tapes, Matt tried to learn all three parts of every song on the tapes, but the task was gigantic, and when he hadn't been asked to fill in for two months, he laid the tapes aside and went on about business at hand.

Six months later, one Wednesday night, he got a call from Mike.

"Can you go with us Friday?" Mike asked. "Eddie has a funeral and can't go."

"Sure, I'll be ready."

Knowing he would sing baritone that weekend, Matt began working on a few songs he thought the Inspirations would sing.

The quartet was singing in Elizabethton, Kentucky, and when Matt showed up at the bus, he asked Mike, "When will we practice?"

"Probably on the bus," Mike said.

The bus left at eight in the morning and as soon as they boarded, the singers sat down and began reading, watching the scenery go by, or whatever turned them on at the moment. No one mentioned practice. After a while, Matt went back to his room and began playing tapes, singing along a bit.

Ronnie popped his head in Matt's door and said, "Don't try to cram. If you don't know a song, don't worry about it. Cramming will make it worse."

"We never did practice on the bus," Matt said, "and as we approached Elizabethton, I became nervous."

"Don't worry," Mike assured him. "We'll probably practice when we get to the gymnasium."

But they arrived just in time to set up and go back to the bus and change, and then they went in to sing.

Over by the bleachers, Martin called the group together to pray. He looked at Matt and said, "Well, Matt, we're not expecting any miracles."

Matt thought but didn't say, "It's a good thing!"

So the Inspirations prayed a little and Matt prayed a lot, and as they were climbing the steps to the platform to sing, Matt tugged at Mike's coattails.

"Mike," he said, "can you at least tell me what songs we are going to sing?"

Mike looked down at him and smiled and said, "Whatever Martin plays!"

"I was in such a daze," Matt said later, "that I don't remember what songs we sang. That's the way it's been ever since. I thought for a while that things had gotten a bit better, but one night they did it again—pulled out another one I'd never sung before."

After that first night, Matt was no longer so excited about singing with the Inspirations. He went back to his room and prayed, "Oh, Lord, I thought this would be fun, but if you'll let me get home I won't worry about it any more."

As time passed and he substituted for members of the quartet, Matt became more comfortable, except that he had trouble getting used to life on the road.

"There was the setting up," he said, "the knockdown, the riding, the hours on the bus, and the long hours of waiting in a town to sing that evening. Sometimes we have to wait all day, just sit around for twelve or thirteen hours to sing thirty minutes that night. That was a real letdown at first. I get excited about singing, but I didn't dream it would be like that.

"And, then, I turned it all around, started preparing myself better for the road, and began to look at it this way: We're allowed the privilege of that thirty minutes. The Lord has really blessed that. The spiritual experience is great. We cut up and goof around all day, but when we get on the platform, the only thoughts that come across our minds are to do our job the very best we can.

"I remember when we sat on the bus one afternoon and watched people gather, and when the gates were opened, people began to run with their lawn chairs. That broke my heart! They had paid to be there, they waited no telling how long, and then they ran to find a good place and sit down. That convicted my heart. To us, we sing a lot of the same songs every night, but to them that's the first time and maybe the only time they'll ever hear us sing.

"This was our only time to make that first impression on some of those people, and to get across the spirit and message of the song. Every night when I go out there, the Holy Spirit reminds me that these people didn't have to come. They chose to come! They could have listened to anybody, they could have stayed at home, they could have done a lot of things, but it will be our only time to reach some of them and we ought to do our best to make our songs mean something to them."

There was more. "We see a lot of country," Matt said, "and we like that. Some of it is educational, but traveling with these guys is a lot more educational."

Matt filled in for a while, and then Ronnie was forced out of singing by his illness, and Matt took the lead singer's job full time.

"My wife and I discussed things many times before I came on full time," Matt said. "She made the statement—and I really appreciate her saying it—that as long as she could tell that the Lord wants me to sing, she'll back that up, and she has.

"I've had to work mainly on saying the words correctly, instead of just running through a song. For a while, as I traveled with them, sang with them, and spent hours listening to their tapes, I didn't realize how much I was learning. But I know now.

"I praise The Lord for the ministry I had at the Open Door church for twelve years," he said. "I appreciate the church's support of my ministry with the Inspirations. The outreach of the Inspirations is unreal in the volume of people we reach. Some people will say, 'Well, I don't like gospel music because some people will go to a concert who won't go to church.' I say that's why I like it. Those people come and listen to us when they won't go to church and through our ministry they may get into church. You never know. Definitely it's not entertainment; it's ministry. Why, many times they have brought people from the hospital to a concert and then taken them directly back to the hospital."

Matt was born in 1966, the same year the Inspirations cut their first record and began singing in all those churches around Atlanta. He was born in Royal Oak, Michigan, about thirty miles from Detroit, to Gordon Dibler and Roberta Carlson, who were divorced when Matt was four.

In his youth, Matt got as good a dose of gospel music as anyone living in Michigan could get. His introduction to the genre came when he was seven or eight, old enough to understand what was going on. The Blackwood Brothers sang in a Methodist church and Matt's mother and grandmother took him to the concert. "I remember thinking I would love to do that," he said later.

As a growing boy, Matt also got to see the Inspirations, then the Cathedrals, and finally the Kingsmen in Detroit. Those were the only quartets he had heard before he moved south to Anderson, South Carolina, at the age of eighteen. But his mother and grandmother had seen to it that gospel music became a major part of his life.

Through his growing up years and part of his teens, Matt heard gospel music at home. "My mother and grandmother bought Inspirations' records," he said. "We had a little snack bar in the kitchen that we would march around singing with the Inspirations. If my mother heard us listening to certain other kinds of music, she wouldn't come right out and tell us not to listen; she would hand us an Inspirations' record and say, 'Listen to this'."

Since Matt was a little boy, he thought about singing with the Inspirations some day, never dreaming that his hopes would come true.

He moved to Anderson so he could attend Tabernacle

Baptist Bible College in nearby Greenville. He enrolled in 1984 and before he was graduated in 1988, two other great things occurred in his life: He was married between his first and second years in school, and during his third year in Bible college, he became pastor of a Baptist church.

He married Paulette Hoyle of Lenoir, North Carolina, near Patterson, where George Younce grew up. Matt and Paulette enjoyed going to many gospel concerts. One of her favorite groups was the Inspirations. On a New Year's Eve, they went to a singing in Greenville where he met the Inspirations. He talked to them, stayed in touch with them, and was ready to sing when Mike called him and told him to come.

Paulette and Matt have two daughters, Sabrina Leanne, born August 14, 1988, and Lindsay Nichole, born June 26, 1991. Sabrina is a good singer who has done well in talent contests. She also plays the piano.

Lindsay keeps the whole family in line, and has begun concentrating on the Inspirations as well. One evening, Eddie Deitz came to the front of the bus, dressed and ready to sing, except that he had not put on his coat. "Put on that coat," Lindsay ordered, "and suck in that gut!" Eddie quickly obeyed both commands the best he could.

Matt has been the object of Inspiration jokes since he joined the group. On Christmas Eve, 1998, he was on the floor playing a game the girls had received for Christmas and his telephone rang. He answered his cordless phone.

"Is this the preacher?" a strange, halting voice asked.

"Yes."

"I can't take it no more," the man said, speaking as if he were in great stress. "I just can't take it no more, people always making fun of me for the way I talk."

Before Matt could say anything, the man blundered on.

"I'm going to blow my head off and kill myself," the voice was strangled, harsh.

Matt sat bolt upright. "Please," he said, "you don't want to do that. Don't do it!"

"Yeah, you're right," the voice said, "I don't want to."

Suddenly, huge guffaws came through the phone to Matt.

"You don't know who this is, do you?" the voice asked.

"No."

More laughter. Then, "This is Jack!"

Matt could hear someone else laughing in the background. That was Archie.

"If I'd known it was Jack," Matt said, "I would have talked him into it."

Later, Archie explained, "Jack was supposed to take his gun and step outside and shoot it, but he chickened out."

"I didn't chicken out," Jack said. "I just got to laughing too hard."

"What made it so bad," Matt explained, "was that three or four years ago I had had that same phone call and it was real. Jack didn't know that. I went out at three o'clock to help that guy, and I thought here he is again!"

Matt realized then that he had become truly a part of the Inspirations. He had been initiated, big-time, mountain style.

# 27

# The Primitives

This is the way most good quartets begin. They start singing because they love it, and after awhile some organization appears within the ranks, and then, if they sincerely sing within the will of the Lord, and sing until He is ready to make room for them, a big break comes along.

It was so with the Primitive Quartet, and the Inspirations were God's helpers in getting them going.

Those who know the Inspirations know how friendly and "down home" they are. Those who don't know them can ask Reagan Riddle or any of the Primitives.

The Primitives are from Candler, ten minutes west of Asheville and sixty miles east of Bryson City. Like the Inspirations, the Primitives are good old country boys, friendly, conservative, strong Christians, very talented, and entertaining with a message in their songs. Salt-of-the-earth, all of them, just like the Inspirations.

In 1972, two sets of brothers, Norman and Furman Wilson and Reagan and Larry Riddle, cousins to each other, went fishing in Fontana Lake, near Bryson City, and camped out for a few days.

Norman was a mandolin player. He called Reagan and suggested he bring his guitar, and they would sing a little after supper. The four had sung with their parents, around home, in church, and other places like that, and not one of the four had ever given a thought to becoming a professional singer.

Each night on that camping trip, the four sang and played, and worked up a couple of gospel songs they liked.

Back home on Sunday afternoon they gathered at the Riddle home and sang the songs, just for fun. Their preacher was there. He patted his foot and gloried in the talent these young men had put to use in the Lord's work, and he suggested the quartet bring their instruments to church that evening and sing the songs for the congregation.

Like the afternoon session, that was a toe-tapping singing also. There were visitors at church that night from North Asheville Baptist Church who liked the Primitives so much they invited them to their church's next monthly singing.

Word spread rapidly and still with no thought of becoming professional, just enjoying themselves and satisfied with what they were doing, the Primitives went from church to church to sing, never charging a dime, because all the fellows were employed and working regularly—and their fame spread locally until they were known by sight.

"We sang that way for about five years," said Reagan Riddle, leader of the group, "and really enjoyed ourselves."

They would have been happy to spend the remainder of their lives working on their jobs and singing for fun.

They became popular at many churches, and now and then a preacher would pass the plate and take a love offering for them. That embarrassed Reagan deeply. They weren't singing for money, but for pleasure, and for a cause. He would tell the preachers, "We don't want that," but the preachers would insist. Reagan held strong, however, and always gave the money back to the church.

In 1977 a severe flood washed parts of their hometown of Candler away. People were killed, homes ruined, employment lost, and the whole countryside felt devastated.

To help in reconstruction and to aid families standing destitute, a benefit singing was scheduled at nearby Enka High School for families that had lost everything. The featured singing group was the Inspirations, and the Primitives were on the program.

Martin Cook was already familiar with the Primitives. He had heard them sing at East Sylva Baptist Church, and he'd liked what he heard.

"They were different," he said. "They had good songs and sang them well." Martin also had some of their records. He especially liked the way they sang such songs as *Rose Among the Thorns* and *On Heaven's Bright Shore.*

The singing turned out well that afternoon. A good bit of money was raised for the destitute families, and Martin thought the Primitives sang exceptionally well.

A week or two later, Martin telephoned Reagan Riddle. "Would you be interested in going out with us to a few more places and sing with us on some of our dates?"

Reagan said he would talk with the others and see what the group wanted to do. This would require more of their time than driving out to area churches to sing.

When the Primitives talked it over, Furman Wilson turned thumbs down. "I can't do it," he said. "I'm not at all interested in going." He had just gone into the ministry and felt a closer tie to home, and he thought that working in the ministry would preclude the time he would need to go singing with the group.

Reagan's brother, Mike, replaced Furman, and the group continued to excel.

"I started helping them arrange their harmonies. I used to meet with them at Barberville Baptist Church, near Waynesville, and help with their songs and their singing," Martin said.

The Inspirations took the Primitives aboard their bus and squeezed thirteen men into a sleeping arrangement. They attached two bunks to the walls up front, and brought aboard several inflatable military mattresses, which they would blow up at night and put on the floor.

In that way, all thirteen men found comfortable sleeping spaces. For a year and a half, they traveled together, sleeping in that makeshift manner.

"We have always had a soft spot in our hearts for the Inspirations," Reagan said. "They're my favorite group and always have been."

To give the Primitives a painless start, Martin asked promoters who booked the Inspirations to book the Primitives also. Most complied, and the Primitives rode the Inspirations' coat tails that first time around the circuit. The two quartets did a program they called "A Night of Inspiration," and things began to click.

"On that first round," Reagan said, "we met so many radio people and promoters who knew us and welcomed us the second time around that we began to get professional dates of our own. The first time we went, they'd never heard tell of us, and they really couldn't have cared less. The promoters added us to the programs because Martin asked them to, and they trusted Martin. But the second time around, we felt that we added a little to the program, and apparently the radio people and promoters felt the same. Once we really got going, we have not lacked for bookings since."

The convincing night for the Primitives came on a Saturday evening in Logan, West Virginia.

"When we started," Reagan said, "we had no idea of becoming the singing group we are. Didn't care a thing about it. Honest, we didn't want that. We had no desire of doing it at all.

"When Martin asked us to go on that first trip with the Inspirations, we met them in Pikeville, Kentucky, and sang there, and then on Saturday night we went over to Logan. Up to that time we had made four records and had sold them on our personal appearances around home.

"A lot of people came to that singing in Logan, and we felt that we had really had a good turn on stage. That night we sold $1,700 worth of records, and I'm telling you what's the truth, that blew my mind. I couldn't believe it."

Martin watched the Primitives' record table through intermission that night, his grin growing ever wider. He had known all along that the Primitives were a professional-quality quartet, dedicated to the task, and that evening he knew they were having good sales.

Reagan told him later how many records they had sold, and Martin saw that night that the Primitives were going to make their mark in gospel music.

"Within a year's time," Reagan said, "the Lord blessed us and we were able to quit work and sing full time. Our sales would sustain us."

In retrospect, Reagan said, "I guess the fact that we hadn't set out to do what we did, that it just happened, made us realize we were in the Lord's will, doing what we were supposed to be doing, and that made the difference."

After that eighteen-month jumpstart the Inspirations gave them, the Primitives bought a bus and hit out on their own.

"We credit the Inspirations with giving us our start," Reagan said. "And we're happy to be singing in the Lord's will, but there was something else that spurred us. One thing that is important to all of us is keeping our mountain heritage alive, and I'm talking about the old-time, shaped-note singing. That's what we do.

"All through the mountains when we were growing up, as soon as a Vaughan or Stamps-Baxter songbook came out, those old-time churches would have a two-weeks' singing school, teach all those parts, and you talk about pretty singing, that was it. It seems like our mountain heritage music is dying out. We're losing it.

"Also, growing up in the mountains, we had to entertain ourselves, and we usually did it singing. That's one reason so many good gospel singers came out of the mountains here; they didn't have much else to do for entertainment. Singing was a favored pastime and sacred music came easiest for us. Everybody enjoyed it, most people lived it, and many participated in it. We enjoyed our music. I hate to see our heritage music die out. We're trying to keep it alive and I think that's important. Our name, the Primitives, dedicates us to that mountain music."

Not that there were ever cross words spoken on the bus, but with thirteen men shoehorned into one coach during those eighteen months, the proximity of so many people, the almost total lack of privacy, the challenge of finding something constructive to do while en route, could have created dissention in both ranks. Each quartet knew it had to have an outlet for emotion, and Martin knew what the situation called for.

He increased physical activity for both quartets.

"We played ball all the time," Reagan said. "Martin really believed in physical fitness. He realized that if he didn't keep us active and see that we got good workouts, we wouldn't get along. He would see to it that we worked off our tension. Almost every day on the road, we would either play softball or basketball or go to a YMCA where we would all work off our anxieties, and then take showers and go our way.

"It worked. Martin is a sharp guy. Lot of country psychology about him. And we had some of the best fellowship during that time."

All the Primitives are grateful to the Inspirations. "I write a lot of our material," Reagan said. "I've written six songs for our next record. But what I would like to do most of all is find a song to fit the Inspirations. I'd give anything in the world to find another *Touring The City*. I would love to be able to write them something like that."

Finally, Reagan sighed, "Sometimes we do get tired of traveling. I remember Archie telling me that he believed we all have points in our lives and careers when we burn out a bit. Archie told me once that if he wasn't afraid the Lord would kill him, he'd be perfectly happy to never leave Bryson City again.

"I enjoy singing as much as I ever did. I enjoy the people. But the miles surely get long."

# 28

# Stage and Studio Work

In most cases, recording a tape filled with songs is not an easy task. Long hours are involved in recording an acceptable tape, usually over two or more days, followed by cutting and editing, dubbing over, reworking almost everything to squeeze the last ounce of pleasure out of the songs.

There are exceptions, of course, but they are rare. The rarest one may have occurred in Warner Robins, Georgia, in 1976, when the Inspirations cut two live albums, their classic *Warner Robins Live*, their 12th anniversary record, on one evening and the next night recorded their *Night of Inspiration* live album, both evenings to capacity crowds.

Marvin Norcross of Word, the Waco, Texas, inspirational publishing establishment, was the producer. When all cameras were placed and ready and the crowd and singers warmed up for the *Warner Robins Live* album, Marvin sought out Martin Cook.

"I want twenty-seven minutes, Martin," he said, and Martin smiled and said, "Okay, Marvin, that's what you'll get."

The Inspirations went on stage as if this were an ordinary singing. They did not have a note written down, they had no cue sheets, no cue cards, not one visible aid.

"We're gonna give 'em twenty-seven minutes, boys," Martin instructed the quartet just before it went on stage. "Give it your best."

So they walked out there, Martin took his seat, Marvin introduced the Inspirations, Martin played an intro, and the guys began to sing—and they sang for twenty-seven minutes on the nose.

"The only thing changed in the studio for that album was Marvin's introduction," Martin said. "He thought he could do it better in the studio. But our singing wasn't touched. You hear it on the tape exactly as it happened on stage, song for song, word for word.

"Most live recordings are not live at all," Martin explained. "The quartet sings through the program, but later in the studio they re-sing the songs and patch them over the originals that they sang on stage. But we didn't do that. That twelfth anniversary album is a classic, and we did it once through on stage. We didn't stop, didn't start any song over, didn't patch, didn't do anything to it."

"It's the same with our videos," Martin added. "They may not be the quality that some of the others are, but whatever you see on the video happened on stage that night. None of it was recorded before, and we didn't go back and redo anything. Maybe we should have, but we didn't. If Archie flubs a word on stage that night, he flubs it on the tape. We feel that's a part of it."

Things work differently in the studio. There the little glitches in the singing are identified and dubbed over. If the quartet mangles a song, the tape stops and the guys sing it again. But there, they are trying to present the best songs they can. On stage, in a live recording, the Inspirations want to give it to the people on tape just as it happened on stage. All the atmosphere is captured on tape.

"If a person watched any quartet make a record," Martin said, "he'd think everything was out of hand. But it isn't. It's just that recording is a hectic business."

At the Inspirations' last recording session, Martin asked Roger Fortner, who once played regularly for the Inspirations and now does studio work on their tapes,

"What can I do to improve our approach to help us do things better in the studio?"

Roger answered, "I don't know how you could improve it. You know what you want, and we know what you want. You don't have to tell us. I don't think you could improve that."

The Inspirations go into a recording session probably better prepared than most other groups. They know which songs they are going to sing, they have worked out the arrangements, and they hope they work.

"Everyone has input into our things," Martin said. "When we finish a song and have it ready for presentation, it's a product of the entire quartet, not just Martin Cook. The boys ask, 'Martin, why don't you just do the arrangements and give them to us to sing? Before we go into a studio to record, send them a tape and let them have the music ready.' But I tell them that it doesn't work that way.

"As we sing in the studio," Martin said, "new thoughts and ideas occur to us, and we listen to everybody's suggestions. There isn't any way we could do all the arrangements beforehand and go in and record them just as they were written."

The Inspirations know what they want when they record, albeit they are always open for suggestions. They know the music they want and the sound they want.

"We've taken talent into the studio for the first time," Martin said. "Roger Fortner, for example, when he was playing for us on stage. Marvin Norcross didn't think he ought to be in there. He wanted studio musicians. But Roger had the talent and the quartet knew it. Roger's first song, *Jesus Is Mine,* became the number one song in the nation. They didn't want Dale Jones to record with us, but his situation was the same as Roger's. He had the talent, and we insisted, and he did an excellent job. They both knew what we wanted; they played a little differently than studio musicians, but it was exactly the way we wanted it, and it turned out for the best."

Kevin Williams, who now plays for Bill Gaither, was taken into the studio the first time by the Inspirations.

"He was scared to death," Martin said, "but he did fine, and now he's a top musician. We got the best out of Kevin that day, and it was something new, something a little better.

"So, we try to make every session a product of everyone who participates. They tell me some of the groups spend the first day arguing about what they're gonna sing. We know what we're gonna sing before we get to the studio, but at the same time, we don't prescribe it.

"Like, the engineer had a good idea on our last session. We came down at the end of one song, closing it by dropping it a couple of steps, and the engineer said, 'Boys, I believe it would sound better if you'd go one more step.' We did, and it did sound better. The whole effect of the suggestion turned out for the best."

To clarify his position, Martin further explained this cooperation between singers, musicians, engineers, and producers. "Don't ever say one of our records is a Martin Cook deal. It isn't. But I do have the final say. Everything you've heard on an Inspirations record, all the way back to the first one, I was the guy who said, 'That's okay.' Or 'that's not all right.' If something doesn't sound good, we're going to change it. We'll either change what we're supposed to be doing and do it better, or if we can't make it sound good, we'll back up and do it another way. That's a thing you have to watch out for in the studio: Something may be perfectly fine and correct, but if it doesn't sound good, you don't need to record it."

Martin is not a martinet, if you'll pardon the pun; he is not a strict disciplinarian, not one who stresses a rigid adherence to the details he puts forward, but someone has to be the boss, and he's been it for thirty-five years. He does not force things down anyone's throat, and he keeps himself on an even keel.

Once, when Martin questioned something in a recording session, someone whispered to Otis Forrest, who plays piano on most of the Inspirations' sessions, "Look out, Otis, ole Cook is mad as a hen," to which Otis answered, "Not Martin Cook. He don't let himself get that way."

Martin takes a similar approach with people. "Everyone has a good side and a bad side," he said, "and it's not always the same every day. I try to keep the good side turned up. If I see somebody's bad side start flipping up, I try to put my foot on it and just let it lie. It's the same way with songs a person sings—how he can sing and how he can't sing. A lot of groups, young groups especially, start trying to copy someone else. That's the most foolish thing you can do, because you can't do the same things well that someone else can, and he maybe can't do the same things well that you can. So whatever you do you need to do well, but you've got to remember that you're not going to have the same strengths as other people."

A little psychology can go a long way, especially in a recording session.

Putting ten songs on tape for a recording is only a small part of the task of bringing out a new tape. The real work comes before the quartet goes into a studio. And sometimes when a song comes out on tape, its writer might barely recognize it.

"With our writers," Martin said, "we reserve the right to make changes in the song—even to rewrite it—to fit our style of singing. Often, the finished version is not recognizable as the song the writer sent in.

"We have sung songs without thinking about pleasing the writer. If you turn his song into a hit, he's going to be pleased anyway. So we're not bashful about changing a song."

"We sing songs," Archie joined in, "as they fit our voices. Maybe we'll let Matt take the melody and try it, and maybe we'll sing it that way. But almost always, when we're learning a song, we'll try it with two different people singing the melody. That's inverting the harmony.

If I take the melody, then Matt and Jack take the harmony below. That's been an asset for us. We've been able to turn a song upside down and make it sing, because that's the way it fits our voices. We can do that because we have the voice range to do it."

"There are times," Martin rejoined, "when we use words that are not correct. We're not teaching English out there. Some words just don't sing. There are some songs that don't record worth a flip the way they're written. You've got to have a good E or a good A. E's, A's, and I's sing. There are some where we use the wrong word or even the wrong pronunciation because it sings. Some are just bad grammar. I'm not trying to excuse that, but we sometimes have to resort to it."

A quartet should try every conceivable word to reach some degree of correctness. One poorly worded song comes to mind, an old song the Blackwood Brothers and other quartets once sang, entitled *Angels Watches Over Me.* The words sang well, but were still poorly chosen, because *Angels Watching Over Me* would have sung just as well and would have been grammatically correct.

Martin continued: "In a song we sing where we say 'I can't even walk without you holding my hand' the grammar is poor. 'Without you,' to be correct, would read 'without your holding my hand,' but the word *your* doesn't sing. It wouldn't sound right, so we changed it to *you* and it sang exactly where we wanted it to. There are a lot of words you can't sing and *your* is one of them."

The Inspirations collect all songs that writers send to them, and prior to recording, they go through boxes of them. They listen to every new song they've received. Songs usually come in with a tape and the words. They prefer the writer to sing a rough version on tape. At times they can't understand the words as the writer sings them, and that's why they ask for the written words.

"The tape of the raw song doesn't matter too much," Martin said, "because we're going to sing it our way anyhow. From what we were sent, you might not even recognize most of the songs we sing, like *Cry for the Children*. We even completely rewrite some of them, like *I'm Taking a Flight*. I put in two days on that song, and if you'd seen what we were sent compared with how the song came out, you would hardly recognize it.

"Same way with *Touring the City*. Harold Lane had written about four verses, and we got the song while we were in Nashville taping the *Jubilee*. Archie took a part of one verse and put it with a part of another and brought it down to two verses and a chorus. Harold had written the song six years before that and had never done anything with it, but our rearranging made a big difference, at least to us. Sometimes, though, we just change a word or two.

"You've got to get your best line where the music sounds the best, too. That line has to be right and the music has to be right, or you've got no song. That's the peak of the thing, the top, and any song is measured by that peak line and what it sounds like."

So songs, like books, are not just written. They are rewritten. And rewritten again. And again. Until they sound right. Writers don't say, "Well, I believe I'll write a book," and sit down and start punching the keyboard. There has to be inspiration, an outline, or at least an idea of what the writer wants to write, and if the story takes off on a tangent and hits a dead end, then he brings it back to Point A and starts all over.

It's the same way with a song. Most—not all, but most—songs are written, rewritten, and rewritten again.

"We get boxes of this material every year," Martin said, "big boxes. We sit down and play a bit of everything. If anybody in the quartet notices something he likes, we make a note of it and come back to it later. If nothing in the song really strikes one of us, we discard it. Then we wind up with a number of songs that we go back and listen to, and we ask, "Does somebody like this song?" In that manner, we narrow the field.

"This may sound too complicated, but if a song doesn't bless a singer, then he can't bless someone else with it. Jack Ham, a Tuscaloosa radio deejay, who has been on the same station for forty-seven years, said he had never played a gospel song that he didn't get something out of when he first listened to it."

The Inspirations narrow their songs down to a manageable number and set about perfecting the songs by actually singing them.

"We don't know at that point," Martin said, "exactly which ten songs will be on the tape we record, but at least we have a set of songs. When we narrow the list to the ten we are going to do, they still aren't set in stone. One might get eliminated and another put in its place.

"We go into the studio with the ten songs we're going to sing, but we don't necessarily come out with the same ten. We may have eliminated one or two, and replaced them with one or two others. We always have a song or two that we're ready to record in place of one we've already chosen.

"To begin with," Martin said, "we have several boxes full of songs. I mean dozens and dozens of songs, and we work away at them until we narrow the list down. We check all the chords and everything ahead of time.

"We have to be very, very careful, because a song in the raw stage may not even sound like a song. We have to recognize that it has the *potential* for a song.

"And when you get tired of the whole business and say, 'There's not a good song in the world,' that's usually when you uncover a gem. Some of them come from someone we've never heard of. *Thank you Lord* came from an old boy we didn't know, but we listened to his tape and liked the potential. All of a sudden, we had a hit with *Thank You Lord*."

Martin no longer plays piano on the Inspirations' recordings. He did for several albums at the start, but now he listens, gauges, and corrects while Otis Forrest, a studio musician from Greenville, South Carolina, who has played for several quartets, plays piano.

"Basically," Martin said, "our studio musicians are the same ones. We use Roger Fortner, who once played for us; David Johnson of North Wilkesboro, who can play anything from a fiddle to a steel guitar; Otis; Mike Riddle of the Primitives on the rhythm guitar; and Tim Compton of Kingsport, Tennessee, on the doghouse bass. That's our lineup and we feel we get the best results from them."

# 29

# Musicians

Like the Cathedrals and the Stamps in later years, the Inspirations never needed much music to accompany their singing. Martin has been such a great rhythm piano player over the years that he could fill in the holes and cracks in a song without help from other instruments.

The bass guitar, one of the first instruments used by professional quartets to complement the piano, was played by Jack or Troy, and later by Myron, and for the most part is the only support the Inspirations have given to Martin's piano playing over the years, except for a period of time from the mid 1970s till the early 1980s.

During those years of numerous big singing concerts, television's Gospel Singing Jubilee, the Singing in the Smokies, the Battle of Songs, and other innovations, the Inspirations employed two musicians to add to their sound. One was a Bryson City boy, Roger Fortner, and the other was a picker from Akron, Ohio, named Dale Jones, the first man the Inspirations ever hired from north of the Mason-Dixon Line until the recent addition of Matt Dibler, a lead singer from Michigan.

Actually, there have been so few changes in Inspiration personnel that few Northerners, or Southerners, for that matter, have had an opportunity to become an Inspiration. Anytime Martin mentions from stage that Matt Dibler was born a Yankee, he is jesting, and the crowd accepts his little anecdote, for they know that where a man comes from makes no difference to Martin or any of the others, as long as that man can sing like an Inspiration. Or pick suitably to accompany them.

That was the case with Roger and Dale. Both made music their livelihood, and both now play for gospel-singing groups they have married into. Proving their mettle, both have become so accomplished with strings that they do session work in recording studios for other quartets. Only the best qualify for that.

Like the rest of the Inspirations, Roger grew up in Bryson City, the son of Elijah and Notabelle Fortner. He came by playing instruments naturally. His dad bought him a guitar when he was nine and he learned to play it by listening to the only station their radio could pick up in Bryson City's mountain fastness, WBHN, the local station. He played along with whatever song the station played, whether gospel, bluegrass, country, or pop. He learned chords that way.

"My brother Jack had a bluegrass band," Roger said, "and I got into that with him. My other brother, Johnny, had a quartet and I played bass for them." He was fourteen or fifteen years old then, and from there, he began teaching himself fancy licks on the guitar.

In 1973, the Inspirations hired him to play bass, and he remained with them eight years, moving to the electric guitar after a while. His great guitar licks still decorate the Inspirations' recordings, for he has gone with them to the recording studio the last half-dozen times they've gone.

When Roger left the Inspirations, he played a few months for the Hoppers, then worked as chief engineer and sessions guitarist for Grand City Recording in Mount Airy, North Carolina, for about four years. After that came short stints with the Greenes and Talleys until he hooked on with the McKameys in 1987.

He has been with the McKameys since, not only because he was good enough to play for them but also because he married Peg and Ruben McKamey's oldest daughter, Connie. She sings soprano in the group and she and Roger make their home near the McKameys' in Clinton, Tennessee, a short distance northwest of Knoxville.

Roger does not profess to be a singer; he is content to pick and place good notes behind good singing, but there were two occasions when he was with the Inspirations that he was forced to sing.

The first came in Mobile, Alabama, where Mike became ill from eating seafood and turned green, blue, orange, and red while Martin poured Coca-Cola in him to settle his stomach. It didn't work and the bus driver took Mike to the hospital while the Inspirations sang.

As they were going on stage, Martin gave Roger the shock of his life: "Roger, you'll have to sing bass!"

Others might have died a slow death at news like that, but Roger was ever up to an occasion. Archie, Troy, and Eddie were the other singers, and Jack was playing bass. That was also when the Inspirations were singing the *Fa Sol La* song, which required good licks from the bass. Without batting an eye, Roger stepped up and sang a credible bass.

"No, I had never sung bass before," Roger said, "at least not like that. But we had to pull it off, and it worked. We came out of that all right, considering."

The next time was in Chattanooga when Mike came down with appendicitis and had to be rushed to the hospital for an emergency appendectomy.

"I remember Martin was pouring Coca-Cola down him again," Roger said, "and Archie was holding Mike's head up and combing his hair.

"So I sang bass again," Roger laughed, "and when I came off stage that night, I had concluded my singing career. That was more singing than I had ever wanted to do."

Today, Roger plays on all the Inspirations and Kingsmen recording sessions. He plays the electric guitar and/or the bass on those stints. He has also recorded with the Talley Trio, the Perry Sisters, with former Harlem Globetrotters' star Meadowlark Lemon on a compilation CD of different country artists. He played for Merle Haggard's *Christmas at Branson* and with Box Car Willie. His career credentials are impeccable.

Once, on a long, boring trip by bus, someone brought a tape recorder aboard. "After watching as many trees go by as we could stomach," Roger said, "somebody asked why we didn't cut a radio tape, and we did. Jack preached, and his fire and brimstone burnt the road. We sang some and cracked jokes. I sat back and laughed a lot. Jack and Troy were the creative minds behind it. We'd cut the tape and then listen to it and horse laugh. It was something to kill time and boredom, and it was an art."

"Did it ever get on the air?"

"No, no, no!" Roger said. "Not that we put anything bad on it, but nobody could appreciate it but us."

Once when Jack was telling a story about a mad bull and was trying to demonstrate his part in it, he needed someone to portray the bull and Roger happened to be sitting nearby. Jack appealed to Roger for help, "Come on, Roger, snort and paw."

"What?"

"Snort and paw. Like a mad bull."

So down on the floor of the bus, Roger snorted and pawed, and everybody laughed.

"We had some crazy times," Roger said. "All those guys had great senses of humor and now and then they relive those times. Sometimes I'll be around Jack and he'll say, 'Come on, Roger, snort and paw'."

Dale Jones grew up loving gospel music. He heard the Inspirations sing in the Akron area several times and "kinda fell in love with them." He really liked the way they sang.

"I was playing steel guitar and looking for a job in gospel music," he said. "I had tried to get a job with the Cathedrals because they lived there in Akron, but with their style, piano and bass was all they needed."

He became friends with the Inspirations, and when they came to sing in Akron, he picked for them on stage. Twice, when he took a vacation, he went on the road and picked with them to see what it was like.

"I loved it," Dale said, "and they must have liked it, too, because they hired me in 1976 and I was with them six years, playing steel and lead guitar.

"They taught me a lot," he said, "in fact, they educated me. You know what I mean, when they got on the bus and you were the greenhorn, so to speak, it was every man for himself. I was the greenhorn, and they made me the butt of many jokes—but it was fun. Anyone who can't take it should never try to ride with the Inspirations."

Dale took lessons and learned how to play the regular guitar, and then taught himself to play the steel guitar. "I love both of those instruments," he said, "and I kinda mess around with the banjo and dobro."

Dale is married to Cyndi Mashburn who sings with her mother and father, Marilyn and Earl Mashburn, as the Mashburns. Marilyn's brother plays bass guitar and Cyndi's brother plays drums, so theirs is a real family group, the Mashburns.

All the Mashburns live in Odenville, Alabama, halfway between Birmingham and Gadsden. Dale and Cyndi live about thirty yards from Marilyn and Earl, so they don't have far to go to drop the baby and be gone. The baby is Collin Matthew Jones, who at this writing is very small.

Dale works in the automobile auction business and Cyndi works in computers. Since they and others of the Mashburns have regular jobs, they are a weekend singing group.

"I do some session work on the side in Birmingham," Dale said. "There's not a lot of gospel music going on down there now, but I do get some work. I'm thankful for that."

As we conducted this interview, Jack walked by and stopped.

"I learned a lot from this old bear hunter," Dale said.

Jack responded: "He was one of my best students."

"He taught Roger, too," Dale laughed.

"That's right," Jack replied, "I taught them all the mischief they know."

"I thought we were talking about guitar," Dale quipped, and then added, "We played a lot of games, football, basketball, softball."

"I was the quarterback," Jack explained, "and Dale was my favorite receiver."

"That's true, and he'd throw the ball out in front of cars, hoping I'd go after it."

Fun and games meant a lot to the Inspirations. All of them.

"Exercise was important to us," Dale said. "Lying around on a bus and eating fast food is not the healthiest existence. The Inspirations never would let me do that."

# 30

# Donald and the Buses

It may sound strange, but when Donald Watkins, Archie's brother, was young and in the navy, and the Inspirations were neophytes in gospel singing, Donald drove the bus. He drove that old Greenbriar van for the Inspirations before they bought their first bus.

Donald was in service from the mid-'60s until September 1, 1971. The navy stationed him at Norfolk, Virginia, only eight hours from Bryson City for one who had a car. It was about eight and a half hours for one who depended on his thumb getting him where he wanted to go. Motorists encountered hitch-hikers frequently in those days, and weren't afraid to pick them up if they had room in the car. Folks especially didn't mind giving servicemen a lift, and every time Donald thumbed home, he wore his sharply-pressed uniform.

His folks didn't see a lot of Donald when he came home for the weekend. Usually he got there in time to hop in the van, later in the bus, and drive the Inspirations where they needed to go.

"Once, they sang in Tupelo, Mississippi," Donald said. "We left Tupelo on the old 4104 and rolled up 441 into Dillsboro (a few miles east of Bryson City) about nine that evening. Mom and Dad were waiting there with my car. They rode the bus back home, and I jumped in the car and headed for Norfolk. I got there about five o'clock

Monday morning, in plenty of time to go to work."

It didn't matter to Donald that he had driven most of the previous day and all of the night. "I had a lot of fun driving the guys around," he said, "and I was young then, and single, and I didn't care.

"I was in Norfolk sixteen months without a car, and I don't remember missing but two weekends coming home. On Sunday afternoon, Daddy would drive me up to Gateway (about three miles east of Bryson City) and I'd hitch-hike from there. Many a time before he could get turned around, I'd catch a ride and be gone."

One Sunday afternoon Donald thumbed a ride with a family from Robbinsville, beyond Bryson City. They introduced themselves and asked Donald where he was going.

"I'm going to Norfolk, Virginia," he said.

"We are, too," the man said. "Our son has just come out of boot camp and has to check in on a ship tomorrow."

Donald rode all the way with them, and when he thanked them for the ride he showed them where to go to find their son.

All together, Donald has driven the Inspirations fourteen or fifteen years since they started singing.

"I came out of service in seventy-one," he said, "took a week off, and started driving them. Drove three or four years and took two years off and David Shuler drove for them. When I came back I drove three or four more years and left again. It was like that all along, but I've been back with them now for seven years."

He is an excellent driver. During his times away from the Inspirations, Donald once drove for a motor line on long-distance hauling, but mostly he worked for himself. He owned his own vehicles, a backhoe, a bulldozer, and a dump truck, and he stayed busy.

"I sold them," he said, "and in 1998 I had a light heart attack and my wife and daughter wanted me to slow down. I have a friend who has a dozer, backhoe, and dump truck, and I help him out sometimes."

Donald said he had had "some close calls" but never an accident in driving the Inspirations a million miles.

When the Inspirations bought a new bus in the fall of 1998 and parked the one they drove more than two million miles, the guys wrote a tribute to the old bus. They named the tribute "The Big I" and it went like this:

*"Purchased new by the Inspirations in the spring of 1971, this Silver Eagle bus served unprecedentedly as our home away from home for twenty-seven years. Many years ago, it became affectionately known as 'the Big I' to us and to our families. It has safely and sufficiently been our means of travel from coast to coast and beyond. Most all of our families have had the opportunity of touring the great country in which we live, and even our border neighbors, Canada and Mexico, while aboard this stately land vessel. It is yet today very capable of extensive and satisfactory excursions across this land of the free and the brave.*

*"The purchase price of this bus new was $57,381. That is about twenty percent of the price of a new bus today. In 1973, the interior of the Big I was completed at a cost of approximately $7,500. Today's cost for the same type job would be about five times that amount. Through the years there have been renovations of the original interior by members who occupied the respective rooms. There is memorabilia of these respective personnel in the areas where they spent much of their time while on the road.*

*"The mileage on the Big I is somewhat a mystery. The speedometer has been changed so many times, it is almost impossible to determine the number of miles it has accumulated. The best estimate is about three million. The number of engines is also a mystery. We can remember at least seven motor changes, but possibly there have been more. The Big I has the reputation of being the coldest bus in gospel music, because of the added air conditioning systems.*

*"The Big I is not, nor has it ever been extravagant, flashy, or phenomenal. It has been used as a medium of*

*transportation of the gospel of the Lord Jesus Christ, and we hope is a great testimony of our faithfulness to Him."*

"The old one," Donald said, "when they bought it new, didn't have power steering. We have added some since. It had a four-speed transmission, and you could burn rubber with it.

"I haven't had this new one in a place yet that I couldn't take off in it. It has full hydraulic power steering, automatic transmission, and what I like is it has the comforts of home: a rest room, microwave, coffee maker, television, and stereo system. We didn't have any of that on the old one. This one sleeps three people more than the old one and it's much easier to cool. We've got a generator on this one."

The new bus is the same length as the old one, but six inches wider and seven inches taller.

# 31

# Marlin

A memory Marlin Shubert will never forget was getting to sing a short, private concert with the Inspirations for Billy Graham and his wife Ruth in their Montreat, North Carolina, home.

"I will cherish that experience forever," Marlin said. "I learned that day what a great and gracious man he was, and he seemed to enjoy our singing. He talked with us man to man, without any hint of his status in world religion."

Indeed, Billy did enjoy the visit. Martin sat at the grand piano in the living room of the rustic, mountaintop Graham home, and Archie, Troy, Jack, Ronnie, Eddie, and Marlin gathered around and sang for the Grahams, who gave them a standing ovation.

A friend of both the Inspirations and Billy's had taken them up the winding track, through the two security gates, to the log home of the Grahams, and Billy was as happy to meet them as they were to meet him.

In March of 1970, the Inspirations sang in the coal-mining town of Jasper, Alabama. On the program with them was the Shubert Family singers of Jasper, including three sisters, Kay, Martha, and Carol Shubert, their brother Marlin, and sister Vera Jo at the piano. Marlin sang bass and dragged bottom that evening, impressing

Martin so much that he asked Marlin if he would be interested in singing with the Inspirations if and when they had an opening. Marlin told him that he might be.

Soon after that, Troy left the quartet and moved to Greensboro, taking a job that would pay him more money, and when Martin called and offered the bass job to Marlin, he took it.

He sang with the Inspirations from July of 1970 till September of 1972 when he quit and moved back to Alabama.

"I just got tired of traveling," Marlin said. "Susan and I had been married fourteen months when I left. Both of us wanted to go back to Alabama, and we did."

"We could understand that," Martin Cook said. "Anybody who has lived in Alabama or has spent a lot of time there would understand. It's a beautiful state that draws its natives back."

When he got home, Marlin joined his father-in-law, Bert Crump, in the automobile business. Six years later, in 1978, they got the Nissan franchise, and in 1987 Marlin launched his own automobile business and remained in it until 1997. A year before that he got his real estate license, and when he quit selling cars he began a successful career in real estate.

Marlin and Susan have two daughters who are now grown, Cristy, born in July of '74, and Kim, born in March of '79. At this writing, Cristy is a graduate of Birmingham Southern College and Kim is a junior at the same school.

Marlin was born April 8, 1949, to Joe and Christine Shubert. Joe has retired from the City of Jasper. Christine was a Hefner, first cousin to Bill Hefner who managed and sang first tenor for the Harvesters Quartet in Charlotte and then served several terms in the United States Congress as representative from the Charlotte district.

Growing up, Marlin had no choice but to sing. The pastime of the Shubert family was singing. Marlin's father and his three brothers and five sisters were convention singers. His grandfather and grandmother sang at conventions all their lives. Joe's three brothers, Johnny, Donald, and Reynold, were singing school teachers.

"I grew up singing," Marlin said. "We started singing as a family group when my baby sister, Carol, was three and I was nine. I sang first tenor then. As far back as I can remember we were convention singers.

"My voice changed when I was thirteen or fourteen, and then it deepened, and I began to sing bass."

It is hard for a professional gospel singer to pull completely away from singing, and Marlin still sings now and then with the Inspirations when they come to the Jasper area.

"I think often of the good times I had with the Inspirations," he says. "I was with them the last year the Singing in the Smokies was in Sylva and the first year it was at the old airport in Bryson City.

"No one can ever question the sincerity of the Inspirations," he said. "I was with them one night in Cartersville, Georgia, when fifty-four people were converted or rededicated as we sang."

When Marlin returned to Alabama he rejoined his sisters in the family singing group and they sang together until his youngest sister developed voice problems. They stopped singing regularly in 1988 but continue to sing on occasions.

The only problem that the Inspirations had with him, Marlin says with a laugh, was that he was a Methodist.

"I grew up a Methodist," Marlin said. "The boys always wanted me to join the Baptist Church. Well, I do go to a Baptist Church now—but I'm still a Methodist."

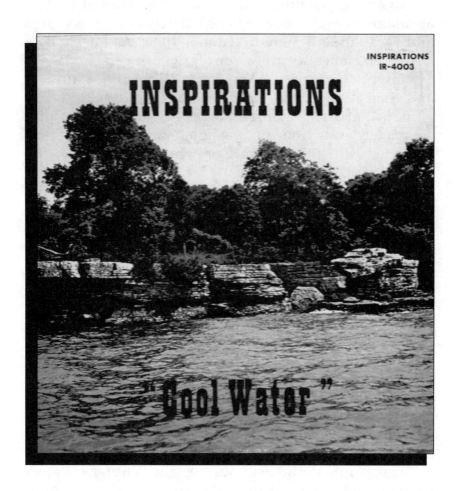

# 32

# Chris

A way back in 1964 when Martin Cook was bringing home four of his students from Swain County High School to sing in his basement in the evenings, Arnold and Mary Smith of Benton, Tennessee, were happily expecting their second child.

The boy was born October 31, 1964—a little Halloween goblin—and the Smiths set about rearing him in the way he should go, taking him to church, instilling in him strong Christian principles, and teaching him that the best way to accomplish what he wanted was to work hard toward a fixed goal.

All of that seems a bit heavy for a newborn baby, but that's only when it began; they continued these strong moral teachings as he grew through childhood to manhood.

Meanwhile, across the state line in Bryson City, Martin Cook and the Inspirations were undergoing the same growing pains, only on a more advanced level. They, too, were living right, going to church whenever the doors opened and the bell rang, adopting strong Christian principles and supporting each other in them, and they, indeed, were working hard toward a fixed goal.

If you said that Chris Smith and the Inspirations were born the same year and were walking a straight and narrow collision course, you'd be right.

In 1978, when Chris was thirteen, he sang in a high school quartet and the quartet's manager took the group to City Auditorium in Chattanooga to hear the Inspirations sing. Chris fell head over heels in love with their music and their ways.

"I had never seen a professional quartet," Chris said, "but something happened to me inside and I felt I needed to sing with them one day."

He bought all of the Inspirations' records and at home in the privacy of his room Chris learned all of their songs. Not only did he learn to sing the melody, he learned to sing each of the four parts in every song on the recordings. He had an excellent voice of exceptional range. He could sing the lead or baritone, both of which were well within his range, and his voice was high enough to reach the first tenor notes and low enough to dig out the bass notes.

He had never had formal music training but had a good ear and learned four-part harmony in his sing-alongs with the Inspirations' records.

He even began to act like an Inspiration. He kept his hair trimmed, dressed neatly, developed good manners, and tried to conduct himself in the way he thought Inspirations should. His parents were extremely proud of their son, and eventually, when Chris' story developed to a climax, the Inspirations learned, if they hadn't realized it before, just how much influence they had over the lives of some people. They learned how some, without their knowledge, looked up to them and made them role models for their lives. They had encountered much the same experience with Mike Holcomb, and Chris Smith helped to indelibilize on the singers hearts how much influence they had on many, many lives.

Chris worked, driving a Coca-Cola truck, soon after he was graduated from Polk County High School. His five-foot, six-inch, 140-pound frame was not strong enough to handle a heavy truck and thousands of heavy Coke crates, so he switched employment to the Olan Mills

Company and became a traveling photographer. That job failed to satisfy him and he soon changed employers again, this time winding up as a printer at Choate Printing Company in nearby Etowah, Tennessee. There he came in contact with the Inspirations again. Choate printed all of the Inspirations' sheet music, and Chris said he printed enough copies of *Wonder of Wonders* to know every note by heart before the music was wrapped for shipping.

In 1984, with a yearning to sing one day with the Inspirations, Chris recorded several songs on a tape, singing all four parts as a one-man quartet. He got a letter of recommendation from his high school principal, attesting to the fact that he was a nice young man of solid moral convictions and good standing in the community.

When he felt he was ready, Chris contacted Martin and asked for an appointment. He gave Martin the letter of recommendation and the tape. He also gave Martin the tape recorder so all he would have to do was press a button and listen to the tape.

Martin made it a point to push the button—and he liked what he heard. The boy could sing! He could sing any part. But the Inspirations didn't have an opening for a singer.

Working purely on faith, Chris quit his job at Choate in December of 1987 and decided to concentrate on singing. He knew deep down that he was ready to sing with the Inspirations at that moment and that he would still be ready at any future date.

On Christmas night, Chris and his mother talked in the kitchen. She said, "Son, I'm still praying, and I believe the Lord will open a door for you."

A few minutes later the phone rang and when Chris answered it, he heard Martin Cook say, "Merry Christmas, Chris, how would you like to do some singing with the Inspirations?"

A bit stunned at this immediate answer to his mother's prayers, Chris said he would, indeed, be available to fill in for any of the singers any time he was needed.

He didn't have long to wait. Archie came down with a sore throat and Chris sang high tenor for a weekend. A few weeks later Troy suffered a back problem and Chris sang lead for a weekend.

All the guys liked him and found they could sing with him very well. The blend was outstanding. He also quickly became one of the fellows, earning the respect of the entire quartet.

Ronnie had returned to the Inspirations two years before Chris began to sing. He came back aboard with the understanding with Martin that he would sing for two years, through 1987. The crush of his studies at Western Carolina University was severe. He was straining to keep up with his studies and sing, and he wanted desperately to finish his education and get into the world of finance. On Thursdays, he got out of his last class at 8:15 p.m., long after the time the quartet should have been rolling down the road. They became pushed to meet their scheduled dates.

Martin and the Inspirations didn't need a month to find the answer to their dilemma. The answer lay just down the road and over the state line in Benton, Tennessee.

So Ronnie left in March of 1988, and Chris joined the quartet to sing baritone, the harmony part, thus fulfilling a ten-year dream of singing with the Inspirations. There wasn't a happier twenty-four-year-old singer in gospel music. Nor one who had worked harder to reach his goal.

"He really makes the other guys sound good," Martin said at the time. "That's what the baritone part is for— to make Archie and Troy sound smooth and slick. Adding him to the quartet was a good stroke for him and for us. When anyone got sick, Chris could sing the vacant part and Ronnie could usually come and sing baritone in an emergency."

Oddly enough, the first date Chris sang with the Inspirations after he joined them was at his alma mater, Polk County High School.

"His coach had made the date a long time before we knew Chris would be with us," Martin said, "and when the coach called about the date I asked him what kind of boy Chris was. The coach told me he was one of the finest boys who ever came through that school and who ever lived in that community. I took that to be an extremely high recommendation of the boy's character because coaches are universally honest in their summation of kids who played for them."

Chris's presence proved valuable in many ways. People would ask which album a certain song was on, and sometimes it's a time-consuming process for someone to find the song by going through all the records.

One evening soon after Chris became an Inspiration, a woman asked Troy, "Which album is *Bound for That City* on?"

Troy answered, "Lady, I don't a bit more know than the man in the moon."

Neither did Archie or Mike, but Chris, who had overheard, spoke up, "Ma'am, *Bound for That City* is on the album *Looking for You*, first song, second side."

The woman bought the album and left happy.

"He saved us a lot of lookin' time," Archie commented.

Because he could sing all four parts, Chris became invaluable to the Inspirations on several occasions.

"Chris could double my part in a certain range," Archie said. "He did the bass high and the first tenor low. We did songs where Chris would do my part and I would sing the lead, and Troy did the baritone. Chris would do my part and people wouldn't know it. We did a lot of switches for one reason or other that people never knew we were doing."

Chris, who remained with the Inspirations two years, was employed only on a temporary basis. He left the Inspirations because of his health, which prevented him traveling full time. He moved back to Tennessee and is now singing as a one-man quartet.

# 33

# Impact on Humanity

The Inspirations' fans are a loyal multitude. Time after time when the quartet visits any town, the same faces will show in the audience. Attendance, however, is not the fans' only contribution.

"Our fans are unique," Martin said. "They are absolutely loyal. They are so loyal in their buying habits, for example, that it sometimes mystifies me. But I'm proud of it when I really stop and think about it. We have a three-hour video of the Singing in the Smokies on which we sing for an hour and other groups sing the other two hours. Then we have all sorts of videos just of the Inspirations. Our fans will buy those individual videos with us singing forty-five minutes when they could get us for an hour and others for two hours for just five dollars more. We consider that a compliment, because it tells us that they want to hear us."

Martin feels that a great part of their appeal lies in the fact that the Inspirations hit the stage singing and leave it singing, with little talk and no commercials in between. "A singer told me once," Martin said, "that when he was a little boy and the Jubilee came on that his mother would tell him, 'Now, get in here and hear this.' So our popularity is built on songs. When you stop doing songs, you're dead in the water. Nothing on stage can take the place of a good song."

Being a fan of the Inspirations—a truly loyal follower—means different things to different people. For some, it is a spiritual loyalty, for others it may be simply a friendly association. No one really knows how many people they have influenced in various ways.

"The Inspirations made me come home one time from a good job," said Sean Winchester, a big country boy from Bryson City, "and they didn't even know it.

"I went to Atlanta and got a good job driving a truck," Sean said. "First time I'd ever been out and away from home. Here I was, a big, old twenty-one-year-old young'un, and the farthest I'd ever been was maybe Knoxville.

"I had a small apartment down there, me and another guy, and that old boy was a party man. He was gone every night, and I'd sit there and watch television or something.

"We didn't have nothing besides our jobs. Our TV stand was a milk crate, and our couch was three cinder blocks, a two by six, and a couple of cushions.

"I was sitting there in late June, I guess, of 1982, watching TV. I'd been down there maybe four or five months, basically by myself. I was so starved for company if I passed a dog on the street I'd speak to it.

"My roommate had gone to bed that night, and I turned the TV to an Atlanta station, and on the news they were showing scenes of things going on and other things that would be going on the Fourth of July. All of a sudden, there was this mountainside in Bryson City on the screen. They talked about the Singing in the Smokies coming up right away, and I perked up.

"They interviewed Archie and showed Martin and then showed the whole quartet singing on stage. They swept around the mountains with their camera, and suddenly a big knot come up in my throat, big tears come to my eyes."

Sean came to his feet and went over and knocked on his roommate's door.

"Claude," he said, "I'll see you."

He said, "You going out tonight?"

"Yeah," Sean answered. "I'm agoin' away out tonight. I'm going home."

"Home?"

"Tell the bossman I'll pick up my check in a couple of weeks; I'm going home."

He climbed in his car and hit the road.

"I drove all the way to Bryson City," he said, "as fast as I could get there."

"You never know who's in the crowd," Martin said, "or listening on radio or television, and what their problems are, but we hear from people all the time who said they heard us sing a song and they really got some help from the message in the song.

"And that's the reason we have striven so hard to maintain our good names through the years. We would never want a kid to say, 'Why am I smoking this cigarette? Because I saw Archie smoking one the other day.' No, sir, that won't happen with the Inspirations. We're so serious about our work that none of us would do a thing to influence anybody in an adverse way."

They care about those who come to hear them sing. They care about the man they pass on the street, and even in the middle of New York City they'll speak to strangers. That is the mountain way. People speak to each other, ask how they're doing, how they feel. They do it because they care. And the Inspirations sit at the head of the class in caring.

Andrew Phipps is a gospel music promoter in Muncie, Indiana. He retired as a school teacher in 1997 after thirty-three years teaching history, government, and economics. His father was a Baptist preacher and music teacher of shaped-note singing in Wayne County,

Kentucky, who moved to Indiana in 1941, and to whom Andrew was born in 1942.

"Singing was a part of our family tradition," Andrew said. "We had enough in the family that we could sing as a quartet, or as a family group, and we sang in church and at funerals, things like that."

In 1973, when he was thirty-one years old, Andrew got a copy of an Inspirations' recording and played it over and over. "My," he thought, "I sure would like to have that kind of gospel singing in our own area." He had heard of other groups, but there was something about the Inspirations' singing that really caught his attention.

"It was down to earth and simple," he said, "the style of singing seemed to have an anointing."

He telephoned Martin Cook and told him that he was a teacher, that he had never done any promotions, but had heard of people who had, and he had heard that a man could lose his shirt, being obligated for all expenses, and that so many negative things could happen.

But he wanted to try, and he and Martin agreed to a date. He asked Martin if he would need to schedule another group, and Martin, thinking perhaps that Mr. Phipps shouldn't obligate himself that much, said, "Well, we can carry the program, unless you just want to have another group." Phipps didn't. He didn't want to obligate himself for money that his family finances couldn't afford to lose.

Came the night of the singing and a good crowd turned out to the Muncie Masonic Auditorium, and Andrew made a little money. He liked promoting, so he scheduled the Inspirations to come back, and he has been promoting them in Muncie since that time.

In 1975 the Phippses found that their two-year-old firstborn son, John Clay, had a malignant brain tumor. The family was devastated, and for the next four years until his death in 1979, John Clay was never really able to walk.

When the Inspirations came to sing in Muncie, they drove the bus to the Phipps home and went in to see John Clay.

After awhile, Martin said, "Archie, why don't you and the boys take John Clay for a ride around the block in the bus. He might enjoy that." He did; he enjoyed it immensely.

In his pocket, Martin had a pocket watch that his dad had given him. "It might have a special attraction or something to him," Martin explained, and he left the watch with John Clay for a year or more, picking it up after the boy's death.

Over the years, Phipps has promoted the Inspirations in Indiana more than eighty times, having them sing in Muncie, South Bend, Fort Wayne, Hammond, Indianapolis, Connorsville, and even over in Dayton, Ohio, a couple of times. "We could have a crowd of six to eight hundred people," he said, "just by promoting the Inspirations. They are that popular up here."

One winter night in the late 1980s, the Inspirations were scheduled to sing in Muncie, and that afternoon the weather turned bitterly cold and impacted the crowd so badly that attendance was down by sixty or seventy percent.

Knowing that Phipps had promoted the singing the best he could—he advertises on radio and television and by posters and mailing lists—Martin, probably remembering Roy Carter and the Chuck Wagon Gang from an earlier day in Bryson City, went in to get his pay, and said, "Aw, Andrew, give me about $250. That'll be all right. It'll get us some fuel and a bite to eat."

And then Martin added, "By the way, was my piano sounding all right? It sounded a little off to me and I'm concerned about it." The auditorium piano hadn't been in tune and during intermission, Martin had gone out and unloaded a piano from the bus bay and set it up for the second half.

"I wonder," Phipps said, "how many managers would have been concerned about their sound on a night like that before that small a crowd."

Martin has made friends for the Inspirations among promoters across the country. "I've known him to turn down dates," Phipps said, "because he thought the Inspirations couldn't help the program—maybe they had been there too recently, or they were not that well known in the area.

"It doesn't hurt the Inspirations to do that. They know Martin can book any date he wants in many places, and Martin is so honest he will not hesitate to refuse an offer to sing if he doesn't feel he can do the promoter some good. And if he does book a date, the Inspirations will be there, short of a calamity. I've never known them to fail to make a date with me in the twenty-six years I've promoted them. Knowing what the Inspirations stand for, and recognizing their honesty, promoters across the country have a deep respect for them."

Phipps admires them for their work ethics. "They'll show up on time and be ready to sing," he said. "And while a lot of groups stand and talk about their recordings and things for sale on their record tables, the Inspirations sing. I took them to Hammond once and I recall that they sang forty songs that evening. I've never known them to have a gimmick of telling the same joke every night or introducing a song with a memorized introduction. They just sing whatever Martin begins to play. They don't have a canned program in their repertoire.

"Too, they have preachers in the quartet, and the entire group is dedicated to their churches. They go about their work with great commitment.

"How could a group like that not have an impact on the people they sing for?"

The Inspirations feel a loyalty to their fans. And most of the time when they need something—say, help at the Singing in the Smokies—they will call on fans to help them, and the response has always been a hundred percent affirmative.

Opal Hice of Marietta, Georgia, was there the night the Inspirations made their professional debut in the Atlanta City Auditorium, June 10, 1966, and she has followed them faithfully for thirty-five years.

"They came on stage singing," she said, "and after their first song we in the audience were so overwhelmed that ovations came in waves. One woman got so happy, she ran all over the auditorium shouting. I told Robert, my husband, that if Archie kept on blessing me, I was going to jump on stage and pinch his little, fat cheeks."

Opal and Robert followed the Inspirations almost everywhere they sang, "and we never regretted a dime we spent on gas, motel rooms, and food." And as long as the Inspirations owned their motel in Bryson City, Opal and Robert reserved the same room for all of the Bryson City singings. When the quartet sold the motel, the Hices rented an apartment in Bryson City and maintained it for more than twelve years so they would be sure of having a place to stay when the Inspirations sang in the mountains.

With the help of the Inspirations, Robert began operating their promotions in the Cobb Civic Center in Marietta. He did all the promotional work and loved it, and the quartet paid him handsomely.

Robert passed away in 1993 and Opal still follows the Inspirations like she always did. She helps in the quartet's office when needed.

"I will always be grateful," she said, "for all the blessings the Inspirations gave Robert and me, and I was grateful when they came to sing at his funeral."

Opal has seen people literally ready to fight to keep their seats at Inspirations singings. "Sometimes someone would take the seat of one who had gone to the lobby," she said. "I remember a little lady in Chattanooga who cracked us up one night. She always sat in the end seat of the front row, and everybody who came regularly knew that was her seat. A guy once took her seat while she was out and when she came back and asked him to move, and he wouldn't, she started beating him over the head with her umbrella."

At one of the sings in Marietta that Robert promoted, a woman came in just a couple of minutes before the singing started and wanted to sit in one of Opal's up front seats.

"Honey, may I see your ticket?" Opal asked. She showed the woman where her seat was located farther back in the house. The woman said, "Well, that lady that sold us our tickets told us to just go sit anywhere we saw empty seats."

Opal said, "Well, I'm sorry this happened," knowing all the time that the ticket-seller told her nothing of the sort. The ticket seller was Opal and Robert's daughter, Amanda. "She would not have told the woman that," Opal said.

At another Marietta sing, a woman came in and gave Amanda a sob story and asked for the money back on their tickets, saying they were unable to attend.

Amanda looked at the tickets and replied, "I'm sorry, but we don't give money back to people who did not pay for tickets." The woman fled from the Civic Center.

"You see," Opal explained, "we had a code on all the tickets we gave away for radio promotions, and that woman's tickets had the code."

There was one other thing Opal wanted to say, but didn't know whether to say it or not. Coaxed a bit, she came right out with it.

"I remember," she said, "the early years and those polyester suits I thought the Inspirations would *never* quit wearing."

A woman once told Martin, "I don't know if I could have made it without this *Thank You Lord* song. My daughter was tragically killed in front of our house two years ago, and I've listened to this song over and over. I listened to it this morning. It has helped me make it through many a day."

"When we did that song," Martin said, "we thought the people on the mountain top enjoying the blessings of God would enjoy it most, but it lifts people up from the doldrums in any circumstance you can think of. I believe *Thank You Lord* has helped people who have lost a child or a husband more than any others. There is no explanation for that, but it's true. Whatever the reason, we're proud of it. And we are extremely proud of all of our fans."

# 34

# The Future is Bright

Ownership of the Inspirations Quartet and the pay each man receives is based on the number of years he has put in.

"For example," Martin said, "I have never received one penny for managing the Inspirations and doing the booking. I draw just the same as anyone else with the same number of years. We look at things like that as part of our ministry unto the Lord.

"I don't expect to be paid extra for either booking or managing. No one gets paid for doing extra chores. We all work at those chores—things like supervising the bus, keeping track of record sales, setting up the P.A. and the record table—to keep expenses down. Every man in the quartet has specific tasks. We learned many years ago that if you hired everything done, you wouldn't have anything left in gospel music. If everyone in a quartet is willing to take on proper responsibilities, if he'll do them, you can cut your overhead tremendously.

"Booking agencies charge fifteen percent to book us. For three years, when he had a booking agency, J.G. Whitfield booked us, including the year of the Battle of Songs between the Inspirations and the Happy Goodman Family.

"Different agencies book us occasionally now. They have always gotten some dates for us. Say, eight or ten dates a year. They'll just call and say, 'Martin, can you do this?' and if we have the date open, we're glad to do it."

Martin has always done most of the booking. He and the quartet feel that no one else knows where the Inspirations need to go better than they.

"That right there," Martin said, "is the future of the Inspirations, knowing where to go and what to do when we get there."

Martin and his family recently vacationed through Maine, New Hampshire, Vermont, New York, and Pennsylvania, and as he passed through New England towns, he saw many places he believes the Inspirations need to go.

"Not only that," he said, "not just those places, but even within a day's drive of our homes, there are places we need to go, places we haven't been. There are so many opportunities that we have not touched, and if you don't go within forty or fifty miles of the homes of most people who have never heard you before, they won't drive any farther than that to hear you.

"If we go into a person's hometown, chances are pretty good that he'll come out and hear us, especially if it's a small town, and he'll bring his family. So there is great potential there. It's something we feel we should do—carry the gospel in song into places that no one has touched."

He continued: "I told the people at the *Singing News* that we were reading our own newspaper too much, that we need to look around a little bit. We're doing a good job with what we're doing—and I include all singing groups in this—but we have to do more. It's almost like witnessing to someone about their salvation; you can't just walk up to a stranger and start talking about being saved with a great amount of success. You need to have some kind of contact before you try to win them to the Lord, and singing is a good way to make that contact.

"That's why I say we've got to go into more places that we've never been. Once people hear gospel music and get to swap howdies with you, they will listen and enjoy it. They're not going to tune in the gospel radio stations— they never have—until they meet some of the singers in person and like them and like their music. Then they'll tune in."

The Inspirations found that they made a host of new friends, including a lot of people who had never heard the gospel sung before, after they appeared on the CBS Weekend News in 1970. "People saw us," Martin said, "because they were watching the news. If CBS had announced that the Inspirations were going to be on, most of those people wouldn't have watched, but they did watch the news, and they saw us, and they liked what they saw."

The Inspirations' five-summer sojourn in Gatlinburg was largely the same. Thousands heard them sing there who had never heard gospel music before, and among the thousands were people from all over the world.

"We are aware of the thousands of people in given areas who don't know what gospel music is," Martin said. "They don't dislike it. They just don't know about it. Dr. Norman K. Myers, former president of Southwestern Community College in Sylva, once said that gospel music is almost like an undercover music. He said a lot of people who like it won't admit it. He said it's the most powerful music in the history of the world, and it is true American music. That's coming from a pretty high source, from the president of a college.

"So the devil has been successful in stigmatizing the most powerful music. The devil has done it. No one else would have been powerful enough to put that kind of stigma to it. But the Lord is more powerful, and if we really did the job for him, that stigma wouldn't amount to as much as it has.

"I'm saying that we need to take gospel music into every nook and cranny of America," Martin said, "and we're going to do our part. That's the future of the Inspirations."

Around 1985, Dr. Myers almost got four million dollars from the state legislature of North Carolina to build a Gospel Music Heritage Center on his college's campus. It would have been more than a museum of gospel music.

It would have been a library of gospel music and a learning center for people who wanted to study the music. It would have contained an archive of memorabilia and historical facts, and would have been a part of a large cultural center."

As often happens, politics knocked the heritage center in the head. Liston Ramsey, state representative from mountainous Madison County, was speaker of the house and was ramrodding the movement through the North Carolina House, but he lost his seat as speaker a year too soon and the legislature dropped the idea.

One immediate thing the Inspirations are doing as of this writing is consolidating all of their efforts into a new headquarters in Inspiration Park.

They have purchased the mountainside that they leased for twenty-six years, and when finished, the quartet office, warehouse, and all other facets of their operation will be in that one place.

"By owning Inspiration Park," Martin said, "we can improve it as we need to and expand our operations as much as we want. We're having eighteen days of singing on the mountain every year, and if we want to expand that, we can. We'll also build new shelters from the weather, and a lot of other things."

In the millennium year of 2000, the Inspirations will team with the McKameys in a package presentation as they did with the Happy Goodman Family in 1974. "We've tried it, and it works," Martin said, "so that's one of the immediate things we're going to do."

The Inspirations are excited about the future, and they feel they stand on a springboard that will launch them into the new millennium in the right way.

"Our country really needs to get back to basics," Martin said. "Living where we are—it's like an Eden in these hills of North Carolina—most of the time we're a thousand miles away from where the ball game's being played, or where a disastrous flood is going on. Oh, I don't mean we're exempt from anything like that. When it rains, the creeks get up—but they're not the Mississippi. I'm not talking about something nobody's ever heard of; I'm speaking of peace and contentment and relaxation that only God can give to man.

"And above all else, we need to learn to say, 'Thank You, Lord.' When we learn to start doing that as adults, children right down the line will start doing the same thing. They won't go to school and open up with a machine gun. They will copy their parents, and that will help them grow up to be outstanding citizens, good people who look out for their neighbors as well as themselves. They'll do unto others as they would have others do unto them.

"Until we do this, the problems with our children are only going to intensify."

The Inspirations feel they can be a part of meeting a great need in this country. "We must have the anointing, the touch of God," Martin said, "and here again I'm talking about that quiet leadership of the Holy Spirit that people enjoy a lot of times without even realizing what it is. For those who truly want it, God will provide opportunities for doing good to combat evil.

"We feel that right now we have the greatest opportunity to help people that we've ever had, and anyone who doesn't want to help people won't spend year in and year out singing gospel songs. You have to love people, and like to help them, and feel that you're helping them. There are just too many opportunities for us to stop singing. I'm speaking for the quartet; all the guys feel this way.

"I never dreamed that the increase in interest and outreach of the Inspirations would be as it has been since around Christmastime last December (1998)."

Martin feels part of this is due to a rising generation of Americans who are not that familiar with the Inspirations, but want to hear more. They are beginning to sit up and take notice.

"We worked in Meridian, Mississippi, recently on the Jimmie Rodgers Memorial program. One of the fellows on the board that operates the center told me that when he was a small boy his mother brought him to hear the Inspirations. He said, 'I see things really turning your way. We have made the turn. We've had all kinds of music in here, and I see more interest in the Inspirations and other gospel groups than ever before.' He said when he was a kid his mom bought one of our long-play albums and it made a difference in his life."

All of the Inspirations feel that they couldn't have accomplished what they have without full family support.

"My wife and children love the Inspirations singing as much as I do," Martin said, "and I can tell you that I love it more than I ever did. I don't care about being away from home unless I'm actually singing. I don't go on the road just to piddle around. When I come home, though, I'm going to stay home until I get ready to go singing again. That's one reason I don't belong to a lot of organizations and go to meetings. I'd love to, but I've been gone thirty-five years. Now, I'm ready to go sing and present the gospel, but outside of that I don't have much interest in going anywhere for anything else.

"What we do does not happen without family support," Martin added. "My wife has never known anything else. Archie's wife has never known anything else. If they had known ten years of some other kind of living, it might not work as well with them. But they grew up in gospel singing and they know what it's all about.

"My son, Myron, was a year old when we started singing and that's all he knows. He has played the bass with us seventeen years. He loves gospel music. He loves everybody in gospel music. He looks on them as his brothers and sisters, and you'd better not say much about them to him. If some of them were meaner than snakes it wouldn't matter to Myron. If they sing gospel songs, they're all right."

God opens the doors for the Inspirations. He has provided the opportunities, and the Inspirations have responded. Without the touch of God's hand, how else could they have had more chart songs on both the *Singing News* and *The Gospel Voice* than any other group? How else could they have been chosen to represent Southern Gospel on that CBS Weekend News report? That spread their name, and fame, if you will, across the country. Later, when people heard their name in faraway places, they knew who they were. In God's book, familiarity breeds opportunity and opportunity calls for response. That's where the Inspirations have risen even above themselves, for they have always responded.

The Inspirations have received showers of blessings, too. For thirty-five years they have made good livings singing the gospel. Martin quit teaching thirty years ago, and the kids who went with him to sing in that old van have never done anything but sing, if you discount mowing lawns and picking blackberries.

"There has always been interest in the Inspirations, wherever we go," Martin said, "but we've never had the kind of interest we are seeing now. Our name is out there ahead of us, and we can go to almost any town and have a reasonably successful singing. We've probably had only one week of singing this year when we didn't make enough money to pay the bills, and that's unusual for any quartet."

Martin is proud of the fact that he has never criticized a person in the quartet for their singing.

"I always try to tell them the right way to do it," he said, "but I've never said, 'Boys, you did a bad job tonight.' Never! I've never called Ronnie Hutchins off to one side and said, 'Ronnie, you didn't get it tonight,' or anyone else in the quartet. That's just my way of operating.

"When I started teaching school," he said, "I coached a little softball and learned that you play with what you've got, not with what you wish you had or what you think you've got. If Eddie has had a hard time singing for two years, I'm not going to belittle him, and every person who has ever sung in this quartet has had a year or two when they just didn't sing well. I guess that's true of every quartet and every singer. But one of the good things about having a quartet is that you'll always have a couple of boys who'll be hitting any time and they take up the slack. You work with what you've got."

Martin judges the Inspirations' personnel and plays within the boundaries of his judgment.

"The Inspirations have a group now with Martin, Archie, Matt, Jack, Mike, and Myron with Ronnie singing occasionally, that can do more things, run more plays, than we've ever been able to.

"Jack is a true baritone singer," Martin said. "You've not seen many baritone singers in gospel music. I don't mean that critically. Most baritones sing a second tenor, a low lead, but Jack is a natural. When he's featured he's singing baritone.

"Eddie and Ronnie were versatile, but if one was singing the low harmony part next to Mike, it was like another lead singer singing low. And if he were to be featured, it may as well have been the other lead singer, because he's singing about the same notes the lead would be singing.

"But Jack sings straight baritone and people love it. He seldom goes above a middle C, and most people wouldn't think about singing in that range and being featured. Except for the first tenor, Jack will sell as many records as anybody in the quartet. There isn't a lead singer in the country who'll sell more records than Jack will. He sings *Where We'll Never Grow Old* and *Jesus, Savior, Pilot Me*—and his singing sells records. He's got one now, *It Wasn't The Nails (that held the Lord on the Cross)*, and he could sing it right now and you'd never guess how many people would come to the table and ask for that song. They'll ask for that as much as for *Two Shoes*.

"Archie is a singer all his own. He's like Johnny Cash, he may not be the best in the world, but he's Archie. You can put him out there to sing *Amazing Grace* or whatever, and people will come and buy it.

"Mike Holcomb is the same way. He'll walk out any time and sing his song and get the people's attention. On the other end, we've got Matt Dibler, who is clean cut, has a neat appearance, and he *can* sing the lead. I've heard few people, maybe Smitty Gatlin, who can make a group sound any better and can sing the notes any prettier than Matt can. He's only been here two years. He won't really hit his stride for four.

"You can put four men together and they won't make melody. They may hit their notes, but won't make melody for four years. They'll get by all right after two, but they won't really make melody with the harmonics you need until about four years."

In retrospect, Martin can see another major reason for the success of the Inspirations.

"We're more like a family than most folks realize," he said. "On more than one occasion, I remember someone coming in and his tie would be missing. We would cut a tie in two and one wear one end and the other wear the other end, and no one knew the difference.

"It's the same with clothing. Somebody would be out of the quartet a year or two and come back and wouldn't have a suit because the suit of the man he replaced didn't fit him. We would make a chain and mix up all of our suits until everybody, including the new member, had suits that fit reasonably well. We're doing that with Jack right now. When we wear our blue suits, Jack wears my coat and Mike's pants. Mike and I have more than one blue suit.

"We used to start out in that old van, and I wasn't much older than the rest, and we would rassle—not wrestle, but rassle. I mean scuffle, roughhousing from the time we left home till we got back. We'd get to a town and head for the YMCA, and if that town didn't have one, we'd find a pool, a lake, a pond, or whatever we could get into, and it was knock-down-and-drag-out. Not fighting, but playing for keeps. In a swimming hole, it was survival of the fittest. That's the reason we get along so well; we have became like brothers."

Some of the quartet's best arrangements come when they're riding down the road and an idea hits someone.

When they got the song, "Up...up...up...up...I'm going up to be with Jesus," they were coming down Schoolhouse Hill in Bryson City on the bus, heading out to sing. Someone started talking about that song. and Archie said, "Boys, why don't we answer this thing?"

The song was just straight up...up...up...up. It really was no song at all, but before they were out of town, they were stair-stepping the song. Someone sang "Up!" and someone else "Up!" and another, "Up!" and the fourth, "Up!" and before they were many miles down the road, they had come up with a pretty good song.

"Your best ideas for music don't come when you sit down for a practice session," Martin said. "That may be your worst time. Like praying. They say, 'We're gonna meet Thursday night at seven o'clock to pray.' That doesn't excite me much. I may be different, but that may be my worst time to pray that week."

The Inspirations know that they are totally unique. They don't sound like other male quartets. They sound more like a family group because they are a family.

"We learned together," Martin continued, "and that's the reason we have that together sound, like a family. Not any of our boys, except Eddie and Mike, have really sung seriously with anyone except each other, and that's why their harmony is so close and natural.

"The Speer Family had that certain sound because they were a family. Same with the Chuck Wagon Gang. Some may have come close to their sound, but they were never duplicated. Or the Goodman Family. Nobody's ever sung like the Goodman Family.

"Eddie and Mike had some trouble singing Inspirations' style, because they learned to sing another way and it is hard to retrain a person. Matt Dibler has never sung any other way. His grandmother put him to singing with Inspirations records when he was a little kid, and right now when Ronnie goes with us I can't tell whether it's Ronnie singing or Matt, and nobody can hear the Inspirations better than I can. I brag on that. No matter where it is, I can hear every piece and every note, and on a lot of our recordings I can't tell who's singing, except for Mike and Eddie. Many times I can't tell if it's Troy or Ronnie on the lead, and I sure can't tell if it's Matt because that's the only way he has sung since he was a kid.

"You can't make an Inspiration out of someone just because he can sing. He'll never sing exactly Inspirations' style. No one can explain that to you. Matt says if a person doesn't really want to be an Inspiration and has sung much any other way, he'll never make it. Those who learned to sing together as Inspirations will hit their notes together and put out a lot of sound."

They will never change their sound—not until all are gone and a whole new set of singers has replaced them. If they are replaced gradually, one by one, perhaps a bit of the original sound will be retained.

Over the years, the Inspirations have meant much to the economy of the mountains, particularly those in the far western end of North Carolina.

"In the early days," Martin said, "a lot of people came to the mountains to hear us, enjoyed the singing and the cooler summer weather, and decided to build summer homes here. When they retired, they moved to those homes permanently. Now, since our singing has become better known across the country, more of our fans are moving into the mountains.

"Fifteen years ago, it was figured that the Inspirations increased the area's economy by five to ten million dollars a year. To find how much value the quartet is to the people of this area now, you'd have to increase that figure according to inflation, at least, and probably more because a lot of mountainsides are filling up with our people."

Some people moved here because of the quartet and opened businesses. There is no way to tell how many families have settled here and no telling how much money is poured into the economy each year because of the Inspirations.

Each year, the Inspirations and others sing eighteen nights in Inspiration Park. The Singing in the Smokies lasts nine nights. The Labor Day Weekend Festival brings people in for three more nights, and on two weekends in October at their Fall Color Festival, the Inspirations attract big crowds for six evenings. Thirty-three different groups sang in sixty-seven appearances in 1999, some of them singing two, three, and four times, and the Inspirations sang all eighteen nights.

Because of those eighteen nights, the Inspirations are one of the nation's largest employers of gospel singers.

The Inspirations mail out thousands of four-color brochures on their singings, listing not only the singing schedule, but long lists of hotels, motels, lodges, bed and breakfasts, cabins, campgrounds, and the telephone numbers of eight different chambers of commerce, all to help people find accommodations during singing times.

To see the future, you sometimes have to look to the past.

Few quartets, with the Statesmen being the most notable exception, have burst upon the scene of gospel music with greater impact than the Inspirations. Six years after their first huge success in Atlanta on that June night in 1966, the Inspirations reached the pinnacle: They were voted the number one singing group in gospel music, and from there they became the dominant quartet of the 1970s, attaining that top position six times during the decade.

So overpowering was their impact that they were voted number one for five consecutive years, 1974 through 1978. Their first top position vote came in 1972 when they stormed the charts with songs like *Joshua, Beyond, Going Up, Bring Your Burdens to Him, Swing Wide the Gates*, and *I'll Wake Up In Glory*, with three of the songs peaking out in the top four.

In those consecutive years at the top they had twelve songs in the top ten, and three of them placed number one in the charts. *When I Wake Up to Sleep No More* remained at the top for eight months of 1974; *Touring The City* was on top five months in late '73 and early '74; and *Jesus Is Mine* stayed on top four months in '76. *Shoutin' Time in Heaven* and *A Rose Among the Thorns* both reached number two in 1977.

In the 1970s three of their songs won Singing News Fan Awards as Songs of the Year, *Jesus Is Coming Soon* in 1970, *Touring The City* in 1974, and *Jesus Is Mine* in 1976.

Individual honors were rampant.

Archie was voted Favorite Gospel Artist, the highest individual honor, three times (1974, '75 and '76) and was voted Favorite Tenor Singer four times (1972, 73, '79, and '82.) Archie also received Gospel Music's most prestigious distinction, The Marvin Norcross Award at the 1999 National Quartet Convention.

Troy was Favorite Lead Singer in 1977.

Eddie won Favorite Baritone three times (1973, '75, and '79.)

Mike was the nation's Favorite Bass four times (1974, '75, '76, and '78.)

Martin was named Favorite Instrumentalist twice (1973 and '76.)

Their dominance continued in placing songs in the charts through the 1980s. In the Top 40 Songs of the Decade (January 1980 through December 1989) compiled by the *Singing News*, the Inspirations had fifty-nine songs, more than any other quartet. The Florida Boys had 52, the Kingsmen 43, the Cathedrals 42, Speers 33, Hemphills 32, Nelons 31, Wendy Bagwell 23, the Hoppers 20, and the Dixie Echoes 19.

In 1984 the Inspirations came off the road for half of each year, and for the next five summers sang alone in Gatlinburg. During those Gatlinburg years, they managed to land eight songs in the charts.

They have sung a lighter schedule through the '90s

than ever before, but they still carry as much weight in gospel singing as any other quartet.

"We've been very fortunate to have had good songs," Ronnie said. "I've always said that it's the song and not the singer that's most important, and I think that's been very evident in the ministry of the Inspirations."

At one time or another during interviews for this book, each member of the Inspirations expressed that same view.

"We've been very fortunate," Martin said, "but we've worked hard to attain what we have. We've set sales records, which proves we're doing what the people want, and we still go to places every year that we've been singing in for thirty years, and our concerts are still as successful in those towns as they've ever been. Over the years we've won about as many awards as we could expect, so there isn't a lot that challenges us any more—except our original goal. That is to be closer to God. We want a double portion of the Spirit of God that Elijah and Elisha spoke of. And, very simply, we want to reach more people who are lost.

"We're always on the lookout for more meaningful songs, because the older we get the more we're concerned about the great needs of our country. We are still hoping for the opportunity to reach people nationwide on a regular basis. That time hasn't come yet, but we feel that it will one day, and when that time arrives, we will be ready."

People often worry about the Inspirations retiring. After all, they've been singing a long time. They have sung much longer than most quartets. But if the Inspirations were giving thought to retiring, would they have bought a new bus?

The Inspirations hope this book will inspire others to sing the gospel, and to sing it well.

# About the Authors

BOB TERRELL is the author of several books on gospel music, including the highly praised history of the genre, The Music Men. He also wrote three books with J. D. Sumner, Gospel Music is My Life; The Life and Times of J.D. Sumner, and Elvis: His Love for Gospel Music. Other Terrell titles include The Legend of Buck and Dottie Rambo, and A Legend Lives On, the story of the Chuck Wagon Gang.

He is a native North Carolina mountaineer, having grown up in Addie, near Sylva, which is only 20 miles up the road from Bryson City. Bob has followed the Inspirations since their inception.

He has written for the Asheville Citizen-Times for 50 years, and all together is the author of more than 45 books on humor, travel, biography, history, and Western novels.

TIM GARDNER served as research assistant for this book. He is a North Carolina mountaineer also, from Ingalls, located in the heart of the Blue Ridge Mountains near Plumtree, Lick-log, Toe River, and Gusher Knob.

Tim is a writer for the Singing News and various daily, weekly, and specialty publications. For years he has been friend, fan, and companion of the Inspirations.